CREATOR CULTURE

Creator Culture

An Introduction to Global Social Media Entertainment

Edited by Stuart Cunningham *and* David Craig

Foreword by Nancy K. Baym

NEW YORK UNIVERSITY PRESS
New York

NEW YORK UNIVERSITY PRESS
New York
www.nyupress.org

References to Internet websites (URLs) were accurate at the time of writing. Neither the author nor New York University Press is responsible for URLs that may have expired or changed since the manuscript was prepared.

Library of Congress Cataloging-in-Publication Data
Names: Cunningham, Stuart, editor.
Title: Creator culture : an introduction to global social media entertainment /
edited by Stuart Cunningham and David Craig ; Foreword by Nancy K. Baym.
Description: New York : New York University Press, [2021] |
Includes bibliographical references and index.
Identifiers: LCCN 2020039531 (print) | LCCN 2020039532 (ebook) |
ISBN 9781479879304 (hardback) | ISBN 9781479817979 (paperback) |
ISBN 9781479837601 (ebook) | ISBN 9781479890118 (ebook)
Subjects: LCSH: Social media. | Mass media. | Creative ability.
Classification: LCC HM741 .C74 2021 (print) | LCC HM741 (ebook) | DDC 302.23/1—dc23
LC record available at https://lccn.loc.gov/2020039531
LC ebook record available at https://lccn.loc.gov/2020039532

New York University Press books are printed on acid-free paper, and their binding materials are chosen for strength and durability. We strive to use environmentally responsible suppliers and materials to the greatest extent possible in publishing our books.

Manufactured in the United States of America

10 9 8 7 6 5 4 3 2 1

Also available as an ebook

CONTENTS

FOREWORD

NANCY K. BAYM

In 2019, Lil Nas X's song "Old Town Road" spent an unprecedented nineteen weeks at the top of the Billboard charts. Was "Old Town Road" social media entertainment? One answer is an easy no. It may have been released independently, but it was quickly rereleased on a major record label. If that isn't mass media entertainment, what is?

But "Old Town Road" came from somewhere. Lil Nas X spent years refining his social media persona, making memes as a teen, spending time on Facebook, Instagram, and Twitter. By the time he bought a beat for thirty dollars on the internet, crafted "Old Town Road," and hyped it through a series of TikTok memes, he already knew how to accrue the kinds of capital that social media value. He'd found the exact balance between being "authentic" and performative that social media audiences desire. He had millions of followers on multiple platforms. His "viral" hit took years of work. His mastery is better understood from a framework of social media entertainment than mass media entertainment.

The success of "Old Town Road" speaks to the liminal status of social media entertainment (for more on liminality, see Elaine Jing Zhao's contribution in this volume). Its (continually updated re)mix of country, rap, rural, urban, meme, video, and song only hints at the boundary crossing at play in the field at large. It's not just genres that are blurring. Social media entertainment, as this volume shows, seems well on its way toward being an industry (or industries?) of its own, yet in many ways it appears as another iteration of (or feeder for) well-established industries. On the one hand, it seems to offer the radical decentralization that can let a kid from a rural state in the United States achieve international fame through self-produced media. On the other hand, it is increasingly concentrated in a handful of corporations that, like media of old, make money by selling their users to advertisers.

As scholars, how are we to make sense of a whole that sits between forms new and old and calls for theories and methods both new and old? This book and its predecessor, Stuart Cunningham and David Craig's *Social Media Entertainment* (2019), along with much of the work cited therein, provide a foundation. We can begin to see the actors—human, corporate, and technical—and the connections between them. There are the creative workers, a category that belies an extraordinary range of motivations, ambitions, and practices. There are audiences, who have relationships not only with creators but with one another and who function as recipients, interlocutors, influences, antagonists, and products that the creators are able to sell to advertisers (for more on this, see Brooke Erin Duffy and Megan Sawey's contribution in this volume). There are communities, online and off, with their own norms, expectations, and modes of self-regulation. There are platforms and the many decision-makers within them, from those deciding business models to those implementing them through algorithms and interfaces and always-fraught content moderation. There are the ever-changing algorithms and the interfaces, continuously creating consequences their engineers didn't anticipate. There are the data, some presented as metrics to influence action, some captured and sold behind the scenes in ways neither creators nor audiences can see, let alone control. There are the old media—the record labels, the television stations, the radio, the film industries, and more, all of which not only persist but exert tremendous regulatory influence. There are new intermediaries, many already having their own rises and falls as mini-industries—the personality curators, the multichannel and multiplatform networks, the Patreons and the Kickstarters. There are the brands and the advertisers, still exerting the same influences that have made creative professions viable while challenging artists' "authenticity" for generations. Social media entertainment is a world of product placement, of sponsorships, of partnerships, of affiliate relationships. There are the nations and governments, with their existing policies and laws, striving to figure out whether and how to regulate this new realm with its slippery boundaries and propensities to make work look like play, to make play into work, and to let intellectual property serve as fodder for others' creativity. And, of course, there are the billions of media artifacts created and circulated to form the "content" of an economy that thinks so little of artistry that it uses that term to describe creative work.

We can also now start charting the industrial and spatial logics on and within which social media entertainment economies operate. We can begin to see different models of production, distribution, work, success, and failure. We can begin comparisons, asking how things work differently when the genre is (to take a few examples from this book) video book reviews, style blogs, or game commentary. We can begin to compare contexts, from the communities that form around individuals and genres to the regions and nations within and across which they form.

Most importantly, we can begin to see the dynamics through which power is exerted and claimed, and it is here where we must be most careful to remember that the approaches we've already built in our decades of understanding how media industries operate still provide insightful lenses for critical assessment. We can see how, despite rhetorics of democratization and examples of youths who find their way out of poverty through media they create on their phones, success in this realm is still elusive, while its pursuit inevitably benefits those who hold power. We see workers beholden to platforms' recommendation systems, algorithmic discrimination, and changing affordances, interfaces, and terms of service into which they have little insight, let alone control, while the guilds and unions that helped create acceptable work conditions for their mass-media predecessors struggle to find footholds. We see the gendering, as the work of creation is dismissed as trivial, while the coding of the platforms on which the creations circulate is valorized as the skillset to which all would-be workers should aspire. We see how people's very selves become products in this economy, as, regardless of what they produce, being "authentic" and forming relationships that feel intimate to audiences become germane to making a living (a topic I explore extensively in my book *Playing to the Crowd*). We see how being "real" can mean becoming a brand that algorithms will find legible. Ultimately, we can see how, as currently constructed, social media entertainment serves capitalist logics above and beyond logics of public good. Here, I hope, we will move beyond description and explanation and find ways to intervene before this new road takes us back to the same old town.

Introduction

STUART CUNNINGHAM AND DAVID CRAIG

What we call *creator culture* is being constructed around the opportunities and challenges that have emerged as established media and communication industries begin to share the content and distribution space with digital streaming and social networking platforms. These structural changes in the media landscape have, in turn, contributed to the rise of an industry and culture populated by native social media entrepreneurs. Creators can be simply defined in the words of the social media entertainment (SME) thought leader Hank Green (2016) as any creator "making all or part of their living making stuff on the internet, or are working toward that goal."

The term signifies a distinction from an earlier phase of online content creation characterized by "user-generated content" (UGC). UGC referred to any form of content generated by users of digital platforms, and early scholarly attention rarely entertained the possibility that such activity might give rise to viable entrepreneurial careers. We believe the term *creator*—which we define rather more fully than Hank Green as commercializing and professionalizing native social media users who generate and circulate original content in close interaction and engagement with their communities on the major social media platforms as well as offline—is the term that captures best what is at stake in this book's mapping of approaches to this emerging culture. Creators are dubbed many things now: influencers, bloggers and vloggers, gameplayers, livestreamers, camgirls, broadcast jockeys (Korea), and, in China, KOLs (key opinion leaders), *zhubo*, and *wanghong*, among others. They can be referred to by platform use: YouTubers, tweeters (Twitter), grammers (Instagram), and snappers (Snapchat). Scholars previously coined terms such as "micro-celebrities" (Senft 2008; Abidin 2016), although by now many of these creators have developed greater cultural influence than mainstream celebrities: think of Zhang Dayi (China), Huda Beauty (Dubai), Chiara Ferragni (Italy), PewDiePie (UK), Ninja (US), to name a few. Terminological profusion is an index of the increasing importance of this field of study. Even Hollywood producers, writers, and show-runners routinely refer to themselves as "creators." Nowadays, some of these terms have gone completely viral. Martha Lincoln (@heavyredaction) tweeted apropos an encounter in a classroom, "A student has just astonished me by writing 'Influencers such as Karl Marx and Friedrich Engels.'"

The creator culture that this volume seeks to define and investigate draws on a range of scholarship in media and communication studies, science and technology studies, and social media, internet, and platform studies. We mapped its industrial dimensions in *Social Media Entertainment: The New Industry at the Intersection of Hollywood and Silicon Valley* (Cunningham and Craig 2019). There, we traced the emergence of a phenomenon emerging outside broadcasting and the digital streaming platforms (for example, Netflix, Amazon Prime Video, iQiyi, and Hotstar). Rather, these creators are native to social media platforms such as YouTube, Twitch, Instagram, Facebook, Twitter, and their Chinese counterparts Youku, Weibo, and WeChat. Conditions of labor are volatile and precarious but also more empowered, in contrast to early careerists in Hollywood and the media industries. SME also represented a significant space for new, and much more diverse, voices with the means for cultural assertion as much as commercial media production. Combined, these factors generated a different globalization dynamic that has scaled with great velocity, enabling multimodal content (posts, vlogs, tweets, grams, snaps, and streams) to travel the world without conventional intellectual property (IP) control and posing new challenges for established media companies and regulatory regimes. In this introduction, we elaborate briefly on the industrial underpinnings and global dimensions of creator culture and then introduce the chapters to follow.

The development of creator culture will have reached the fifteen-year mark by 2021, starting with the launch of YouTube, Twitter, and Facebook and their Chinese counterparts around 2005. YouTube has been a critical platform for creators, particularly after acquisition in 2006 by Google, introducing features and services that empowered, and often inhibited, creators, but always in service of the shifting interests of the platform. A short list includes content management systems, programmatic advertising, partnership agreements, programmable channels, mobility, subscription platforms, community pages, ecommerce and merchandise integrations, online mobile payment systems, and livestreaming. There are similar stories of strong growth of native content creation on platforms such as Twitch, Instagram, Facebook, and even Twitter.

The reality is multiplatform for most creators, although the materiality of platform affordances generates real differences in practice: an Instagram beauty vlogger is different from a YouTube content creator, as is a Twitch gameplayer, a Snap storyteller, or a Momo showroom host. In turn, the commercializing practices of creators operating in this industry reflect a diverse portfolio of revenue streams across platforms, in established media as well as off media. Vital to our understanding is that these conditions extend across all social media platforms, many of which have integrated comparable forms of modality (video), monetization (programmatic advertising), and partnership agreements with their native creators.

China's alternative creator industry is a wild card that may upset the accepted understanding of the way cultural influence flows globally. *Wanghong* means "popular online" or "internet famous" and carries connotations that can embrace the entire industry or refer to celebritization as a problematic process, as well as describing the specific subcomponent of Chinese creator culture on livestreaming platforms. China's industry features a highly competitive platform landscape, incubated through regulatory protection and fueled by a rising middle class, and offers more diverse and potentially lucrative opportunities for creators than its Western counterparts. When *wanghong* makes the leap past the Great Chinese Firewall, Western entertainment hegemony may be imperiled. And there are vibrant creator cultures in numerous places around the world that are little beholden to face-offs with old Western hegemons or, for that matter, emerging Eastern ones.

Studying the Social Media Entertainment Industry

"Does the world really need one more field of study?" Jennifer Holt and Alisa Perren (2009) ask this question in introducing their field-setting volume *Media Industries: History, Theory, and Method*. Our answer would be that as industries and cultures change, so fields of study need to change. *Creator Culture: An Introduction to Global Social Media Entertainment* introduces readers to "ways of seeing" social media entertainment from perspectives that critically assess claims for its relation to, yet differentiation from, well-established media forms and institutions traditionally within scope for media studies, as well as differentiation from the agendas now established within social media studies. This volume does not seek to impose a uniform perspective; rather, our goal is to stimulate in-depth, globally focused engagement with this industry and establish a dynamic research agenda attractive to scholars, teachers, and students, as well as to creators and media professionals across the media, communication, and social media industries.

The scholarly foundations of the volume draw on diverse, interrelated disciplines, theories, analytic frameworks, and methodologies. Holt and Perren, in looking to define media industries studies, argued that the field relied on knowledge generated in cultural and creative industries, mass communication, sociology and anthropology, media economics and industrial analysis, political economy and cultural studies, journalism, film and TV studies, and cultural policy. Together with these influences, we suggest that studying the creator culture developed by social media entertainment requires disciplinary input from internet studies, social media studies, and science and technology studies.

There are many productive differences in approach and perspective in the chapters to follow. But what everyone agrees on is that social media entertainment (or whatever contributors call it) is a *thing*. But what sort of the thing is it? Is it an industry? And, if so, what kind of an industry? Nitin Govil poses an interesting question of great relevance to our project when he notes that "most studies proceed from a general understanding of what an industry comprises, with a tacit sense of its boundaries and capacities." One of the "entrenched yet under examined presumptions" of studies of media industries is the "obviousness of its object" (Govil 2013, 173). Govil attributes the fact that the Indian film industry was finally granted official industry status by government only after decades of lobbying principally to the lack of reliable statistical data. An industry that innovatively made the most of its informality had ultimately to embrace formalization to advance. Popular and political ambivalence about the industry had to give way in order for it to be placed on proper legal and financial footing. Govil argues that "we need to broaden the range of practices that count as industrial" and that we need "a more dynamic sense of industries as social and textual arrangements . . . and other dramaturgies of interaction, reflection, and reflexivity" (176).

In this spirit, we posit three basic criteria for considering SME as an industry: size and scope, differentiation from neighboring industries, and degree of formalization.

Gaining *authoritative, independent data on the scale and economic value* that platforms and creators derive from SME is almost impossible at this stage of its evolution as an industry. And any data that can be derived will date quickly, given that growth year on year in these early growth stages is remarkable and remarkably global. Data that are made available are mostly from single platforms, whereas creators' revenue sources typically involve multiple platforms and strategies including crowdfunding, licensing, and direct brand deal making. Platforms have more than one revenue stream from which creators may or may not benefit, but publicly revealing the full story would risk flights of, and fights between, creators and expose platforms' accounting practices. It is always better, think platforms, to impose nondisclosure agreements and deal separately or even purely algorithmically with creators.

YouTube's referencing of creator statistics is classic "spin." A typical statement from Google CEO Sundar Pichai in 2019 touted the ever-increasing monetization opportunities that YouTube provides for creators. "The number of channels with more than 1 million subscribers doubled in 2018," he said, "and the number of creators earning between $10,000 and $1 million from YouTube AdSense grew 40% year-over-year. (Currently, there are upwards of 5,000 channels with at least 1 million subscribers.)" (Weiss 2019). (That figure had grown to more than 16,000 in late 2019.) Who qualifies to be a "partner" has changed semi-regularly, programmatic advertising revenue splits vary between "premium" and "nonpremium" creators, and YouTube has introduced new revenue sources: subscriptions, memberships, e-commerce, and virtual goods. Compared to other platforms' public accounting of creator practice, however, YouTube is relatively transparent. Another exception to the deep opaqueness may be Amazon-owned Twitch. Its platform blog offers explicit dollar figures for aspiring Twitch partners and declares over 27,000 partners as of October 2019, albeit with no indication of total revenue across revenue streams including advertising, virtual goods, and subscriptions.

Attempts to track economic value across multiple platforms and allied funding sources are legion but almost always unverifiable and must be taken under advisement, as they usually come from vested advertising and marketing interests. Business journalists' accounts of the "influencer economy" vary from $1 billion in 2018 (Adweek 2019) to $10 billion in 2020 (National Public Radio 2019). Researchers wanting to dig deeper into such figures would need to ask if they are limited to influencer marketing without programmatic advertising, focused exclusively on the brand-rich environment of Instagram only, and limited to the advertising verticals of beauty and lifestyle alone.

It is possibly even more difficult to be assured of data clarity in China's alternative creator universe. The "*wanghong* economy," according to industry data firms like CBNData, may have eclipsed China's film industry at near US$10 billion in 2016 and was worth US$15 billion a year later (Asia Pacific 2018). Or this could even be the "$24 billion Chinese industry you've never heard of" (Youmshajekian 2019).

The value proposition that third-party data firms such as Social Blade, Tubefilter, and Captive8 offer to the industry is to combine data across platforms and revenue portfolios and package such information as the basis for creators' sales strategies for securing paying customers. However, their estimates are limited without direct access to creators' platform application programming interfaces (APIs), which are repositories of more sophisticated measures such as indicators of "engagement." According to Social Blade, the leading DIY beauty vlogger and queer political activist Ingrid Nilsen makes between $155 and $2,500 a month, $2,000 to $30,000 a year, but none of these data points recognizes her multiyear "glambassadorships" with the likes of Clairol or bareMinerals, which are almost certainly orders of magnitude greater than these figures.

For nearly a decade, *Forbes* has tracked the highest paid influencers, creators, and YouTubers via a mix of qualitative and quantitative methods, in partnership with social insight firms, across multiple platform data sources, coupled with economic assessments of endorsements and offline businesses. In 2011, *Forbes* generated a list of the top "social media influencers"—primarily social media marketing experts operating on Twitter—derived from an "Identified Consumer Count" metric developed by a data firm called PeekYou (Shaughnessy 2011). By 2017, *Forbes*'s list had grown to over one hundred "influencers" across multiple platforms and content verticals like pets, fitness, and gaming; the list was to be published quarterly (O'Connor 2017). *Forbes*'s efforts proved unsustainable. Its 2019 list was reduced to the top ten "YouTube Stars," led by eight-year-old Ryan Kaji of Ryan's World, with $26 million in revenue, based on "data from Captiv8, SocialBlade, and Pollstar as well as interviews with industry stars" (Berg 2019). The dramatic changes in method and outcome in these lists reflect the difficult conditions under which scholars and students must work to assess the scale and economic value of the industry.

Creator advocates have also invested resources seeking to influence political and policy understanding about the scale and scope of the industry on a (US) state-by-state basis. *America's New Creative Economy* is a US-centric analysis of the creator economy funded by the Re:Create Coalition—a creator-focused NGO—prepared by a team of economists. While the lead economist informed us that the report is full of "heroic assumptions" (Shapiro 2018), nonetheless, the report suggests that upward of 10 percent of the US labor force is making some form of revenue by harnessing social media platforms (Shapiro with Aneja 2018). The second report, published in 2019, revealed sustainable growth of creator income at a rate of more than 17 percent per year and growth to more than $1 billion in the size of this economy (Shapiro with Aneja 2019). (We revisit the Re:Create Coalition in chapter 14.)

Comparing and *differentiating* SME from neighboring industrial formations is a constant challenge, as it morphs rapidly. Its history, as we see it (and as set out in Cunningham and Craig 2019, 37–62), shows three distinct phases. Its first phase begins centrally with YouTube providing open access to share content and foster community, thus distinguishing itself from digital TV portals. A distinct second phase is marked by the increased competition from second-generation platforms and the rise of multiplatforming. These were the "New Tubes" consolidated, acquired, internally launched, and feature-enhanced by the SME majors, Google/YouTube, Facebook/Instagram, Twitter/Periscope/Vine, Amazon/Twitch, and Snapchat. In turn, this enhanced platform landscape fostered new types of creators (for example, Snappers, Grammers, Viners). We are now in a third phase, arguably marked by the "Adpocalypse" in 2017 and the increased challenges confronting creators as the platforms face a rapidly growing crisis of governance, first in the European Union, then in other jurisdictions, and now increasingly in the United States. The 2019 backlash toward child creators was deemed the "second Adpocalypse," signaling, for some observers, that the "Golden Age of YouTube is over" (Alexander 2020).

In our previous work on the subject, we say, "Vital to grasping the significance of SME is understanding how social media entertainment platforms operated as both content delivery systems and networked communication technology" (Cunningham and Craig 2019, 32). SME creator culture is being developed and practiced at the intersection of the digital and the social, the interpersonal and the mass, and established and emerging media industries, and studying it means drawing on several disciplinary traditions, as we aim to show in this book.

SME is *both* a content *and* a communication industry; creators *both* produce and distribute content *and* manage communities. Nancy Baym makes clear with respect to the broader phenomenon of new media that they blur boundaries between established communication subdisciplines (interpersonal, group, mass) as well as blurring the linear conception in mass communication media of one-to-many production-reception:

> One of the most exciting elements of new media is that they allow us to communicate personally within what used to be prohibitively large groups. This blurs the boundary between mass and interpersonal communication in ways that disrupt both. When people gather online to talk about a television show they are a mass communication audience, but the communication they have with one another is both interpersonal, directed to individuals within the group, and mass, available for anyone to read. If, as increasingly happens, conversations and materials these fans produce for one another are incorporated into the television show, the boundaries between the production and reception of mass media are blurred as well. (2015, 4)

We have distinguished SME from mass-media frameworks and mainstream screen industries in our previous work (Cunningham and Craig

2019, 8–15). There, we stress the differences between the "born digital," "network native," and "mobile friendly" social platforms on which SME operates, on the one hand, and traditional media, on the other. We point to the pro-am status of the SME creator, the new genres and formats invented, the open intellectual property protocols under which it circulates globally, and the centrality of community development and maintenance as the core *work* in creator culture.

From the perspective of the interpersonal (and group) communication subdisciplines, SME can be viewed from the perspective of the perceived elitism of mass media and its "powerful subversion": "the gatekeeping function of mass media is challenged as individuals use digital media to spread messages much further and more widely than was ever historically possible" (Baym 2015, 11). Just as synchronous person-to-person and small-group communication developed early in the internet's history (Baym 2015, 15), so the video log, or vlog, was, and has continued to be, fundamental to the early commercial internet and to SME. The centrality of livestreaming to contemporary SME reaffirms communication as much as content defines creator culture.

As we outline in the concluding chapter of this book, much scholarship has focused on the downsides of *formalization* of previously amateur content-production culture on social media platforms. (Chapters 5, 9, and 12 also engage with issues of industry formalization.) Instead, we argue there that SME has developed rapidly and that its current shape and future prospects require greater attention to industrial formalization. As we have just seen, one of the key distinguishing features of SME is the (previously) amateur status of creator culture. This has made SME one of the outstanding examples of what Ramon Lobato and Julian Thomas (2015) stress are the innovations that informal media practices have contributed to the institutionalized media industries. A formalizing industry that begins to regulate itself effectively and accepts, where appropriate, the necessity of state regulation is a sign of a maturing industry advancing from its days as the "Wild West" (Mann 2014). As Govil reminds us, one of the key dynamics that inhibit the advance of an industry through appropriate formalization is the degree of acceptance of its bona fides in popular opinion and by the state. Critical scholarship can support this recognition and thus the sustainability of creator culture.

The Chapters to Come

The purpose of this book is to provide resources for understanding, studying, and researching creator cultures in the emerging industry of social media entertainment. We have organized the chapters under three broad heuristic domains, or approaches, through which readers can make sense of the formation of creator cultures in this new industry configuration and the theoretical, methodological, cultural, social, textual, policy, and political issues it raises. These approaches—"Frameworks and Methods," "Genres and Communities," and "Industries and Governance"—form the part structure of the book. Readers will find that there are inevitable and productive cross-referencing of these approaches within many of the chapters. As we introduce the contributing chapters here, we also suggest many links between and across these domains that will encourage you to explore deeper into the field and "connect the dots."

Frameworks and Methods

As we have seen, because SME creator culture sits at the intersection of the digital and the social, the interpersonal and the mass, and established and emerging media industries, it has attracted a range of disciplinary approaches and perspectives. In part 1, several frameworks and methods are explored.

Chapter 1, by Jean Burgess, introduces platform studies, establishing the importance of platforms to creator culture and giving an overview of the platformization of the web, the consequences for media power, and the sometimes supportive, often adversarial, but always political, relations between creators and platforms. It then gives an overview of the field of platform studies before discussing three distinctive but complementary approaches to researching platforms in general and YouTube in particular. These approaches are characterized by critical and qualitative perspectives on issues such as the role of algorithms, computational digital methods using platform APIs, and hybrid methods such as the "app walkthrough." The chapter concludes with some guidelines on the way these methods can be combined to help empower creator communities by enhancing and amplifying their knowledge of how platforms work.

Feminist studies of creator culture are featured elsewhere in this volume (chapter 7, by Duffy and Sawey) but are the structural framework through which Zoë Glatt and Sarah Banet-Weiser, in chapter 2, examine the work of feminist YouTube content creators in the context of popular feminist economies of visibility and an interrelated theoretical analytic of "productive ambivalence." YouTube has been celebrated by many people as a platform that has enabled far more diverse screen representations of race, gender, and sexuality than television and film media do, as is undoubtedly the case. However, feminist YouTube creators have to navigate what are often contradictory pressures in order to gain visibility and earn a living, such as appealing to commercial brands while maintaining their political integrity and cultivating authenticity with their audiences. The work of feminist content creators on YouTube is complex, and so a reductive explanatory frame is resisted. With the analytic of productive ambivalence, this chapter aims to complicate the dominance of popular feminism online by asking, to what extent are professional YouTube content creators able to present more radical versions of feminism or else pushed to fit into neoliberal brand culture in order to gain visibility and income?

In chapter 3, Brent Luvaas discusses the affordances and limitations of autoethnography as a method of social media research. Describing his own experiences as a street style blogger, the chapter introduces the experiential modes of data gathering that autoethnography enables as well as the emotional toll that such methodologies can inflict. Autoethnography provides embodied ways of knowing that no other form of social scientific research can provide. But it also entails affective and existential risk. Becoming what we study is a process not easily undone. And it is one whose ending is not easy to predict. As Luvaas was becoming a blogger, bloggers were becoming something else: social media "influencers" who leverage their personal brands across platforms. To perpetuate his blog, he had to become an influencer too, an identity about which he remained deeply ambivalent.

Carlos A. Scolari, Damián Fraticelli, and José M. Tomasena, in chapter 4, produce a case study of a SME genre rarely discussed: book reviewers on YouTube ("BookTubers"). The case study traces the progressive professionalization of Spanish-language BookTubers and their battles with the book industry while at the same time engaging in a master class on semiotic and discursive analysis in the European tradition. Good examples of discourse analysis of creator production to compare and contrast with this chapter can be found in chapters 2, 7, 9, and 10.

Critical media industry studies (CMIS) is a middle-range approach that seeks to account for both structure *and* agency, power *and* resistance, in media industries. Using CMIS as a framework, chapter 5, by David Craig, Stuart Cunningham, and Junyi Lv, adopts a creator-centric optic to illustrate the interdependencies among industrial, social, technological and economic, and political vectors in Chinese livestreaming. As a state-protected and surveilled industry, China's livestreaming has more genres, revenue models, and participation compared with Western formats. The authors find highly advanced e-commerce integration on platforms that have underpinned livestreamers' *economic* sustainability. However, this enhanced sustainability has to be placed against the *social and political* precarity of the ever-present possibility of state action upholding "social morality."

Chapters in this section (and elsewhere) are careful to highlight the range of methods used to research SME and creator culture: document analysis, interviewing, and textual and discourse analysis are commonly used methods, but we also encounter ethnographic, autoethnographic, and computational digital methods as well as hybrid critical and qualitative methods such as the app walkthrough.

Genres and Communities

Apart from this section's treatment of major SME genres gameplay, fashion and lifestyle, and toy unboxing, you will find analysis of other genres elsewhere in the book: book reviewing in chapter 4, livestreaming in chapter 5. Comedy, satire and prank formats are discussed in this section in chapters 9 and 10.

Hector Postigo's chapter 6 notes that scholars of media industries and other creative cultures have often reported research findings through the lenses of qualitative data (interviews and participant observation), interpretation, and analysis. This chapter describes immersive research methods that Postigo used while studying creative communities on YouTube. But the chapter sits in this section because it also gives us one of the richest—dare we say, most authentic—accounts of the sheer skill, commitment, and hard work demanded of creators in the genre of video gameplay commentary (one of the core SME genres). Postigo also says that the chapter yields findings and methods that are transferable to studying other creator communities. The chapter explores the concept of "authenticity" as a useful (or not) heuristic for understanding what exactly creative communities, like the one featured in this chapter, are trying to portray as they present themselves and their products to audiences. Chapters 3 and 6 make a compelling duet regarding the power and challenge of ethnographic method.

Brooke Erin Duffy and Megan Sawey look at Instagram content creators and their main genre, fashion and lifestyle. Their chapter 7 shifts the conceptual focus of social media influence from labor to service. Instagram-based influencers are beholden to three distinctive groups—audiences, advertisers, and the wider creator community—that exert competing demands on their time, energy, and creative output. After exploring how the provision of service to these groups shapes the cultural experiences and valuations of influencers on Instagram, Duffy and Sawey ultimately locate the power in the hands of the platform itself. It is instructive to compare this account of creator agency with the strongly positive account in chapter 10 and the analytic of "productive ambivalence" advanced in chapter 2.

Jarrod Walczer, in chapter 8, studies the way toy unboxing creator communities have survived the ElsaGate scandal and KidPocalypse of 2017 (in which trusted children's brands were spoofed, satirized, and subverted on YouTube with much panic and scrutiny). To do this, they have had to self-organize and more radically brand themselves as progressive purveyors of quality YouTube-native content for kids. Nevertheless, questions remain as to whether these creator-centric communities are just a second coming of old-style multichannel networks. This chapter profiles both pocket.watch and Family Video Network, asking whether these new organizations are bent on profitability and mass acquisition or whether they represent a new type of community-management and creator-governance formation. Creators seeking to take greater control over the volatile platform environments they work in through self-governance is a theme also taken up in chapter 14.

The creator cultures forming around social media entertainment are thoroughly global, regional, and nationally specific in extent and diversity. Chapter 9, by Sangeet Kumar, Sriram Mohan, and Aswin Punath-ambekar, insists on a regional frame "beyond the nation" as the primary organizing category for the production and circulation of SME culture. In the peninsular region of South India, there is a well-entrenched Hindi-Urdu circuit of cultural exchange between India and Pakistan on YouTube that has advanced a "regional imaginary," often based on affinities of language, cultural idioms, and social similitude, and has enabled dialogue and cultural exchange across fractious national borders.

Mohamed El Marzouki maps the field of creator culture in the Middle East and North Africa in chapter 10. He begins by outlining social, political, and technological developments that furnished the conditions of possibility for the rise of youth digital media culture across the Arab world, including the deteriorating socioeconomic conditions of youth in light of decades of political authoritarianism and state monopolies on media and cultural institutions. The chapter examines the political purchase of youth digital media culture in relation to the online and offline microeconomic processes and monetization schemes that young social media creators engage in to sustain their digital media ventures.

Industries and Governance

In chapter 11, Elaine Jing Zhao exemplifies how a focus on creator culture can illuminate and ground an industrial framework. As the internet opens up pathways to fame and notoriety in an environment of super-charged transformation, *wanghong* (internet famous) has become arguably even more of a cultural and socioeconomic phenomenon in China than elsewhere and constitutes a rapidly growing part of Chinese social media entertainment. The chapter critically examines *wanghong* through multiple layers of liminality: between the professional and amateur, between authenticity and performance, between public and private, and between being celebrated and being disciplined. The theme of creator labor is a constant in the book, and you will encounter it in several chapters; the specificity of China is also considered in chapter 5.

Chapter 12 is a study of the industrial culture of Chilean advertising as it is changing to accommodate SME creators. Deploying the Bourdieusian notion of cultural field, Arturo Arriagada argues that creators and advertising agencies work together as dual markets within the industry.

These markets can be approached as a field where actors compete to legitimize their forms of knowledge, expertise, and taste classifications for the promotion of brands and products. Creators and advertising agencies appear to have a mutually constitutive influence: while creators challenge the power of advertisers by configuring a type of labor, based on knowledge of platforms and promotion, that validates the online content-creation economy, advertisers must accommodate and learn to respect creator authenticity as the basis for extracting value from their relationships with follower communities.

In chapter 13, Jeremy Shtern and Stephanie Hill place social media content creators in a historical frame and under the scrutiny of political economy. The return to sponsorship as a popular model of funding social media entertainment revives a controversial media monetization practice that previously jeopardized consumer trust in advertising and attracted scrutiny from both the public and regulatory agents from as early as the 1930s. This chapter considers sponsored social media content in this historical context, examining how it creates power for advertisers by commodifying social media audiences and analyzing the ways in which media policy and industry regulation currently provide oversight. The extent to which the viability of creator culture hinges on consumer trust, and how effective government and industry standards act as guarantor, quality assurer, and occasional regulator of trustworthiness, is at issue. Shtern and Hill's approach to advertising and to regulation can be profitably compared to those in chapters 12 and 14, respectively.

Stuart Cunningham and David Craig, in chapter 14, offer a creator-centric account of industrial, governance, and rights issues in SME. Social media entertainment is characterized by what appears as a gross power asymmetry between platforms and creators: world-leading and globe-spanning hegemonic organizations, weak intermediary structures, and a "workforce" that is young, globally dispersed, and composed of mostly sole traders. However, this chapter, theoretically framed by a Foucauldian understanding of power as relational and contingent and insights from network economics, suggests a more supple account of power and some progress in collective action and advocacy in the representation of creator rights. The interests of creators are examined in the "top-down" context of the exercise of platform governance and efforts, by platforms and the state, to improve it. Those interests are also canvassed from the "bottom up"—how creators and creator advocacy are organizing and acting collectively to improve prospects for creators in this emerging industry.

"The World Only Spins Forward"

Between delivering this manuscript in 2019 and responding to its review in May 2020, the world tilted on its axis with the global pandemic, COVID-19. The pandemic has killed hundreds of thousands, wreaked economic havoc, and heightened political unrest, leaving our lives quarantined and social practices virtualized. Traditional media industries are both reeling and benefiting from such huge disruption. Live entertainment, theatrical distribution, theme parks, and scripted production are shuttered, while streaming video portals and online video games proliferate as vital services to locked-down populations across the globe. The SME industry has been boosted as audiences crowd online; chapter 5, for example, notes that China's *wanghong* industry has become a vital engine for sustaining the growth of China's digital economy. This book, introducing the emerging field of studies of creator culture in the SME industry, is supremely timely. As creator cultures evolve by responding during and after this crisis, the work we present here analyzes, questions, and contextualizes, while fundamentally registering the importance of, an emerging industry with digital participation and citizenship at its core. To quote from Tony Kushner's (1995, 290) *Angels in America* as it anticipates the end of the AIDS crisis, "The world only spins forward. We will be [digital] citizens. The time has come."

REFERENCES

Abidin, Crystal. 2016. "Visibility Labour: Engaging with Influencers' Fashion Brands and #OOTD Advertorial Campaigns on Instagram." *Media International Australia* 161 (1): 86–100. doi:10.1177/1329878X16665177.

Adweek. 2019. "How to Determine Instagram Pricing for Influencer Marketing." *Adweek*, July 27, 2019. www.adweek.com.

Alexander, Julia. 2020. "The Golden Age of YouTube Is Over." *The Verge*, April 5, 2020. www.theverge.com.

Asia Pacific. n.d. "Chinese Internet Celebrities or Who Are Wang Hong?" July 5, 2019. https://as-pacific.com.

Baym, Nancy. 2015. *Personal Connections in the Digital Age.* 2nd ed. Cambridge, UK: Polity.

Berg, Madeline. 2019. "The Highest-Paid YouTube Stars of 2019: The kids Are Killing It." *Forbes*, December 18, 2019. www.forbes.com.

Cunningham, Stuart, and David Craig. 2019. *Social Media Entertainment: The New Industry at the Intersection of Hollywood and Silicon Valley*. New York: NYU Press.

Govil, Nitin. 2013. "Recognizing 'Industry.'" *Cinema Journal* 52 (3): 172–76. doi:10.1353/cj.2013.0019.

Green, Hank. 2016. "Introducing the Internet Creators Guild." *Medium*, June 16, 2016. https://medium.com.

Holt, Jennifer, and Alisa Perren. 2009. "Introduction: Does the World Really Need One More Field of Study?" In *Media Industries: History, Theory, and Method*, edited by Jennifer Holt and Alisa Perren, 1–16. Malden, MA: Wiley.

Kushner, Tony. 1995. *Angels in America: A Gay Fantasia on National Themes*. New York: Theatre Communications Group.

Lobato, Ramon, and Julian Thomas. 2015. *The Informal Media Economy*. Cambridge, UK: Polity.

Mann, Denise. 2014. "Welcome to the Unregulated Wild, Wild, Digital West." *Media Industries* 1 (2). doi:10.3998/mij.15031809.0001.206.

National Public Radio. 2019. "The Money and Trade-Offs Involved in the Influencer Economy." *All Things Considered*, June 10, 2019. www.npr.org.

O'Connor, Claire. 2017. "Forbes Top Influencers: Meet 30 Power Players Making a Fortune on Social Media." *Forbes*, April 10, 2017. www.forbes.com.

Senft, Theresa. 2008. *Camgirls: Celebrity and Community in the Age of Social Networks*. New York: Peter Lang.

Shapiro, Robert. 2018. Cofounder and chairman, Sonecon. Interview with David Craig, August 3, 2018.

Shapiro, Robert, with Siddhartha Aneja. 2018. *Unlocking the Gates: America's New Creative Economy*. Re:Create Coalition. www.recreatecoalition.org.

———. 2019. *Taking Root: The Growth of America's New Creative Economy*. Re:Create Coalition. www.recreatecoalition.org.

Shaughnessy, Haydn. 2011. "Who Are the Top 10 Influencers in Social Media?" *Forbes*, December 2, 2011. www.forbes.com.

Weiss, Geoff. 2019. "YouTube Hits 2 Billion Monthly Users, as Number of Channels with 1 Million Subscribers Doubled Last Year." *Tubefilter*, February 5, 2019. www.tubefilter.com.

Youmshajekian, Lori. 2019. "The $24 Billion Chinese Industry You've Never Heard Of." *UNSW Newsroom*, June 21, 2019. https://newsroom.unsw.edu.au.

PART I

Frameworks and Methods

1

Platform Studies

JEAN BURGESS

Why Study Platforms?

From the 2010s on, online creators and communities have become increasingly dependent on a relatively small number of digital media *platforms* (or, in Chinese, *ping tai*), which are in turn owned by some of the largest companies in the world. The social media entertainment industry (Cunningham and Craig 2019) is coextensive and symbiotic with these proprietary platforms. The biggest players include Google and YouTube (owned by Alphabet), Tencent Video and WeChat (owned by Tencent), iQiyi (controlled by Baidu), Twitter, WhatsApp and Instagram (owned by Facebook), and Facebook itself. They are all part of a commercial digital media ecosystem that is also populated by visual blogging platforms like Tumblr, livestreaming platforms like Twitch, short-video entertainment platforms like TikTok, and a plethora of niche content and crowdfunding platforms like Patreon. No doubt by the time you read this book there will be many new players, and some of the existing ones may well have departed the scene.

With regard to technology, this platform-centered situation is a significant shift away from the relatively decentralized online ecosystem that characterized the Western digital media of the late 1990s through to the middle of the first decade of this century, in which a variety of competing social networking services and DIY websites or blogs coexisted on a single, shared platform (the World Wide Web), built in turn on the public internet. Today, the most powerful digital media platforms are far more likely to run on their own, relatively closed quasi-operating systems, which tend to be used not on the open web but via proprietary apps on mobile devices. This dramatic shift is a consequence of what has been called *platformization*, defined by Anne Helmond as "the rise of the platform as the dominant infrastructural and economic model of the social web" (2015, 1), a rise that was achieved by extending the reach of and connections between social media platforms and by creating data flows and interfaces with other websites. It is through this process that a handful of companies have been able to diversify their services while concentrating their economic and cultural power over the internet. It is no exaggeration, for example, to say that in much of the world, Facebook has built a proprietary network of applications, data, and advertising that exists parasitically on top of the public internet. The Chinese platformed digital media environment has developed largely in parallel to and apart from the global internet and has its own distinctive characteristics and modes of governance (Wang and Lobato 2019).

But platformization goes beyond the internet and social media—indeed, much of the media and cultural environment now operates under a "platform paradigm" (Burgess 2015). As David Nieborg and Thomas Poell argue, platformization has resulted in "the penetration of economic, governmental, and infrastructural extensions of digital platforms into the web and app ecosystems" (2018, 4276) and hence into other industry sectors that rely on the web, especially the creative and cultural industries. In using the term *platform paradigm*, I mean not only that platforms like YouTube or Facebook have a lot of power within the information sector and creative content industries but also that their *logics*—their ways of operating and their systems of value—are more deeply reshaping our society and culture. Here I draw on José van Dijck and Poell's (2013) idea of "social media logics," in turn built on David Altheide and Robert Snow's (1979) concept of "media logic," defined by van Dijck and Poell as "a set of principles or commonsense rationality cultivated in and by media institutions that penetrates every public domain and dominates its organizing structures" (2013, 3). Van Dijck and Poell identify four principles for social media logics: programmability, popularity, connectivity, and datafication.

While all four of these principles or logics are relevant to content creators, of particular relevance to the rise of platforms is *datafication*—the extraction and collection of digital traces of cultural practices and social interactions so that they can be sorted, aggregated, analyzed, and deployed for strategic purposes. These data are exploited and shared, not only internally by single platforms like Facebook and YouTube, but also across a far more extensive ecosystem of social media companies, advertisers, and third-party intermediaries. Metrics based on these data—measures of audience engagement compared across content items, for example—can in turn shape the activities of media organizations and content creators. In the context of news, recent research has explored how mainstream news organizations are transforming in response to the social media metrics on which they increasingly depend, in a process of "institutional isomorphism" (Caplan and boyd 2018). This process of institutional isomorphism is leading, among other things, to the new forms of explicitly social-media-centered journalism associated with outlets like *BuzzFeed* and *Junkee* (Hurcombe, Burgess, and Harrington 2018).

I discuss later in this chapter how creators have played a major role in building the cultures and audiences of platforms, but it is also true that platforms have the power to make or break the careers of creators. Platform logics shape what counts as value (for example, in the form of audience attention or engagement) and how that value is measured (whether by clicks, subscriptions, watch time, or a combination of these). Platforms convert those measurements into semiautomated decisions about which content is pushed to audiences and the extent to which that content can attract advertising revenue. In order to maintain high levels of visibility, creators have to work out how to engage with each platform's features, policies, audience analytics, and data tools. As well, they must understand how a platform's various automated and semiautomated protocols for content presentation, curation, and moderation (often referred to by creators and commentators as "the algorithm") affect how likely audiences are to encounter and engage with their work. In Crystal Abidin's (2016) research with Singaporean influencers on Instagram, for example, she discusses this work of optimizing for visibility as "visibility labour." These symbiotic, affective, and often fraught relationships with platforms, data, and metrics are particularly significant for those creators whose activities are centered on a particular platform (for example, those who identify as YouTubers) as well as for those for whom social media platforms are a distributed means of audience engagement and community building but who primarily identify according to their own creative practice (for example, as fans, gamers, musical artists, or influencers). Platforms, then, are powerful cultural shapers, and the workings of platforms are of material concern and intense interest to creators; but their architectures and operations are difficult to observe.

Platforms also play a major role in governing the forms of creativity and social interaction that take place through them. They set rules about what content and behavior are allowed, even amplified, and what content and behavior are not allowed or discouraged. They enforce and change these rules through a variety of technical and policy measures, for reasons that are not always explained and that do not always seem fair to creators and user communities (Gillespie 2018; Suzor 2019). Meanwhile, creators are busy interpreting, adapting to, and in some cases deliberately subverting and gaming these platform rules and their various mechanisms of enforcement.

The other side of the story is that platforms are also partly built, shaped, and influenced by creator communities and the various creative practices and social norms they have developed. In fact, many of the features and conventions of social media platforms were collectively created by users and only later implemented by the platform. In YouTube, the vlog format, video replies, and hyperlinking between videos and channels are early examples (see Burgess and Green 2018); for Twitter, it is the hashtag, retweet, and reply feature (Burgess and Baym 2020). As other contributions to this volume show, while we cannot understand the dynamics of labor or content governance in creator cultures without taking platform power into account, creator communities are themselves by necessity very actively engaged in debates, discussions, and peer education about the hidden workings of the platforms on which their cultural practice—and, especially in the case of social media "entertainers," their livelihoods—depend.

Additionally, while the platform paradigm and its accompanying logics are general tendencies, not all platforms are the same. The designs and features of particular platforms differ in important ways, and so too do the cultures of use (the social norms and creative conventions) that have come to be associated with each of them. We might think, for example, about Twitter's distinctive mixture of social chatter, political antagonism, and global news and compare that with the cultures of visual creativity, self-expression, and coded entrepreneurialism that many people would associate with Instagram or the deep integration of professional entertainment, user-generated content, and e-commerce in Chinese video platforms like iQiyi (Wang and Lobato 2019). These differences between platform cultures are the result of the coevolution of particular user populations (with different combinations of ages, geographies, and identities), platforms' business models (their ways of operating and generating revenue), and platforms' affordances (their features and the practices these features invite). Twitter started as a geeky personal-status-update tool built for mobile and evolved into a global platform for news and debate, but its feature set has always focused primarily on text, news, and conversation; Instagram started out as a hip, mobile photography app and became a favored social platform for a diverse and global community of visual communicators. This particularity of platforms is why digital media scholars do not usually (or should not) discuss social media culture in general but instead work carefully to closely observe the distinctive cultures and conventions—the "platform vernaculars" (Gibbs et al. 2015)—of Twitter or of Instagram or of YouTube.

To study creator cultures in digital media, then, is also inevitably to study how platforms work, how creator communities are shaped by or work with their specific architectures, interfaces, and affordances, and how these creator communities in turn influence, negotiate, and resist platform cultures. Focusing particularly on YouTube, the remainder of this chapter provides an overview of platform studies approaches, a detailed discussion of how such approaches can be used to study platform-based creator cultures, and some guidelines on how these methods can be combined to help empower creator communities by enhancing and amplifying their knowledge of how platforms work.

Critical and Qualitative Approaches to Platform Studies

Platform studies is an umbrella term for holistic approaches to those entities that are understood and represent themselves as digital media platforms. Platform studies concern the technologies, interfaces, and affordances, ownership structures, business models, media- and self-representations, and governance of these entities, positioning these elements in a coevolutionary relationship with the platform's diverse cultures of use (for an extended example applied to Twitter, see Burgess and Baym 2020).[1]

Of course, even the labeling of entities like YouTube or Facebook or WhatsApp *as* platforms should be approached critically. As Tarleton Gillespie (2010) has so clearly shown, the power of the concept lies in its multivalence, or multiple meanings. That is, platforms are both *computational architectures* on which features and services (including advertising as well as third-party apps) can be built and *discursive spaces* for cultural expression and audience engagement. Exploiting these multiple meanings, the companies that own the platforms are able to appeal simultaneously to multiple sets of stakeholders, even those whose interests are not aligned—offering value to advertisers, entertainment to audiences, and infrastructures and audiences to creators, while representing themselves to regulators as neutral intermediaries—as technology companies rather than media publishers (Napoli and Caplan 2017). These contradictory discursive appeals to diverse stakeholders reveal the struggles between competing interests within platform companies and user cultures—struggles in which the most actively involved creators are both literate and highly invested.

There is also a growing number of book-length scholarly works that take particular platforms as their objects of analysis and take quite a holistic approach. The Polity Press series Digital Media and Society is the source of several rich examples, including Instagram (Leaver, Highfield, and Abidin 2019), Twitter (Murthy 2018), and my own book on YouTube (Burgess and Green 2009, 2018). In the study that led to that latter book, Joshua Green and I brought together media discourse analysis, document analysis of the YouTube company and platform itself, and an empirical exercise that, with the aid of a basic web scraper, collected thousands of videos and used them to explore the results and shaping effect of YouTube's metrics of popularity. Using this video corpus as a base, we were able to use YouTuber video testimony to investigate how creators were engaging in debate and activism with respect to the platform's emerging cultural economy. We could already see how creators were inventing new genres (from YouTube Poop to reaction videos), debating future directions (like YouTube's partner program and deals with mainstream media), and contesting norms (whether to fan flame wars or to promote a more supportive participatory culture on the platform). In short, we saw how they, alongside the developing businesses of online video and internet advertising, were shaping and contesting YouTube's distinctive creator cultures and user conventions—its platform vernaculars (Gibbs et al. 2015).

Given the increased role of automation and data-driven systems in platform operations as well as advertising and their role in defining and extracting value, platform studies also increasingly incorporates various critical approaches to platform protocols and algorithms. Karin van Es's theoretically driven forensic examination of the category of the "view" in the YouTube attention economy establishes that, "although content on YouTube is measured in various ways (through clicks and other forms of engagement), it is monetized through views" (2020, 234). Although "the view interconnects YouTube, advertisers, creators, and MCNs," van Es argues, "it is YouTube that decides how to count views and which content to monetize": "advertisers, creators, and MCNs have rather limited means to hold YouTube accountable for its procedures" (234–235). Van Es concludes that the view "helps to legitimize hierarchies on the YouTube platform," and "these hierarchies concern, and impact, participation, financial compensation, visibility, and popularity" (235).

Sophie Bishop (2018) has drawn on Taina Bucher (2017) and others to critically examine YouTube's algorithms and their impact on creators (in this case, influencers). Bishop very usefully outlines the two, intertwined approaches necessary to understand this aspect of how platforms shape culture: first, "what algorithms are doing" and, second, "what content creators think an algorithm is doing, that is to say, how YouTubers believe the YouTube recommendation algorithm operates," and thereby "how perceptions of its value systems are consciously or unconsciously incorporated into vlogging practices" (2018, 73). Bishop (2018) examines YouTube's algorithmic logics of visibility, arguing that the platform works actively to make the vast proportion of its diverse content *less* visible. Connecting this approach with creator experiences, Bishop (2019) has also explored how vernacular understandings and public discourses about the YouTube algorithm, which she calls "algorithmic gossip," work to shape individual creator "self-optimizing" practices and collective creator culture.

As Bishop's work shows, incorporating creator knowledges and experiences into platform studies is important, because their practices are visible and can be highly influential, not only over other users but also over the platforms themselves. Bucher provides a concrete example of this in her study of the YouTube Reply Girls, "a group of young women who rose to a brief moment of YouTube fame in 2012 for using their cleavage-baring bodies as thumbnails to drive traffic" (2018, 127). This technique worked for a brief period of YouTube's history, when one of the platform's features was the ability to create video responses, thumbnails of which would appear on the website in the right-hand column, alongside the original video. While video replies originated as a social networking and fan practice, YouTube's display algorithms would prioritize the more popular replies in the "related" or "recommended" videos section, incentivizing users to draw as many clicks to their video replies as possible. As Bucher explains, "the Reply Girls had found a way of exploiting the recommendation algorithm by employing various engine optimization tactics to drive traffic to their videos" (128): by displaying cleavage in the thumbnail (or "cover" image) for their videos and posting them as replies. Understandably, the videos attracted not only large numbers of clicks but also "massive down-votes by frustrated users who felt deceived or irritated by the proliferating cleavage-baring images popping up in the related feed" (128)—but the algorithm computed these down votes not as dislike but simply as "engagement" and promoted them even more. The Reply Girls' practices, intended to game the algorithm by feeding it what it seemed to want (clicks and views), may have played an important role in changing it: in 2012, YouTube announced it was changing its focus from clicks and view counts to maximizing for "watch time" and repeated viewing (Bucher 2018, 129). For Bucher, this case demonstrates the complex, dynamic, and multisided nature of power in algorithmic platforms:

If one side of the story entails content creators having to monitor the systems while feeling like a "slave to the algorithm," as the YouTuber Taryn Southern suggests, the flipside is that platform providers have to be alert as well. Power and resistance are part of the same operation, and the question is, How and with what effects are they exercised by different actors in the algorithmic assemblage? (Bucher 2018, 139–140).

As these examples show, in incorporating an understanding of creator activities, perspectives, and voices, interviews are very useful, but equally useful is public discussion about platform-specific controversies (like the algorithm changes that Bucher discusses), which can often be found in the technology press or indeed in content posted by creators around particular events and controversies occurring on the platform. Direct-to-video testimony by YouTubers and other content creators is a rich source of insider perspectives and contested community norms around content standards and commercial dimensions of life as a YouTuber.

Computational Digital Methods Using Platform APIs

Since the later part of the first decade of this century, researchers in a range of disciplines have had increasing access to public social media data and to ever-more-powerful computational methods and tools that can be used to analyze and visualize these data. These methods and tools make it possible to track large-scale patterns of platform use. For example, tracking the frequency of tweets over time on a particular hashtag can help us understand the intensity of public conversation on a topic; mapping the networks of links between Facebook pages can assist researchers in observing the emergence and clustering of political interest groups. Within critical media and communication studies, such approaches go beyond scientific observation: rather, they deliberately and reflexively use platforms' own affordances and tools—that is, the "methods of the medium" (Rogers 2013)—to critically investigate and generate public oversight of their operations and societal influence.

It is no surprise that people wanting to study platform cultures have turned to computational digital methods, because platforms are very large and complex and because they are internally ordered and structured, making large-scale data collection and analysis feasible. This makes it far easier to observe patterns across millions of tweets or YouTube videos than it was in earlier periods of web history, when similar approaches required researchers to scrape and analyze thousands of individual web pages, each with its own unique structure and design. Advances in software tools and the availability of training to use them have also made these methods accessible to humanities and social science scholars, and increasingly digital methods have become embedded and normalized in doctoral programs and even undergraduate courses.

A key affordance of platforms for research purposes has been their application programming interfaces (APIs)—encoded protocols that instruct one software application about how and within what limits it can access data from another. In our case, a software program that wants to extract metadata about YouTube channels or videos can do so—and be reasonably confident of complying with YouTube's terms of service—by connecting directly to YouTube's databases using one of the YouTube APIs. It is important to note here that while public APIs have been used extensively by researchers, they have been traditionally provided by platforms for commercial rather than public purposes. In the Web 2.0 era of the early to middle part of the first decade of this century, APIs were offered by social networking sites and user-created content platforms as a way to attract third-party tech developers to build additional features or external enhancements for the original websites, thereby improving the product and growing the audience overall.

In doing digital methods, which requires deploying the "methods of the medium" in a critical way, it is very important to appreciate how the structures and strategies of platforms can shape the questions and methods that can be used to investigate them. The choice of which kinds of information are encoded as data, the way that platform data is structured, and the rules attached to data access to public APIs both enable and inevitably influence empirical research questions and analytical techniques—that is, different platforms not only have different affordances for creators and users but have different research affordances as well. The Twitter APIs enable extensive research into time-series analyses of public discourse on a particular topic because they provide precise time stamps for each tweet and because they contain textual data that can easily be mined for hashtags. It is also common in Twitter research to map topical conversation networks because they provide data points relating to the identities of original posters, mentioned users, and replying users, with the tweet itself the unit of analysis. The YouTube APIs enable research into the comparative popularity of videos and creators because they provide view and interaction counts on videos and sub-scriber counts on channels.

Usable tools built on the Google-provided YouTube APIs, such as Bernhard Rieder's (2015) YouTube Data Tools (YTDT), have made it relatively straightforward for nontechnical researchers to access and analysis metadata that can be used to observe and investigate YouTube as a cultural system. However, the real added value for studying creator cultures comes from interpreting these data with the aid of situated, critical knowledge about creator and audience practices in the context of specific genres, communities, or issues. YouTube's "ranking cultures" were studied by Bernhard Rieder, Ariadna Matamoros-Fernández, and Òscar Coromina (2018) using a large-scale computational analysis of which videos related to particular topics were ranked as most relevant by the YouTube search algorithm, combined with a qualitative analysis of the video content. They found that different topics exhibited very different patterns of video ranking trends (or "morphologies"), with some controversial topics looking more "newsy" and unstable with regard to which videos and creators ranked most highly and others looking more stable, with predictable actors ranking at the top. The authors conclude that "YouTube's search function is highly reactive to attention cycles" but that "YouTube-native" content and creators appear to successfully negotiate these attention cycles, with "the overall presence of often (far) right leaning YouTube personalities" indicating that the platform "arranges search ranking in a way that allows highly active 'niche entrepreneurs' to gain exceptional levels of visibility" by "feeding on controversy and loyal audiences." Through a combination of digital methods and literacy in YouTube's platform vernaculars, the authors were able to "get a glimpse at complex ranking cultures that reward platform-specific strategies and audience activation through strongly opinionated expression" (Rieder, Matamoros-Fernández, and Coromina 2018, 64).

In another study, Dhiraj Murthy and Sanjay Sharma combined "social network analysis, qualitative coding, and thick data descriptive methods" to interpret comments posted on a small corpus of videos associated with the provocative music group Das Racist (2019, 191). Contrary to commonsense understandings of YouTube, in which "comments are often perceived as individual, random insults or only generalized ex-

pressions of 'hate,'" the study was able to discover that "racialized expressions also involved networked interactions" in which "hostile ideas"
were "passed through multiple parts of the comment network," both
across different videos' comment spaces and within the comment spaces
of a single video (191). The authors' findings would not have been possible either through the use of network analysis *or* through a close reading of a sample of comments alone; both were needed.

Digital-methods-enabled research has established shared approaches
and methods, largely due to the shared reliance on platform APIs and
the internal data structures of the social media platforms in question
(as discussed earlier with regard to Twitter conversation networks and
time-series analyses, for example). This has created some orthodox approaches and a common vocabulary, but it also entails an increasingly
problematic dependency on free access to data provided by the same
large proprietary platforms that we are attempting to study critically. For
example, the new "computational legal studies" approaches developed
by Nicolas Suzor and colleagues (2020) use Google/YouTube's and Twitter's own APIs to collect data on and observe the patterns in platforms'
content moderation and their public justifications for these decisions—
one of the most politically sensitive areas of platform governance and
one that is very difficult to get data on in any other way.

At the time of writing in 2020, the future of data-driven digital methods is far from certain. From the mid-2010s onward, the trend for corporate digital media platforms has been toward a far less open, more
centralized approach to innovation, alongside the growth of user data
markets—which has made the provision of open data access less appealing to platforms. At the same time, platforms are under increasing
scrutiny both because of the cultural power they have and their role in
extreme speech and the rise of Far Right subcultures and because of
growing concern around the exploitation of user data for commercial
ends without regard to privacy. As a result of these combined historical
trajectories, platform companies have gradually been restricting access to
their APIs or shuttering them altogether. These developments have had
a negative impact on creative methods and tools development and, as we
have argued elsewhere (Bruns et al. 2018), threaten public oversight of
platforms at the very moment when societal concern about their reach
and potentially harmful consequences is the highest it has ever been.

Since the operations of platforms are becoming such an acute issue of concern for creators, as well as a key site of public discourse and controversy, efforts to understand and maintain public oversight of platform protocols and algorithms are more important than ever. To forge ahead with platform studies, then, researchers will need to find ways of combining the systematic observation of platforms' activities with insights into the experiences and vernacular expertise of creators, ideally delivering value back to creator communities by sharing knowledge and analytical tools. But given the progressive lockdowns and lockouts affecting data-driven digital methods, scholars will need to get creative and to deploy forensic investigative approaches that do not always depend on platform-provided data access via APIs. The future of platform studies is hybrid digital methods.

Hybrid Digital Methods

Hybrid digital methods still use the "methods of the medium" to study platforms and their cultures of use, but they blur the boundaries between so-called quantitative and qualitative methods, use both computational and manual techniques for gathering and analyzing data and other materials, and do not necessarily rely on platform APIs. These hybrid methods are needed in order to follow the theoretical framework for the study of platforms that I established earlier in this chapter—that is, that platforms gain their distinctive characters, and change over time, through the coevolution of technologies, business models, and cultures of use (in terms of the focus of the present volume, this means creator cultures). It is therefore necessary that these different aspects be studied together and with regard to the relations among them and not separately.

An example of a hybrid digital method is the app walkthrough (Light, Burgess, and Duguay 2018). The app walkthrough allows researchers to systematically and forensically step through a platform or app interface, enabling the close observation of symbolic appeals to users, design logics, and traces of data flows, against the background of the platform's ownership structures and business model. The method can be very useful both for coming to grips with the particularities of a platform and for situating it in social, political, and economic contexts. For example, in Wang and Lobato's (2019) discussion of how Chinese video-sharing services throw into question some of the assumptions of Western platform studies, they used the app walkthrough method to examine the iQiyi interface, identifying and drawing out key distinctive elements of the platform for further critical discussion. They highlight that, contra many themes in Western critical platform studies, iQiyi does not demonstrate a trend to algorithmic personalization at an individual level and instead favors a busy aesthetic, presenting a plethora of content to users. This analysis leads the authors to observe that "iQiyi seeks to integrate its diverse audience into a common, shared, stable online television experience—in which all viewers are offered the same news, current affairs and celebrity gossip—and to didactically guide viewers towards useful content" (Wang and Lobato 2019, 365). They point to an overarching cultural logic of paternalism rather than the more familiar (to Western observers) logic of individual cultural taste. The authors conclude that "the structural integration between new and old media takes a visible form in iQiyi's interface, which rejects the Silicon Valley model of algorithmic curation in favor of a newspaper and broadcast-like organizational structure," providing "an important counterpoint to dominant strands of media theory in which platforms are associated with fragmentation, personalization, and individualization" (367). This insight is only made possible through the combination of media industry and interface analysis and requires close forensic investigations of the platform interface.

The app walkthrough can also be conducted in a qualitative social research setting, working with app users or, in the case of studying creator culture, with creators such as YouTubers or Instagram influencers. Such approaches have been discussed and modeled in depth in the study of Facebook users by Brady Robards and Siân Lincoln (2017), as well as in the context of dating-app users by Kristian Møller Jørgensen's (2016) "media go-along" method, which uses co-observation of users with mobile in hand as part of ethnographic work. In both cases, close attention is paid to the app's features and affordances at the same time as research participants are encouraged to reflect on their own practices and in particular the way those practices and the app or platform itself have changed together over time.

In *Twitter—A Biography* (2020), Nancy Baym and I undertook such a project. We used a hybrid method called the "platform biography" to tell the story of how Twitter's interface, business model, and architecture both shaped and was shaped by its user cultures. We gathered existing scholarly research on early Twitter's features and users, and we mined tech-industry materials, Twitter's official blog, and hundreds of mainstream news articles about Twitter. We drew on popular company histories of Twitter, such as the journalist Nick Bilton's book *Hatching Twitter*. We relied heavily on the Internet Archive's Wayback Machine to uncover earlier iterations of the Twitter website's interface and terms of service, as well as the many still-live blogs where early Twitter users discussed its culture, conventions, and norms in the early years. Most importantly, we undertook oral-history interviews with a small group of Twitter users, combining semistructured conversations with "scrollbacks" (Robards and Lincoln 2017) through their own archives. Through this combination of methods, we discovered that Twitter's distinctive platform culture and the struggles over that culture's direction were intimately connected to its core features: the @ (reply or mention), the # (hashtag), and the RT (retweet). When we drew all these data sources together, we saw the dynamic and often fraught interplay among stakeholders and sociotechnical actors, working together to incrementally shape Twitter's culture and to recast its possible futures. Our study showed that ideological struggles over whether the platform should be for socializing or for news have shaped the internal and external struggles over Twitter's social purpose and transformed its technical architecture, in turn transforming it into a platform that prioritizes debate and news over intimacy and fun.

Conclusion

One of the biggest challenges for researchers who want to understand the platformed media environment is also one of the biggest challenges for creators who rely on those platforms to make a living: platforms are by design relatively closed systems whose interfaces and user experiences are personalized to individual users, so it is difficult to achieve a shared or collective understanding of how they are operating and in whose interests. As some of the examples in this chapter have shown, artful combinations of critical interface analysis and ethnographic work can help to build a more holistic picture of platform culture and histories. There is much more yet-to-be-realized potential for hybrid methods— particularly the combination of ethnographic, creator-centered approaches with critical and computational digital methods—for example, conducting walkthroughs alongside creators to explore their metrics dashboards or using data visualizations of YouTube channel networks or patterns in video recommendations as prompts in interviews. The benefits to both researchers and creator communities could be significant: participatory, co-research approaches can empower creators with data about platform-wide trends and additional opportunities to engage in debates about platform logics and the broader political economy of digital media; at the same time, researchers have much to gain from being able to access the particular forms of insider knowledge about platform operations and logics that creators accumulate and share over time through their platformed labor, creative experimentation, and community-building activities.

NOTE

1. In the context of videogames, there is a parallel discussion around the establishment of a specific subfield called "platform studies," which has been accompanied by complex intradisciplinary debates (for details, see Apperley and Parikka 2018).

REFERENCES

Abidin, Crystal. 2016. "Visibility Labour: Engaging with Influencers' Fashion Brands and #OOTD Advertorial Campaigns on Instagram." *Media International Australia* 161 (1): 86–100. doi:10.1177/1329878X16665177.

Altheide, David, and Robert Snow. 1979. *Media Logic*. London: Sage.

Apperley, Thomas, and Jussi Parikka. 2018. "Platform Studies' Epistemic Threshold." *Games and Culture* 13 (4): 349–369. doi:10.1177/1555412015616509.

Bilton, Nick. 2014. *Hatching Twitter*. London: Hodder and Stoughton.

Bishop, Sophie. 2018. "Anxiety, Panic and Self-Optimization: Inequalities and the YouTube Algorithm." *Convergence* 24 (1): 69–84. doi:10.1177/1354856517736978.

———. 2019. "Managing Visibility on YouTube through Algorithmic Gossip." *New Media & Society*. doi:10.1177/1461444819854731.

Bruns, Axel, Anja Bechmann, Jean Burgess, Andrew Chadwick, Lynn Schofield Clark, William H. Dutton, Charles M. Ess, et al. 2018. "Facebook Shuts the Gate after the Horse Has Bolted, and Hurts Real Research in the Process." *Internet Policy Review*, April 25, 2018. https://policyreview.info.

Bucher, Taina. 2017. "The Algorithmic Imaginary: Exploring the Ordinary Affects of Facebook Algorithms." *Information, Communication & Society* 20 (1): 30–44. doi:10.1080/1369118X.2016.1154086.

———. 2018. "Cleavage-Control: Stories of Algorithmic Culture and Power in the Case of the YouTube 'Reply Girls.'" In *A Networked Self and Platforms, Stories, Connections*, edited by Zizi Papacharissi, 125–143. London: Routledge.

Burgess, Jean. 2015. "From 'Broadcast Yourself!' to 'Follow Your Interests': Making Over Social Media." *International Journal of Cultural Studies* 18 (3): 281–285. doi:10.1177/1367877913513684.

Burgess, Jean, and Nancy Baym. 2020. *Twitter—A Biography*. New York: NYU Press.

Burgess, Jean, and Joshua Green. 2009. *YouTube: Online Video and Participatory Culture*. Cambridge, UK: Polity.

———. 2018. *YouTube: Online Video and Participatory Culture*. 2nd ed. Cambridge, UK: Polity.

Caplan, Robyn, and danah boyd. 2018. "Isomorphism through Algorithms: Institutional Dependencies in the Case of Facebook." *Big Data & Society* 5 (1). doi:10.1177/2053951718757253.

Cunningham, Stuart, and David Craig. 2019. *Social Media Entertainment: The New Intersection of Hollywood and Silicon Valley*. New York: NYU Press.

Gibbs, Martin, James Meese, Michael Arnold, Bjorn Nansen, and Marcus Carter. 2015. "#Funeral and Instagram: Death, Social Media, and Platform Vernacular." *Information, Communication & Society* 18 (3): 255–268. doi:10.1080/1369118X.2014.987152.

Gillespie, Tarleton. 2010. "The Politics of 'Platforms.'" *New Media & Society* 12 (3): 347–364. doi:10.1177/1461444809342738.

———. 2018. *Custodians of the Internet: Platforms, Content Moderation, and the Hidden Decisions that Shape Social Media*. New Haven, CT: Yale University Press.

Helmond, Anne. 2015. "The Platformization of the Web: Making Web Data Platform Ready." *Social Media+ Society* 1 (2): 1–15. doi:10.1177/2056305115603080.

Hurcombe, Edward, Jean Burgess, and Stephen Harrington. 2018. "What's Newsworthy about 'Social News'? Characteristics and Potential of an Emerging Genre." *Journalism*. doi:10.1177/1464884918793933.

Jørgensen, Kristian Møller. 2016. "The Media Go-Along: Researching Mobilities with Media at Hand." *MedieKultur: Journal of Media and Communication Research* 32 (60). doi:10.7146/mediekultur.v32i60.22429.

Leaver, Tama, Tim Highfield, and Crystal Abidin. 2019. *Instagram: Visual Social Media Cultures*. Cambridge, UK: Polity.

Light, Ben, Jean Burgess, and Stefanie Duguay. 2018. "The Walkthrough Method: An Approach to the Study of Apps." *New Media & Society* 20 (3): 881–900. doi:10.1177/1461444816675438.

Murthy, Dhiraj. 2018. *Twitter: Social Communication in the Twitter Age*. 2nd ed. Cambridge, UK: Polity.

Murthy, Dhiraj, and Sanjay Sharma. 2019. "Visualizing YouTube's Comment Space: Online Hostility as a Networked Phenomena." *New Media & Society* 21 (1): 191–213. doi:10.1177/1461444818792393.

Napoli, Philip, and Robyn Caplan. 2017. "Why Media Companies Insist They're Not Media Companies, Why They're Wrong, and Why It Matters." *First Monday* 22 (5). doi:10.5210/fm.v22i5.7051.

Nieborg, David, and Thomas Poell. 2018. "The Platformization of Cultural Production: Theorizing the Contingent Cultural Commodity." *New Media & Society* 20 (11): 4275–4292. doi:10.1177/1461444818769694.

Rieder, Bernhard. 2015. "YouTube Data Tools." Computer software. Version 1, no. 5. https://tools.digitalmethods.net.

Rieder, Bernhard, Ariadna Matamoros-Fernández, and Òscar Coromina. 2018. "From Ranking Algorithms to 'Ranking Cultures': Investigating the Modulation of Visibility in YouTube Search Results." *Convergence* 24 (1): 50–68. doi:10.1177/1354856517736982.

Robards, Brady, and Siân Lincoln. 2017. "Uncovering Longitudinal Life Narratives: Scrolling Back on Facebook." *Qualitative Research* 17 (6): 715–730. doi:10.1177/1468794117700707.

Rogers, Richard. 2013. *Digital Methods*. Cambridge, MA: MIT Press.

Suzor, Nicolas. 2019. *Lawless: The Secret Rules That Govern Our Digital Lives*. Cambridge: Cambridge University Press.

———. 2020. "Understanding Content Moderation Systems: New Methods to Understand Internet Governance at Scale, over Time, and across Platforms." In *Computational Legal Studies: The Promise and Challenge of Data-Driven Legal Research*, edited by Ryan Whalen. Cheltenham, UK: Edward Elgar.

van Dijck, José, and Thomas Poell. 2013. "Understanding Social Media Logic." *Media and Communication* 1 (1): 2–14.

van Es, Karin. 2020. "YouTube's Operational Logic: 'The View' as Pervasive Category." *Television & New Media* 21 (3): 223–39. doi:10.1177/1527476418818986.

Wang, Wilfred, and Ramon Lobato. 2019. "Chinese Video Streaming Services in the Context of Global Platform Studies." *Chinese Journal of Communication* 12 (3): 356–371. doi:10.1080/17544750.2019.1584119.

2

Productive Ambivalence, Economies of Visibility, and the Political Potential of Feminist YouTubers

ZOË GLATT AND SARAH BANET-WEISER

I'm gonna talk about my responsibility as a YouTuber, as an Internet cousin, as someone you just know from within the confines of this screen, of this box, of this device, of the 1s and 0s—you know what I'm saying—of the algorithm that brought me to you. What's my responsibility to you?
—Evelyn from the Internets (2017)

Evelyn from the Internets is one of many YouTube content creators who use their platform to express progressive political values, as well as to entertain viewers, to brand herself (Evelyn sells a variety of merchandise with her "Magical Black Girl" slogan), and to promote products from sponsors. In this particular video, Evelyn talks about what her responsibility is to her followers. She says she wants to "feel all these feelings" with them but also discusses how her job is not to engage in "Internet rage" about the world. Though she notes that these kinds of reactions are justified, she positions herself as a "Capri Sun when you are thirsty," aiming for her content to be refreshing, light, and enjoyable. Clearly her answer to the question that titles the video, "Do I Have to Be an Internet Social Justice Warrior?!," is no. She ends by saying that this video is sponsored by Audible by Amazon and recommends the African American author Ta-nehesi Coates's book *Between the World and Me* as part of her sponsorship.

Evelyn is just one of many YouTube content creators who emphasize contemporary political issues and controversies around gender, race, and sexuality. While others are not as explicit as Evelyn on the question of a YouTuber's responsibility to their followers, we begin with this example because we are interested in the relationships that are constructed and assumed between feminist content creators and their followers and the way feminist politics partly form the parameters of these relationships. Of all the social media platforms that have garnered attention in the past decade for the promises of widespread access for ordinary individuals, perhaps none has achieved the kind of visibility that YouTube has, as the world's most popular site for online video. Here, entrepreneurial content creators are harnessing the platform to build their own brands within the emerging social media entertainment industry, or SME (Cunningham and Craig 2019). Feminist content is a well-established genre on YouTube, in which creators post political and social commentary on topics such as intersectionality, politics, gender, and sexual identity alongside comedic, lifestyle, and personality-driven fare. While looking to advance feminist cultural agendas, these creators are situated within an economy of visibility (Banet-Weiser 2018), incentivized to adopt certain norms and trends if they wish to garner likes, views, and subscribers. We situate these creators, and their content, within the cultural context of popular feminism. Popular feminism is part of a larger context of what Catherine Rottenberg (2018) has called "neoliberal feminism," where corporate- and media-friendly feminist expressions achieve a heightened visibility, and expressions that critique patriarchal structure and systems of racism and violence are often obscured (McRobbie 2009; Rottenberg 2018; Banet-Weiser 2018). In other words, many of these creators both advance and profit from popular feminism: brand-safe feminist discourses that dovetail comfortably with neoliberal agendas. Seeing and hearing a safely affirmative feminism, in spectacularly visible ways, often eclipses a feminist critique of structure; the visibility of popular feminism on YouTube is important, but it often stops there, as *visibility*. That said, the platform has also provided a cultural space for more marginal groups and radical left-wing politics to flourish; the visibility of diverse, LGBTQ, and gender-fluid identities on YouTube far outstrips its broadcast-media counterparts.

YouTube has been lauded as a utopian space for ordinary users outside the greedy hands of corporate gatekeepers, as it simultaneously has been vilified as the height of narcissistic self-branding, threatening "authentic" media production with its insatiable appetite for young, superficial content creators. As with every development of a new technology, a utopic/dystopic discourse frames YouTube's creation and reception, and, we argue, as many scholars have about emerging media technologies, this framing does not help push us forward to a more nuanced analysis of the cultural impact of YouTube. Here, we attempt such a nuanced analysis by positioning feminist YouTube content within what Jean Burgess and Joshua Green (2018) have called a "cultural system," one that provides both openings and foreclosures for specific kinds of cultural and political participation. We situate our analysis within the broad context of popular feminism, comprising neoliberal feminist images, expressions, and practices that circulate with speed and reach on multiple media platforms (Banet-Weiser 2018).

Specifically, we theoretically frame our analysis within the popular feminist economies of visibility and, following the feminist theorists Clare Hemmings (2018a) and Lauren Berlant (2008), an interrelated theoretical analytic of productive ambivalence, to analyze content creators in a cultural, economic, and social context of popular feminism. The work of feminist content creators on YouTube is complex, and we resist a reductive explanatory frame here. YouTube has been celebrated by many people as a platform that has enabled far more diverse screen representations of race, gender, and sexuality than television and film media, as is undoubtedly the case. However, feminist YouTube creators have to navigate what are often contradictory pressures in order to gain visibility and earn a living, such as appealing to commercial brands while simultaneously maintaining authenticity and relatability with their audiences (Cunningham and Craig 2017). With this framework of ambivalence, we aim to complicate the dominance of popular feminism online by asking, To what extent are professional YouTube content creators able to present more radical versions of feminism or else pushed to fit into neoliberal brand culture in order to gain visibility and income?

The Context of Popular Feminism: Economies of Visibility and Productive Ambivalence

We examine YouTubers who can be positioned within a broad context of "popular feminism," which Banet-Weiser (2018) defines as a contemporary feminist media environment that relies on the (relatively) broad accessibility and reach of digital and social media to circulate particular feminist messages. Part of the "popular" of popular feminism indicates that some versions and iterations of feminism will become more visible than others, and because popular feminism often depends on the affordances of capitalist media platforms for circulation, the versions that have the most heightened visibility are typically those that are aligned with capitalist logic (see also Rottenberg 2018).

But another element of popular feminism involves the various power struggles on popular cultural terrains (such as YouTube), where different expressions and practices compete for dominance. We see these kinds of navigations within feminist YouTubers, where some of the most "popular" (defined by numbers of followers) are precisely those who create content about topics that have less visibility in mainstream media, such as trans and queer issues. Again, the political potentialities of YouTube as a platform for social change are often framed within a utopic/dystopic binary: either it is described as a space where freedom of expression reigns, unfettered by corporate gatekeepers, confidently leading to social change, or it is a completely colonized media platform with the sole purpose of capital accumulation. Remaining within this binary is unproductive, not least because it both over- and underestimates what media platforms can do as a starting point for social change. That is, because media platforms are structured by algorithms organized by capitalist logic, it does not make sense to insist that they enable freedom of expression. On the other hand, capitalism is not always organized in predictable and stable ways, so media platforms such as YouTube can exploit this instability. As the second-most-popular website in the world, preceded only by its parent company, Google (Collins 2019), YouTube is undoubtedly a central player in the current social media ecosystem. Since its inception in 2005, YouTube has accumulated over 1.9 billion logged-in users each month, 500 hours of content uploaded every minute, and over 1 billion hours of content watched daily (YouTube, n.d.). Yet, when digital media platforms such as YouTube become so central in such a rapid period of time, it is tempting to definitively claim what YouTube *is*. In a time of information glut, constant media circulation, dis- and misinformation, and political upheavals, we often reach for certainties about media and what they apparently can do with regard to political and social change. We seek to provide distinct parameters around media platforms, as if having control over the theoretical definition of media platforms and media use will allow us to have control in other realms of cultural life.

We argue, however, that the ambivalence we see framing many feminist content creators on YouTube offers conflicting and often contradictory feminist politics, and it is precisely these conflicting views that we find the most productive to make sense of contemporary feminist politics. As Clare Hemmings points out in her work on feminist ambivalence, feminist politics often disavow feminism even as they retain critiques of gender relations; this contradiction is often "the result of a complex set of negotiations all gendered subjects make and that cannot always be resolved" (2018a, 75). Contemporary popular feminist politics achieve a heightened visibility, which competes with an equally heightened visibility of popular misogyny, increasing normalizations of racism and white nationalism, and the emergence of the Far Right across the globe. Rather than insist that feminist content creators are either enabling or inhibiting feminist politics, or rather than insist on the *certainty* of feminist politics on YouTube, we follow Hemmings in her resistance to the notion that such politics can be completely "knowable." As Hemmings argues, "The uncertainty that characterizes feminist and queer understandings of gender, race, and sexuality in the present is easily obscured through propositions of certainty about precisely these central concerns. In imagining that we know how to ameliorate gendered, racial, and sexual inequalities, or indeed what gender, race, and sexuality *are*, it is easy to miss the profound ambivalence about these terms and the inequalities or pleasures that cluster around them" (2018b, 1).

We see this kind of political ambivalence in a battle with what Banet-Weiser has called an economy of visibility. Economies of visibility describe the ways in which visibility of particular identities and politics, such as gender, race, and sexuality, circulates on multiple media platforms. While this visibility is important for public awareness, it also potentially becomes an end in itself, such that "visibility is all there is" (Banet-Weiser 2018, 21). That is, through what Herman Gray (2005) has called a "politics of representation," to be recognized in a media economy becomes a kind of politics. This kind of recognition typically defies a reading of political ambivalence; the image or visibility of politics is the beginning and the end of those politics. Yet these analytics are interrelated; as Hemmings points out, a political ambivalence "runs counter to a rights-based approach that characterizes the twentieth century as one of increased recognition (or a lament about lack of recognition, or misrecognition), focusing attention instead on what is lost through a politics of certainty" (2018a, 6). While recognizing that there are blurred boundaries between political ambivalence and economies of visibility, we nonetheless analyze feminist YouTubers within this typology, finding that while there are some similar messages across different feminist YouTube channels, there are also those who are seeking increased recognition and visibility within a capitalist framework and some who are better characterized as politically ambivalent, more complex and contradictory. Following Hemmings, we seek to "foreground the importance of current complexity, despite our desire to have resolved both past and present paradoxes" (2018a, 18). We hope to tease out the tensions, identifications, and disidentifications within the analytics of political ambivalence and economies of visibility by investigating some contemporary creators on YouTube as they navigate two intersecting approaches to feminist content creation: (1) *transactional,* working within a popular feminist economy of visibility concurrent with capitalist logics, and (2) *transformational,* the ambivalent process of attaining visibility within YouTube's attention economy as a route to radical social change.

Content Creation as Transactional

In a short period of time, being a "YouTube star" has become a career aspiration, especially for young people. Unrealistic expectations about making money sustain this aspiration of YouTube stardom; in reality, according to Bloomberg, 97 percent of all aspiring YouTubers probably will not make it above the US poverty line, which is about $12,000 a year, and only 3 percent actually make a living wage (Stokel-Walker 2018a). YouTube is fundamentally structured by an attention economy, wherein the careers of content creators across every genre live and die by the same set of metrics: views, watch time, subscribers, and likes. There are many ways in which content creators make money, and the received wisdom in the online video community is that a diversity of revenue streams is essential for success, due to the unpredictability of the industry as a whole. AdSense revenue, brand collaborations, selling merchandise or books, live shows and appearances, crowdfunding on Patreon, and spreading earnings across different platforms are all part of a well-rounded income. YouTube is a highly transactional platform, and content creators are required to cultivate appealing (that is, normalized) self-brands, loyal audiences, and popular content, all while keeping up with the frenetic pace of content output favored by YouTube's infamous algorithm. Burnout has been one of the most discussed issues in the YouTube creator community, a reflection of creators' precarious and stressful working conditions on a wildly overcrowded platform with opaque systems for both the recommendation and demonetization of videos (Stokel-Walker 2018b).

The creators we position within this transactional framework are those who circulate on an economy of visibility; they merge "safe" feminist politics with corporate sponsorship, and they build their own brand through supporting corporate brands. In essence, YouTube content creators are jack-of-all-trades entrepreneurs within a highly competitive industry, simultaneously videographers, editors, on-screen talent, brand ambassadors, merchandise producers, marketers, and PR reps, and they must find ways to monetize their content if they wish to sustain careers in SME. In other words, the transactional element of content creators is not only about actual cash but also about building a flexible self-brand, one that might find traction in the broader social media network. The *self* here is not seen as a stable entity rooted in some kind of essentialist human nature or psychoanalytic conception of unconscious identity formation but rather as something produced by dominant cultural narratives "intent on constant innovation and flexibility" (Hearn 2008, 197). Alison Hearn argues that in recent years practices of branding have moved away from the direct marketing of particular products to a more ambient and abstract attachment of feelings and associations to objects that may then condition consumer behaviors. A brand is no longer just a simple commodity but rather an "entire virtual context for consumption" (199). Branding is a broad system that validates the neoliberal project: "In a world marked by increasing flexibility and flux, branding works to fix, albeit temporarily and tentatively, cultural meaning around consumption, producing aestheticized modes of justification for life under capital" (199).

To borrow a phrase from Andrew Wernick, YouTubers become commodity signs that "function in circulation both as . . . object(s)-to-be-sold and as the bearer(s) of a promotional message" (1991, 16). You-Tubers' incomes are diverse, based on advertising revenue calculated by viewer figures, sponsorship deals, and broader projects such as merchandise and book sales. But in order to receive any of these revenue streams, YouTubers must first sell themselves by cultivating an appealing personal brand (Glatt 2017). Every self-brand must have a narrative; as Banet-Weiser wrote in 2012 about YouTube, "The almost inevitable presence of commercial brands as structuring narratives for YouTube videos indicates that self-presentation does not imply simply *any* narrative of the self, created within an endlessly open cultural script, but one that makes sense within a cultural and economic recognizable and predetermined images, texts, beliefs, and values" (2012, 66). While the platform has grown tremendously since 2012, it remains true that there are thousands of YouTubers (a career that barely existed in 2012) who post content about their everyday lives, trials, and tribulations, creating narratives of the self. It also remains true that most of these narratives, particularly the ones that are monetized, continue to make sense within the logics of consumer capitalism. Brooke Erin Duffy (2017) calls this kind of economic activity "aspirational labor," describing a context where women largely populate many of the most visible genres of social media production, when digital media in general is crucial to the heightened visibility of popular feminism. As Duffy theorizes, the successes of only a very few women in digital spaces mobilizes a general ethos that "everyone" can be creative and succeed (McRobbie 2016; see also Littler 2018 on the myths of meritocracy). In an article in *Millennial Money* offering advice about becoming a YouTube star, the author Grant Sabatier (who describes himself as a "Millennial Millionaire") encourages people to become YouTubers with the enticing promise of "getting paid to do something you love, receiving praise from millions of fans, working with a flexible schedule, and enjoying other countless perks of being a You-Tube star" (2019).

An archetypal example of this transactional framework is Melanie Murphy, a thirty-year-old content creator from Dublin, Ireland. She has been on YouTube for seven years and has over 649,000 subscribers to her channel (as of May 2020). While Murphy does not brand herself as a feminist, she (and her content) clearly fall within the popular feminist genre, in that she intersperses general life vlogging content with discussions about issues such as her bisexuality, dating life, mental health, body image, and sexual health/periods. For example, her 2018 video "Vulva/Vagina Chat + Routine! (Periods, Shaving, Odour & More)" begins with Murphy saying she is doing a follow-up video from a previous one that "did really really well and you guys seemed to like it." She then says, "And just like that last video, this one is sponsored by Always, who are the global leader in vaginal hygiene products. I've used Always since I was a little girl. I love the brand." She continues by mentioning Always's participation in the End Period Poverty campaign and ends with an enthusiastic "I *love* Always and how much they protect my underpants. 'Cause I don't own too many pairs of underpants." With this beginning, Murphy accomplishes a number of things: she reassures her followers that she listens and responds to them by creating a follow-up to a popular video on her channel; she announces her sponsorship with Always and legitimates both the brand and her own sponsorship by mentioning the company's work in a feminist campaign; and she presents herself and the video as down-to-earth, not a shill for a corporation but just a simple woman who likes to protect her underpants. The thirteen-minute video is largely educational about feminine hygiene, detailing the differences between the vagina and vulva and mentioning tips for cleansing, shaving, and maintaining female genitalia. This video exemplifies the cultural norms of intimacy and authenticity that are vital aspects of the creator-audience relationship, as many scholars of YouTube have noted (Banet-Weiser 2012; Bishop 2018; Cocker and Cronin 2017; Cunningham, Craig, and Silver 2016; Cunningham and Craig 2017; Jorge, Marôpo, and Nunes 2018; Raun 2018). Audiences are savvy about content creators being paid by brands to sell products, but even within that context, transparency and authenticity are valued. As Banet-Weiser wrote in 2012, principles of contemporary branding authorize branding the self as authentic, "because self-branding is seen not as an imposition of a concept or product by corporate culture but rather as the individual taking on the project herself as a way to access her 'true' self" (61). YouTube creators must be careful only to engage in brand-sponsored videos that dovetail with their own self-brands, particularly in the case of politically or ethically motivated content, so as not to undermine the trust they have cultivated with their viewers and appear "inauthentic." It is mutually beneficial for content creators and corporate brands to do collaborations such as this.

Content creators offer brands like Always greater exposure and cultural capital with younger audiences, while brands offer creators a certain legitimacy, as well as exciting content to film and of course significant remuneration. For creators who are able and willing to attract brand collaborations, these sorts of campaigns tend to be far more lucrative than AdSense revenue, merchandise sales, or crowdfunding.

Feminist content creators interpret and renegotiate YouTube's systems and structures and come up with what Michel de Certeau (1984) would call "tactics" to earn income in ways that preferably align with both their values and their self-brands. There is a tension here for feminist content creators between needing either to fit into the brand-friendly logics of YouTube (via lucrative brand collaborations, sponsorships, and ad revenue) or else to make money through alternative means (such as crowdfunding, merchandise sales, or separate employment). Crucially, in this chapter, we are not critiquing any individual creator but rather the structural factors of this industry that embraces certain people to partake in neoliberal brand culture while denying this opportunity to other, more marginal identities. On YouTube, brandable feminist expressions are those that connect social change with capitalism, those that are politically unthreatening to the status quo, and those that emphasize individual attributes commensurate with neoliberal self-reliance, such as confidence, gumption, and entrepreneurialism.

While the competitive and hierarchical structure of YouTube's attention economy blends smoothly with neoliberal logics, and the financial incentives for fitting into brand discourses are enticing, the extent to which individual feminist content creators embrace these values varies greatly. Some resist the pressures to ally with corporate culture or else are too radical to be accepted by it and therefore have to earn income via other means, most often through crowdfunding and selling merchandise. With this in mind, we now move on to what we term the *transformational* axis, a deeply ambivalent process whereby creators attain visibility within YouTube's attention economy as a route to radical social change.

Content Creation as Transformational

Within the general context of transactional content creation on YouTube, we can also see how some productions work to transform hegemonic power relations. Part of this transformational element involves the relative openness of the media platform; for example, the media scholar Aymar Jean Christian founded a web TV platform, Open TV, to develop queer, intersectional television as a way to advance our thinking on networked representation, challenging the notion that television development must be large scale in order to restructure representation. Platforms like Open TV and particular subsections of YouTube demonstrate that it is possible to successfully distribute independent media production, original series, vlogs, and other formats that are created by marginalized communities, including queer, transgender, non-White, and female producers. However, the notion that some YouTube content creators can work to transform hegemonic dynamics of power regarding gender, sexuality, and race does not mean an uncritical embrace of YouTube's political possibilities. Rather, we see these content creators articulating politics and positionalities that are not as easily brandable as some forms of popular feminism, while deploying a variety of tactics to circumvent the oppressive elements of YouTube's systems in order to be able to earn a living. Utilizing the combined analytics of political ambivalence and economies of visibility, in this section we turn our attention to the ways in which some of the YouTube creators who represent more marginal identities and radical politics on the platform are trying to cultivate their self-brands and careers under conditions of precarity.

As explored in the previous section, only certain feminist expressions and politics on YouTube are easily brandable and able to merge with market logics, while other, more marginal identities face additional obstacles in the pursuit of a sustainable career in this industry. Nowhere is this marginalization made clearer than in the ongoing struggles that LGBTQ+ YouTube creators have had with their content being demonetized and age restricted due to not being "advertiser and family friendly," despite YouTube presenting itself as a champion of the LGBTQ+ community (see, for example, Hunt 2017; Khaled 2019). At a panel called "Not Suitable for Advertisers" at VidCon USA 2018, the world's biggest annual conference for online video, one of the authors of this chapter witnessed a discussion between creators deploring YouTube for valuing the interests of advertisers above those of its LGBTQ+ creators as a result of the infamous Adpocalypse. In 2017, in response to brands pulling their advertisements from the platform because they were being paired with unsavory videos, YouTube tightened the algorithmic system that identifies content deemed to be "advertiser friendly," leading to a huge wave of user-generated videos being demonetized and deselected for recommendation to viewers. Creators reported videos with any reference to LGBTQ+ issues being automatically demonetized and age restricted, resulting in a loss of revenue for creators and, vitally important, a loss of visibility. One creator said a friend of theirs had decided not to come out on YouTube for fear of algorithmic discrimination, particularly appalling considering that the LGBTQ+ community has long been an integral part of YouTube culture. At this panel, creators discussed the various tactics they were employing to overcome this structural inequality and regain visibility and income. One creator said that they had started to remove any reference to LGBTQ+ issues in the tags and titles of their videos to avoid algorithmic penalization, but, as they noted, this had the adverse effect of rendering their videos unsearchable to their target audience. For a platform fundamentally structured by algorithmic recommendation systems, making particular identities invisible as a result of pressures from advertisers raises serious questions about the role of YouTube as a curator of public discourse (Gillespie 2010).

A common approach employed by marginalized creators is to minimize their reliance on YouTube's advertising and recommendation systems by cultivating alternative revenue streams via community crowdfunding (predominantly on Patreon but also on tipping apps such as PayPal and YouTube's own "sponsor" feature) and selling merchandise. Thirty-year-old American creator Natalie Wynn, also known as ContraPoints, provides a particularly interesting example. She is a trans creator who posts exquisitely produced long-form video essays on topics such as gender, philosophy, the alt-right, and race, with an aim to "counterbalance the hatred toward progressive movements that is so common online" (Wynn, n.d.). Wynn has been celebrated as a creator who is exceptionally good at communicating progressive politics with misogynistic and alt-right audiences (Cross 2018). As Wynn states in her Patreon description, "Stylistically, I try to appeal to a wide audience and avoid merely preaching to the choir. I try to make the videos I'd want to watch: well-produced, informative, funny, and entertaining" (Wynn, n.d.). She has had remarkable success on YouTube, with over 916,000 subscribers (as of May 2020) and around one million views per video, despite refusing to conform to YouTube's algorithmically encouraged cultural norm of posting a high volume of content. She posts only one video a month, a far cry from the multiple uploads a week recommended for increasing visibility, and actively chooses not to participate in brand sponsorships. As she tweeted back in November 2017, "People ask all the time whether my videos are demonetized. Yes. Pretty much all of them are, and many are also age-restricted. I don't complain about it though because I'm the queen of Patreon." As she continues in a comment, "The age restriction is more of a problem because it negatively affects view count" (Wynn 2017). In response to the discrimination that Wynn faces with regard to visibility and income, as a result of her channel's radical and progressive subject matter, her business model relies instead on selling merchandise and crowdfunding on Patreon, where she has 12,400 patrons who give her monthly donations (there are tiers of $2, $5, $10, $15, and $20) in exchange for exclusive perks such as access to monthly "Ask Me Anything" streams and "immortality in the credits of each new video" (Wynn, n.d.). Aside from generating revenue, the benefit of having an active Patreon community is that it divorces the creator-audience relationship from YouTube's recommendation system, which is notorious for not notifying subscribers when new content is released.

While ContraPoints is an example of a radical feminist creator who has managed to cultivate a successful and relatively stable career on YouTube without completely allying with neoliberal brand culture, this is challenging to achieve and not always possible. It depends on capturing the attention of a large audience and converting this creator-audience relationship into a financial transaction whereby the audience feels moved to donate money. In other words, while these types of creators may resist some of the ad-centered business model of YouTube, they are not anticapitalist. Indeed, there are many progressive creators who occupy a more ambivalent position, whereby they attain visibility and income in part by collaborating with corporate brands, as a route to radical social change. Kat Blaque is a Californian black trans creator who has been posting videos on YouTube for more than ten years and an example of one of the more radical feminist creators on the platform. She is known and loved by her community for her outspoken and "real" approach to controversial subject matter such as transphobia, misogyny, racism, and sexual violence. Much like Wynn, Blaque has faced demonetization on the platform because her content has not been deemed "advertiser friendly," and as a result she has also attempted to gain income directly from her audience. As she reminded her followers in February 2019 via Twitter, "My last two videos were demonetized. If you support my stuff, remember you can always tip" (Blaque 2019a), and she goes on to list her Venmo, Cashapp, and PayPal profiles, as well as her Patreon page.

However, Blaque has found herself and other "LeftTube" creators (the community of left-wing YouTubers who make political commentary and philosophical content, also known as "BreadTube") receiving critique from audiences for producing anticapitalist content while also seeking remuneration via crowdfunding, selling merchandise, and sponsorships. During the process of writing this chapter, Blaque most fortuitously posted a twenty-four-minute video as part of her weekly "True Tea" series, titled "Why Is Left Tube So Sponsored? | Kat Blaque," in which she responds to these critiques. In her usual style of transparency, she explains that it is expensive and precarious to work full-time as a YouTube content creator and that she is barely earning enough to pay rent and buy food for herself. "I don't think that it's fair to chastise people living under a capitalistic system for using capitalism to survive," she argues. "I'm an artist. . . . If you like what I do, you support what I do, then you shouldn't shame me for wanting to make it" (Blaque 2019b). She concedes that there are valid arguments to be made, particularly when it comes to sponsorships, but that creators do not always have the luxury of choice:

> I'm going to try to do some sponsorships that are always in line with my morals, but maybe I'm not going to be able to have that decision. This is the unfortunate reality of being a creator, right? This is how we make our income, this is how we make our living, by allowing people to sell things on our content. I would love to do that in a way that feels very seamless, in a way that seems very natural. I want to be sponsored by things that I do believe in. I don't want to sell you bullshit. I really, truly don't. [But]

I'm not going to prevent myself from making a smart business decision that's going to ultimately feed me and keep me doing this. (Blaque 2019b)

In the description below the video are her usual links to three different tipping platforms, Venmo, Cashapp, and PayPal, as well as to her Patreon page and merchandise store, and information for how to hire her as a public speaker.

We understand creators like Kat Blaque and Ash Hardell, a popular nonbinary creator who makes educational content about trans issues, sexuality, and mental health and who regularly engages in brand sponsorships (recent collaborations include Adam and Eve's gender-nonconforming lingerie, Dollar Shave Club, and Verizon in conjunction with the LGBTQ+ nonprofit PFLAG), as occupying deeply ambivalent, and at times contradictory, political positionalities within YouTube's economy of visibility. These creators are seeking recognition within a capitalist framework, while also using this platform to promote progressive, intersectional, and queer politics. As we have explored, this is in large part a problem of structural inequality, whereby creators are marginalized and forced to overcome algorithmic invisibility and demonetization as a result of their radical content and positionalities.

The Limits of YouTube

In a video titled "Do I Have Privilege?," the queer feminist creator and LGBTQ+ advocate Rowan Ellis (2018) breaks down the concepts of privilege and intersectionality. She explains that while she is marginalized as a queer woman, she is still the benefactor of white, able-bodied, middle-class privilege. The concepts of privilege and intersectionality are foundational to the argument we have presented in this chapter. Those who slot easily into popular feminist "brand-safe" discourses, namely, white, heterosexual, cis-gendered, and middle-class women, face significantly less adversity in their plight to build sustainable careers as content creators. Those who represent more radical positions and marginal identities, particularly creators who inhabit multiple intersections of marginality, such as Kat Blaque, face far greater barriers to earning a living and achieving visibility in the social media entertainment industry. The work of feminist content creators on YouTube is complex, requiring the navigation of often contradictory pressures. Our point in analyzing these videos as "transactional" or "transformational" is not to say that there are defined borders that separate these two aspirations but rather to say that it makes more sense to think about the feminist politics of YouTube creators within a framework of political ambivalence. To return to Hemmings, approaching identities such as gender, race, and sexuality as "knowable" denies the ways that all identities are always problematic and pleasurable, often at the same time. All of the feminist content creators mentioned in this chapter aspire to be transactional, if not actually to make a living, then to build a self-brand. YouTube's algorithm is designed to render some content more visible than others, and the logic of this asymmetry is based on profitability. In line with this logic, videos that are "brand safe" and have preroll advertisements on them get offered up to a wider audience than those that do not. In this way, content creators are steered not only toward making content that is aligned with corporate culture in order to earn AdSense revenue but also toward being promoted algorithmically, in other words, to be seen. We started this chapter by asking to what extent professional YouTube content creators are able to present more radical versions of feminism or else pushed to fit into neoliberal brand culture in order to gain visibility and income. The answer we have arrived at is, as promised, deeply ambivalent. While we have seen the emergence of exciting queer, intersectional, and progressive political content on YouTube working to transform hegemonic power relations, this content is fundamentally built on a platform designed with the capitalist logics of competition, hierarchy, and inequality. So, while some content creators aspire to be "transformational"—to change social norms, to challenge discrimination, to disrupt systems of power—as long as this kind of transformation is also transactional, there is a limit to its progressive potential.

REFERENCES

Banet-Weiser, Sarah. 2012. *Authentic™: The Politics of Ambivalence in a Brand Culture.* New York: NYU Press.

———. 2018. *Empowered: Popular Feminism and Popular Misogyny.* Durham, NC: Duke University Press.

Berlant, Lauren. 2008. *The Female Complaint: The Unfinished Business of Sentimentality in American Culture.* Durham, NC: Duke University Press.

Bishop, Sophie. 2018. "Anxiety, Panic and Self-Optimisation: Inequalities and the YouTube Algorithm." *Convergence: The International Journal of Research into New Media Technologies* 24 (1): 69–84. doi:10.1177/1354856517736978.

Blaque, Kat. 2019a. @Kat_Blaque Twitter post, February 17, 2019. https://twitter.com/kat_blaque/status/1097255564629860354.

———. 2019b. "Why Is Left Tube So Sponsored? | Kat Blaque." YouTube video, July 31, 2019. www.youtube.com/watch?v=-rjao8RY8Sk.

Burgess, Jean, and Joshua Green. 2018. *YouTube: Online Video and Participatory Culture.* 2nd ed. Cambridge, UK: Polity.

Cocker, Hayley, and James Cronin. 2017. "Charismatic Authority and the YouTuber: Unpacking the New Cults of Personality." *Marketing Theory* 17 (4): 455–472. doi:10.1177/1470593117692022.

Collins, Jerri. 2019. "The Top 10 Most Popular Sites of 2019." *Lifewire*, June 24, 2019. www.lifewire.com.

Cross, Katherine. 2018. "The Oscar Wilde of YouTube Fights the Alt-Right with Decadence and Seduction." *The Verge*, August 24, 2018. www.theverge.com.

Cunningham, Stuart, and David Craig. 2017. "Being 'Really Real' on YouTube: Authenticity, Community and Brand Culture in Social Media Entertainment." *Media International Australia* 164 (1): 71–81. doi:10.1177/1329878X17709098.

———. 2019. *Social Media Entertainment: The New Intersection of Hollywood and Silicon Valley.* New York: NYU Press.

Cunningham, Stuart, David Craig, and John Silver. 2016. "YouTube, Multichannel Networks and the Accelerated Evolution of the New Screen Ecology." *Convergence: The International Journal of Research into New Media Technologies* 22 (4): 376–391. doi:10.1177/1354856516641620.

de Certeau, Michel. 1984. *The Practice of Everyday Life.* Translated by Steven Rendall. Berkeley: University of California Press.

Duffy, Brooke Erin. 2017. *(Not) Getting Paid to Do What You Love: Gender, Social Media, and Aspirational Work.* New Haven, CT: Yale University Press.

Ellis, Rowan. 2018. "Do I Have Privilege?" YouTube video, January 21, 2018. www.youtube.com/watch?v=WZPK57Qv7jo.

Evelyn from the Internets. 2017. "Do I Have to Be an Internet Social Justice Warrior?!" YouTube video, January 31, 2017. www.youtube.com/watch?v=AxJDnDRbu6M.

Gillespie, Tarleton. 2010. "The Politics of 'Platforms.'" *New Media & Society* 12 (3): 347–364. doi:10.1177/1461444809342738.

Glatt, Zoë. 2017. "The Commodification of YouTube Vloggers." Master's thesis, Digital Media, Goldsmiths, University of London.

Gray, Herman. 2005. *Cultural Moves: African Americans and the Politics of Representation.* Berkeley: University of California Press.

Hearn, Alison. 2008. "'Meat, Mask, Burden': Probing the Contours of the Branded 'Self.'" *Journal of Consumer Culture* 8 (2): 197–217. doi:10.1177/1469540508090086

Hemmings, Clare. 2018a. *Considering Emma Goldman: Feminist Political Ambivalence and the Imaginative Archive.* Durham, NC: Duke University Press.

———. 2018b. "A Feminist Politics of Ambivalence: Reading with Emma Goldman." *Revista Estudos Feministas, Florianópolis* 26 (3): 1–11. doi:10.1590/1806-9584-2018v26n358564.

Hunt, Elle. 2017. "LGBT Community Anger over YouTube Restrictions Which Make Their Videos Invisible." *The Guardian*, March 20, 2017. www.theguardian.com.

Jorge, Ana, Lidia Marôpo, and Thays Nunes. 2018. "'I Am Not Being Sponsored to Say This': A Teen YouTuber and Her Audience Negotiate Branded Content." *Observatorio* 2018:76–96. doi:10.15847/obsOBS0001382.

Khaled, A. 2019. "A History of YouTube Undermining Its LGBT+ Creators." *Medium*, June 5, 2019. https://medium.com.

Littler, Jo. 2018. *Against Meritocracy: Culture, Power and the Myths of Mobility*. New York: Routledge.

McRobbie, Angela. 2009. *The Aftermath of Feminism: Gender, Culture and Social Change*. London: Sage.

———. 2016. *Be Creative: Making a Living in the New Culture Industries*. Cambridge, UK: Polity.

Murphy, Melanie. 2018. "Vulva/Vagina Chat + Routine! (Periods, Shaving, Odour & More) | ad." YouTube video, October 13, 2018. www.youtube.com/watch?v=NQ9AC-NX0GA&t=38s.

Raun, Tobias. 2018. "Capitalizing Intimacy New Subcultural Forms of Micro-Celebrity Strategies and Affective Labour on YouTube." *Convergence: The International Journal of Research into New Media Technologies* 24 (1): 99–113. doi:10.1177/1354856517736983.

Rottenberg, Catherine. 2018. *The Rise of Neoliberal Feminism*. New York: Oxford University Press.

Sabatier, Grant. 2019. "How Much Do YouTubers Make? (A Lot!)." *Millennial Money*, July 10, 2019. https://millennialmoney.com.

Stokel-Walker, Chris. 2018a. "'Success' on YouTube Still Means a Life of Poverty." *Bloomberg*, February 27, 2018. www.bloomberg.com.

———. 2018b. "Why YouTubers Are Feeling the Burn." *The Guardian*, August 12, 2018. www.theguardian.com.

Wernick, Andrew. 1991. *Promotional Culture: Advertising, Ideology and Symbolic Expression*. London: Sage.

Wynn, Natalie. 2017. @ContraPoints Twitter post, November 12, 2017. https://twitter.com/contrapoints/status/929786834292527104?lang=en.

———. n.d. ContraPoints Patreon home page. Accessed August 13, 2019. www.patreon.com/contrapoints/.

YouTube. n.d. "YouTube for Press." Accessed August 13, 2019. www.youtube.com.

3

Affect and Autoethnography in Social Media Research

BRENT LUVAAS

The Affective Pull of Social Media

It is a recurrent fantasy: social media suicide. A permanently darkened smartphone screen. Blissful, cellular silence.

I start with the "professional" apps: LinkedIn, Academia.edu. Those will be easy. I never really cared much for them anyway. Their nagging notifications in my email inbox, designed to trigger my professional anxieties, get immediately tagged as "junk." Then, I move to the more personal ones: Twitter, Tumblr, Pinterest, Facebook. Those will be harder. They have supplied as many micropings of dopamine as they have waves of existential dread. I might miss them. I might find my finger hovering over my smartphone screen with no destination to go to. The dead time in the supermarket line might feel just a little bit deader.

Then comes Instagram. It, I imagine, will be the hardest of all, a seven-year archive of my photographic work relegated to the digital dustbin. Instagram has provided me with more dopamine spikes than all the other social media platforms combined. And crashes too. It gives, and it takes away. But Instagram is making it easier for me to imagine its absence from my life. With each new change to its algorithm, my follower engagement decreases, and the less engagement I get for the images I put up, the less desire I feel to post them. Instagram is like a critically ill relative I have been watching slowly die for years. I am already well into my mourning.

Finally, I scour my identity from the social media dead zones: MySpace, digg, del.icio.us, Friendster. I am not even sure I can log into those accounts anymore, my user names and passwords long ago forgotten, along with the Yahoo, AOL, and grad-school email accounts I might use to retrieve them.

This is not an original fantasy, I know. Websites like Just Delete Me provide detailed instructions, ranked from "easy" to "impossible," on how to remove oneself from even the most obscure social media account. Apps like Offtime, Moment, and BreakFree promise relief from the constant rejoinders to participate. Every few weeks, a new celebrity, like Eddie Redmayne, Cardi B., or Justin Bieber, publicly declares their exodus from social media, followed by their triumphant return. Kanye West has quit his accounts multiple times already. Even his partner, Kim Kardashian, queen of Instagram, who rakes in millions of dollars every year through her social media accounts alone, made the 2018 New Year's resolution of spending less time on social media. She made that resolution, of course, on social media. In the wake of the Cambridge Analytica scandal, the Huawei and ZTE scandals, and all the other recent what-the-hell-is-Facebook-doing-with-my-data? scandals, "#DeleteFacebook" is trending (again) on Twitter as I write this paragraph.

It is hardly an unattainable fantasy either. I could delete all of my social media accounts right now. No one would stop me. Few people would even notice I had done so. Though I suspect my email inbox would be hit with a barrage of "desperate" pleas from the platforms in question: "Are you SURE you want to delete Facebook?" "So and so REALLY wants to connect with you on LinkedIn." I would get a sick thrill from imagining these companies' suffering (though I would recognize, of course, that the bots that auto-delivered the messages experience no such thing).

I am, you will notice, not currently carrying out this fantasy. I am not committing social media suicide. I am writing this book chapter instead. I have found no shortage of things to do instead. My research requires me to be on social media, I tell myself. I have no choice. But then I suppose I could be studying something else, something other than Instagram influencers or digital photographers, something that does not require me to spend hours a day on these platforms. The fact is, something seems to be keeping me from going through with the plan. Some unaccountable hunger, perhaps? Some (probably) misplaced anxiety? FOMO? Addiction? Structural dependency? Jodi

Dean (2010) has described this compulsion through Lacanian terms as "drive." The communicative capitalism intrinsic to the online environment has us caught in an endless feedback loop of posting and liking. Alice Marwick (2013) and Brooke Erin Duffy (2017) have connected it with the obligatory status-seeking behavior of aspiring creatives in a precarious labor market. Today, we have little choice but to view ourselves as brands, forever in need of promotion (Banet-Weiser 2012). Sherry Turkle (2011), and many others, have described it through the language of addiction. Those pings of dopamine we get when someone "likes" our posts have us hooked. We can never get enough. And yet we can never quite find satisfaction through them either. Whatever it is, it seems to be working. I seem to be staying on social media.

This, I would suggest, is the one thing, above all others, that social media theorists like me (or Dean, Marwick, Duffy, and Turkle, for that matter) strive to uncover. *It* is what lies at the heart of our research, that affective, embodied *something* that compels us to connect and stay connected, that keeps us glued to our phones, even when we would rather not be, tumbling the depths of Facebook's newsfeed without even realizing we are doing it. I have gone after this *something* in my own work by facing it directly in myself. I invite it in and stare it down. That has not always been a good idea.

Let me back up a bit to explain. Back in March 2012, I started a blog called *Urban Fieldnotes* (www.urbanfieldnotes.com). I was interested in the phenomenon of "street style blogs," those informal websites, like Streetgeist (www.streetgeist.com), FaceHunter (www.facehunter.org), and On the Corner (www.onthecornerstreetstyle.blogspot.com), where photographers post their pictures, in the standard blog format of reverse chronological order, of "cool-looking" people from cities around the world, and I wanted to find some way of studying street style blogs in greater depth. As a cultural anthropologist, my methodological tool of choice has always been ethnography, the method of directly immersing oneself in the community one studies, learning how that community thinks and acts firsthand, and participating in its activities, to the extent possible, for oneself. Ethnography usually requires its practitioners to go somewhere. Clifford Geertz went to Bali, Margaret Mead to Samoa. Once there, they do their best to become members of the community, carefully attending to the lifeways and practices of the people they study. But where does an ethnographer studying street style bloggers go? There is no offline community of street style bloggers to live among and immerse oneself into. Sure, I could have done "digital ethnography," that nebulous, emergent methodology attracting no shortage of millennial graduate students these days. A number of social scientists have advocated such an approach, treating online platforms as field sites (Boellstorff 2008; Bonilla and Rosa 2015; Hine 2015; Nardi 2010; Pink et al. 2016), online communities as regular old-fashioned ones. Regardless of the individual merits of these studies, I was not convinced digital ethnography would suffice in this case. Immersing oneself in a "virtual world" like Second Life is one thing—there are "places" there, virtual cities, houses, and nightclubs, where avatars gather and interact (see Boellstorff 2008)—but immersing oneself in a street style blog is quite another. There are images there. There are comment threads. But there is no "place"—and no obvious community to inhabit it. What would it mean to do a digital ethnography of street style blogs? Would it just be lurking on other people's blogs, reading comments, viewing images? This hardly felt like the immersive fieldwork experience I was looking for. It was too disembodied, too abstract. It might have yielded good data—as any other sort of textual analysis could—but it would not have yielded good *ethnographic* data. It seemed to me there was only one possibility for *ethnographically* studying street style blogging: I would have to start a street style blog myself. I would have to *become* the kind of person I was studying. In other words, I would have to carry out the project *autoethnographically*.

This is how I got involved with social media as a researcher. A few months after I set up my street style blog, I set up attendant social media accounts on Facebook, Tumblr, Pinterest, Twitter, and Instagram. At first, their function was simply to advertise the blog, but they gradually began to take precedence over it. Eventually, they displaced it. Likewise, my rationale for using them slowly, almost imperceptibly, disintegrated. My social media accounts were meant to be research instruments, but they did not stay that way, eating up more and more of my free time and blurring the boundaries between research and personal investment. For social media autoethnographers like me, this boundary is exceedingly difficult to maintain.

This chapter confronts the affordances and limitations, pleasures and pitfalls, of using autoethnography as a method of carrying out research into online creator culture. Describing my own experiences as a street style blogger, I discuss the affective and experiential modes of data gathering and theory making that autoethnography enables—the practical, embodied knowledge, the technical know-how and skills, the intimate details of contracts and collaborations that our interlocutors are often hesitant to share with us—as well as the emotional toll that such methodologies can take on their practitioners. Autoethnography, this chapter argues, provides embodied ways of knowing that no other form of social scientific research can match. But it also entails affective and existential risk. We get caught up in the processes we attend to. We begin to believe the hype of the platforms we study. We feel for ourselves the affective pull we theorize.

Becoming what we study is a process not easily undone (see Luvaas 2019). When we immerse ourselves in social media, even to study it, we are *immersed* in social media, just like everyone else who chooses to actively engage the apps they download to their phones. To assume the critical distance of a researcher does not make us immune to social media's affective pull. Moreover, becoming what we study is a process whose ending—if there is an ending—is not easy to predict. As I, for instance, was becoming a blogger, bloggers were becoming something else: social media "influencers" who leverage their personal brands across platforms and monetize those brands through advertisements, affiliate links, and collaborations (see Abidin 2016). I had to become an influencer too, or something approximating it, an identity about which I remain deeply ambivalent. It is this ambivalence, over time wearing down into fatigue, that makes me fantasize about an escape plan I have little intention of enacting.

This chapter chronicles that ambivalence and the eventual dissolution of my blog and the street style project it brought about. It is as much a warning as a testimonial. Deliberate becoming is now a critical ingredient of all of my projects. I can no longer imagine doing research without it. But it is also one that raises the personal stakes of social science. Autoethnography is not a commitment one should take on lightly. It requires an attentiveness to self that exacerbates the already self-obsessed nature of social media. My fantasy of social media suicide is a fantasy of moving beyond that continuous, compulsive self-awareness, of retreating to the neutral, "objective" ground of another popular fantasy: that of the detached observer (Clifford and Marcus 1986). In social media research, there are no detached observers. We all have personal stake in the phenomena we are observing. Autoethnography, at least, provides a medium for interrogating that stake further.

Becoming a Blogger

Autoethnography, like the social media we study, is an unstable, heterogeneous thing. When Karl Heider first used the term back in 1975, he was referring to the self-generated accounts of Dani schoolchildren in New Guinea. Autoethnography, or "auto-ethnography" as he wrote it, was automatic ethnography, autochthonous ethnography, accounts of a people generated by the people themselves, without the trained insights of an anthropologist. By the late 1970s and early 1980s, the term had shifted in meaning to refer to "native ethnography," the work of ethnographers studying "their own" people (Hayano 1979; Strathern 1987). It was only in the wake of the "crisis of representation" (Clifford and Marcus 1986) in the mid- to late 1980s that the current meaning of autoethnography came into use. Convinced that all ethnographic writing revealed more about the writers of the ethnography themselves than it did about the people they were documenting, a generation of anthropologists began to experiment with the practice, reveling in its self-revealing potential, expanding its literary ambitions. Anthropologists like Kathleen Stewart (2007) and Ruth Behar (1996) made explicit use of personal narrative and emotion in their work. They exposed their own positionality. They breached the former barrier between "subjective" and "objective" observations. Since the 1980s, to acknowledge one's personal biases has become standard practice in nearly all ethnographic work. The question becomes, then, Where is the line between "ethnography," as it has been practiced for the past few decades, and "autoethnography," as a distinct, reflexive methodology? I also do not know where that line lies, but I do not see any particular value in locating it. My work could just as easily be described as ethnography or autoethnography. Participant-observation takes the self of the researcher as a given. It already includes the self in its narrative. But there is a spectrum of ethnography/autoethnography within contemporary ethnographic work, ranging from acknowledgment of personal perspective to an exclusive focus on that perspective. I describe as "autoethnography" ethnography that explicitly focuses on the self as its object of study. And as the self is an unstable, continually becoming thing, so must autoethnography be the study of personal becoming (see Biehl and Locke 2010).

I do not know exactly when I started becoming a street style blogger. You could say it began when I put up the first post on *Urban Fieldnotes* in March 2012, but the process was well under way before then. I had been reading street style blogs for a couple of years already. I had been planning my own posts in my head. And blogs take on a confessional tone I had already made a feature of my academic work. Blogging, you might say, was a natural transition.

I can, however, tell you when I first started thinking of myself as a blogger. It was a couple of months after the project began. I attended my first, and only, meeting of the Philly Style Bloggers Meetup group in University City, Philadelphia. The event was sponsored by Google Hangouts, a video feature, new at the time, that allows multiple parties to communicate at once, the video equivalent of a conference call. Several of Philadelphia's most prominent fashion bloggers were in attendance: Sabir M. Peele of *Men's Style Pro*, Jared Michael Lowe of *The Lowe Factor*, Fajr Muhammad of *Stylish Thought*. There was sushi and crackers, bottles of two-liter soft drinks. I introduced myself as the anthropologist and street style blogger behind *Urban Fieldnotes*. We exchanged Instagram handles the way accountants hand out business cards. Soon each of us had several new followers.

As the spokespeople for Google Hangouts were setting up their equipment, a new blogger entered the room. Not recognizing me, he asked if I was with Google. Before I could reply, one of the bloggers I had just met answered on my behalf: "No, he's one of us." One of us! Those few words transformed me—at least in my own head—from interloper to participant. I was not just using my blog to understand the phenomenon of blogs; I *was* a blogger.

This meant something specific to me at the time. It meant I was a co-producer of internet culture, part of an expansive network of avid amateurs, deterritorializing the landscape of fashion (Findlay 2017). These were fanciful and romantic sentiments, no doubt. But they were *shared* sentiments, a mediatized "structure of feeling" (Williams 1977) forging a dense emotional constellation (Döveling, Harju, and Sommer 2018, 4) between us. Such sentiments are the raw material autoethnographers call "data."

Becoming a blogger meant embodying those shared sentiments. It meant I felt for myself the pressing feeling of *needing* to post. It meant my blood pressure elevated as I checked my Google analytics. It meant I got a small high from each new like I amassed on Instagram. It meant I had *stake* in establishing a following and growing my readership.

Becoming a blogger also meant assuming a position within a particular set of material/economic relationships. It meant that I became an entity recognizable to marketing algorithms. Various PR agencies contacted me throughout my project. They still do. I get invites to fashion-related events in Philadelphia, New York, and even occasionally Paris and Milan. Marketing agencies take certain small financial risks on my behalf, provide me the occasional gift card or jacket in the hopes that I might say something nice about them on my blog or Instagram. Sometimes these expectations are clearly articulated or formalized. Other times they are not. The larger economic system in which social media and blogs are entangled is one that continually blurs the difference between personal and promotional (Luvaas 2013), just as autoethnography blurs the difference between experience and data. This is both the strength of autoethnography as a research tool and its critical limitation.

The "Data" of Autoethnographic Research

I was wandering Philadelphia with my camera several months into the blog when I got my first advertising request via email. American Apparel, the now bankrupt and scandal-ridden clothing company based in downtown Los Angeles, wanted to post a banner ad on my blog. If people clicked on that banner, it would take them to American Apparel's website. If they then made a purchase, I would get paid a small fee. My contract with American Apparel prevents me from disclosing the exact amount of that fee, but suffice it to say, it was not much. This was not a substantial investment of capital on America Apparel's part. It only paid on the condition that it made money off the transaction. There was, in other words, zero risk on the company's behalf. There was, however, risk on my behalf. I had to work hard to ever get paid for my contribution to the company's profit, write an invoice, and send nagging emails to its marketing manager. After a year and a half of hosting the ad, I had earned some $250 off it. It hardly seemed worth the visual real estate it took up and the toll it took on my identity. Am I really the kind of person, I asked myself, who advertises American Apparel on my blog? You know, the company with the sleazy CEO and the retro porn aesthetics? Is that who I am today? Eventually, I deleted the banner ad and cut off the relationship, eager to distance myself from its (failing) brand. But now at least I understand how banner advertising works. I understand the kinds of arrangements bloggers have with brands, the nuts and bolts of their "partnerships." And I did not have to force another blogger to violate the terms of their contract to tell me. I also understood the weight on one's personal identity that hosting an ad entails. Bloggers have told me that the criteria by which they determine whether a potential advertiser is a good fit with their blog's brand is whether they "like" it themselves. Do they feel a personal connection with it? Does it describe something meaningful about them? In the absence of some clear method of determining whether a particular brand is an authentic representation of a blogger's identity, they depend instead on a gut-level feeling. Does it feel like who I am? Does it resonate in some deep sense? American Apparel was not resonating with me. It felt like a stain I wanted to scrub off.

I gathered similar data on the details of blogging contracts through freelancing for online fashion magazines. Many of the street style bloggers I had been following as part of this project had begun to sell their images to third parties as early as 2007. Scott Schuman, the blogger behind *The Sartorialist*, was a pioneer in this respect. Establishing an ongoing relationship with the men's fashion magazine *GQ*, he created a new revenue stream for amateur bloggers, looking to make some additional income from their hobby. Tommy Ton, Phil Oh, Tamu McPherson, and a slew of other bloggers soon followed suit. Street style blogger became a professional aspiration. Well-known street style bloggers like Adam Katz Sinding were able to quit their day jobs and do street style blogging full-time. By 2012, I had met and interacted with a number of these bloggers on the sidewalks outside New York Fashion Week. The links between these bloggers and various industry publications were well established by then. They were enjoying comfortable lifestyles, with lofts in SoHo and Williamsburg and a closet full of designer clothes. But they were notoriously close-lipped about their contracts with magazines. Photographers tend not to talk about how much they get paid per image. In part, it is a status issue. No one wants anyone else to know if they are making less than others. In part, it is a legal issue. Bloggers have signed nondisclosure agreements, sealing their lips about terms and conditions. It is to the advantage of publications not to announce their standard rates. There is always someone willing to work for just about nothing. And just about nothing, I soon discovered, after working with magazines and websites including *Racked*, *Kenton*, *Refinery29*, and *BET*, is what most magazines initially offer.

For an eight-hour day of shooting, followed by several more hours of editing and whittling down to fifty images, it is perfectly normal for a blogger to receive as little as $50, and $100 is fairly routine for a more experienced blogger. By the end of my time freelancing, however, I was receiving as much as $1,000 for a weekend. It took me six weeks of regular following up to get paid for that, though. I quickly discovered that freelancing in the world of social media entertainment requires almost as much time chasing down income already earned as it does earning income in the first place. Whatever fantasies I accumulated during my time as a blogger of entering into the fashion industry "for real" were dashed by my brief flirtations with being employed by it. Exploitation is still standard practice when it comes to freelance fashion labor, and this extends into the unpaid or barely paid labor of the fashion blogosphere (see Duffy 2017). Blogging, regardless of whatever media-driven fantasy of instant success surrounds it, is hard work.

But as previously mentioned, my autoethnographic methods did not only yield financial data. I also learned a great deal about the embodied knowledge blogging requires. This embodied knowledge, in turn, became the basis for my theorization about the practice of blogging. For autoethnographers, "*theorizing* is an ongoing, movement-driven process that links the concrete and the abstract, thinking and acting" (Jones 2016, 229). We theorize through a continual back-and-forth between lived, embodied experience and a sort of self-imposed exile from that experience. Theory becomes neutral territory, a space of intellectual retreat. And yet, once we are back in the action, back in the embodied forward motion of life, it comes with us, a spectral outline that alters the shape and feel of what we see and experience. As the "critical auto-ethnographer" Stacy Holman Jones puts it, theorizing becomes a way of "engaging *with* the world as shifting, partial, unfinished, and animated by feeling and imagination" (2016, 231).

In my case, theorization of the practice of blogging was a process of beginning to understand and put a name to the kinds of bodily knowing that street style bloggers undergo. Street style blogging, first and foremost, is about identifying "cool" people on the streets and taking pictures of them. That sounds easy enough, but try standing on a street corner in your hometown and waiting until someone cool enough to appear on a street style blog passes by. And not just cool—this person has to reflect your own personal version of cool. To use blogging lingo, they have to further your "brand" (Findlay 2017), to embody all the aesthetic characteristics that your readership and following, accustomed to your personal brand, will find appealing. That is how you get likes. That is how you build followers. And you have to make all of these determinations before a person passes out of sight, so that you can stop them and ask them to pose.

For me, the natural response to such criteria is paralysis. What does cool look like? I wondered. And how do you recognize it? Is that guy cool? Or that guy? Is that woman's vintage bomber jacket cool, or was that only cool a few years back? And whose cool are we talking about here anyway? The fashion world's cool? A middle-aged, once-hip college professor's version of cool? These sorts of thoughts go nowhere quick. I have nothing like the expertise required to be a trend forecaster or critic. I lack insight into popular sentiment. Better to simply follow the advice of other street style photographers I had interviewed: just photograph what you like. But what do I like? Black-clad, bearded baristas? Hip hop gender-benders in oversize clothes? Punk-rock hairdressers in hand-me-down leather jackets? It turns out, I like all of the above, but my first few weeks out on the streets of Philadelphia, camera in hand, I had no idea what I liked. The more closely I looked at my likes, the more they retreated from view. I had to learn how to react automatically, and bodily, to the people passing by, to *know* they were people I wanted to shoot for reasons I was never quite able to articulate. I had to instantiate an instant, intuitive instrument of knowing. I would come to call this intuitive instrument, tongue slightly in cheek, my *style radar*.

My style radar, I began to understand over time, is a form of bodily *hexis* (Bourdieu 1980), an intuited knowledge that nonetheless echoes the biases and power relationships embedded in the fashion industry. I cultivated my style radar by consuming innumerable online images, reacting to them, forming opinions of them, and then going out onto the streets and allowing those images and opinions to work on me like an internalized blueprint of "cool." My style radar, then, may be prearticulate, and it may be uniquely configured to me, but it does not emerge in isolation, reflecting instead an aesthetic landscape in which I was already immersed, with or without my conscious awareness. When I "liked" something and captured that affect as an image, I either reinforced or challenged an existing set of aesthetic preferences put forward by the larger fashion industry. Looking back on my images now, it is easy to see how most of them did more reinforcing than challenging, even when the experience at the time felt little more than an allowing of my "likes" to assert themselves. Like a model scout or casting agent, I had internalized a set of racialized and gendered norms that further perpetuated the fashion status quo (Sadre-Orafai 2008). But in gaining distance from them, beginning to see them within a larger social milieu, these internalized norms became the raw material of theory.

It took months to develop my style radar, and once I had, I found it difficult to turn off. I picked people out of a crowd in an instant, evaluated the relative coolness of colleagues, conference presenters, other parents at my daughters' elementary school open houses. It clouded my daily thoughts, overwhelmed my aesthetic judgments. This feeling, this embodied affective response to the people around you, *this* is what it feels like on an everyday level to be a street style blogger. How would I have known that if I had not experienced it for myself? By what other means than autoethnography could I have gathered such valuable, experiential data and begun to parse it out as theory?

The same can be said for the more technical details of the job: camera settings, aperture, shutter speed, lens diameters, the appropriate position to stand—or, more accurately, crouch—in order to get the shots that the top bloggers are putting on their Instagram pages. These are important things for an aspiring street style blogger to be thinking about. The answers change depending on current trends in street style photography, but at the time I started the project, they were relatively straightforward:

Aperture equals between F1.4 and F4, depending on how shallow you want your depth of field; shutter speed should be a minimum of 1/60 of a second for a posed portrait, but better to go above 1/250 of a second. For those candid motion shots that Tommy Ton and Adam Katz Sinding are so fond of, you better go above 1/1000 of a second. And do not even think of taking those shots with a camera incapable of shooting off ten frames per second! The top bloggers, when I was in the midst of my project, were shooting with Nikon D3s and D4s, Canon 1Ds and 5Ds. These cameras are perhaps best known for sports photography. In the early days of street style blogging, bloggers often claimed that the cameras they used did not matter. Anyone could take the kinds of pictures they took, with any old camera they picked up on the internet. The supposedly democratic nature of street style blogging depended on these claims. My autoethnographic data, however, contradicted them.

I know what cameras and settings to use to produce street style photographs of the sort popular on the top street style blogs because I have tried them out myself through endless trial and error. I know what cameras and settings to use because I have shot beside other street style bloggers, comparing notes about what we are doing and how, on the sidewalks of New York Fashion Week. I have come to know those cameras and settings intimately. I no longer have to think about them. They are part of my embodied knowledge. They, like the style radar I cultivated, are part of who I am. This is what autoethnography affords the social media researcher. It is also what makes it so existentially dangerous.

Experiential Overflow

Flash-forward to September 2016 at a "VIP preview" of the opening of a new wing of the King of Prussia Mall in suburban Philadelphia, the largest mall, with regard to overall retail space, in the United States today. Gucci, Louis Vuitton, Diane Von Furstenberg, Rag & Bone, and COS were all moving in, among many other retail brands, and the who's who of Philadelphia fashion influencers were all there to witness it. So, strangely, was I.

Over a glass of welcome champagne, I hugged the new arrivals before they took their seats on the plush couches near the valet service. That is what we do: hug, like old friends getting together to visit, rather than mild social media rivals, canvassing the same digital turf. It was a familiar routine. I had gotten to know it well. These were my people, and they treated me as such. But they were in a league of fashionista far above me. In an oversized black T-shirt and pair of faded indigo skinny jeans, I felt badly underdressed. It was a feeling I had gotten used to over the previous several years.

We were toured, champagne in hand, from one store to the next. As we did so, we were showered with coupons and gifts like aristocrats bestowed blessings from their subjects: 50 percent off our first purchase at one store, a silver bracelet at another. Rag & Bone upped the ante with a $250 gift card. Our hosts, managers and marketers from Simon, the parent company that owns the mall, told us repeatedly how awesome we were and provided us with plenty of opportunities to take selfies for our social media feeds. Dozens of selfies transpired (none by me, I might add).

I enjoyed myself that night. I drank champagne and a cocktail or two, relished the appetizers and the gifts, and plotted how I would spend my Rag & Bone gift card when I returned the following week. Rag & Bone, in the parlance of bloggers, was very "on brand" for me, all tailored, military-influenced simplicity. And yet I could not manage to forget what we were doing there: shilling someone else's merchandise. The Marxist-trained academic in me could not quite let that fact go. Sure, there was no explicit requirement to post anything from the event on our social media feeds, but there seldom was. We all knew the deal. We all knew what we had signed on for. Post for your swag. You promote me, and I'll promote you. That expectation took its toll on me. I could feel it in my gut. I could feel it on my conscience. This was not a new feeling for me. In fact, I had recently completed my book on street style blogging, and I talked about this feeling at length in it. The book was already out by the time I received my invitation to the King of Prussia event. I had little new to gain from this feeling. There was, in other words, no clear research agenda—autoethnographic or otherwise—for my attending this event. I had no questions I was pursuing. I had no unfinished business to resolve. No, I attended out of habit and personal vanity. The invitation had flattered my ego, and so here I was.

That night, I realized my blog project was dead—at least to me. It was no longer teaching me anything new about the street style phenomenon or the nature of social media culture. I had already learned to take street style photographs competently. I had already learned how to "partner" with brands and produce "content" they found valuable. I had learned to schmooze at influencer parties, knew the names and faces of the blogging elite. I knew what it felt like to have your number of followers expand exponentially. I knew what it was like for them to contract unexpectedly. And I had developed a theoretical model around this embodiment of brand culture that helped me understand and make sense of it. Perhaps more accurately, I realized that my blog project was undead, an empty shell of a research instrument that continued to lurch forward, dragging its arms along the ground, without any actual legs to stand on. By then, I was posting for the positive feedback. I was blogging for the fringe benefits. I was caught in the circuits of drive (Dean 2010). Any research benefits it might potentially reap were now a secondary consideration. But this game I had inadvertently entered into, this tit for tat, I'll-scratch-your-back-if-you-scratch-mine marketing blitz of social media influence, was not one I wanted to play anymore. It was too far from the starting point of the project. It was too alien to the anthropologist I had trained to be. It was not who I wanted to be anymore.

Sarah Banet-Weiser (2012) has argued that the key emotional attribute of today's brand culture is ambivalence. We attempt to break free from the hypercommodification of everyday life by clinging to brands that promise an escape from that hypercommodification. We seek authenticity even where we know we can never find it, in the very branding of everything that makes authenticity impossible. My fellow bloggers feel that ambivalence. They seek out more "meaningful" and engaged modes of connection with brands, eschewing simple commodity relationships by only wearing and advertising via their blogs those brands that they feel a "genuine" affinity toward. They blog, one could argue, as a means of taking ownership over fashion, instead of letting fashion take ownership over them. Blogging inserts them into the fashion world as active agents, rather than passive recipients. And yet, in the final analysis, what they do as bloggers is wear and advertise brands. The logic of branding has so structured their practice that they can think of no means of escaping it other than more branding. At the King of Prussia event, I felt that brand double bind wrapping around my chest, constricting by breath, exacting a sort of commodity claustrophobia I desperately wanted to escape.

I never did post anything on my social media feeds from that night. I could barely bring myself to like the posts featuring me or the other "influencers" present. A month or so later, I stopped posting to *Urban Fieldnotes* altogether. I let its Instagram gallery, Twitter feed, and Facebook page sit idle.

How do academics know the difference between what they do for the acclaim of their colleagues and what they do out of their own genuine interest? I have never been able to parse that for myself. Do I study what I study out of genuine "passion" for the subject or because I have received positive feedback for what I have done on that subject so far? The same question applies to the business of social media influence twofold. It is difficult, if not impossible, to tell the difference between something you like because you like it and something you like because your followers like it. And it is even harder to tell if you like something when someone is rewarding you—whether financially or socially—to like it. Do I like the $300 jacket you just sent me with a barrage of compliments in the accompanying card? Sure, I do. How could I not? I like being liked.

The emergent industry of social media influence is an industry of affect-for-hire. Influencers are rewarded for their tastes, their likes, their emotional response to something their clients, and their followers, approve of. These social expectations then become embodied, inseparable from an influencer's sense of self. Over time, as I carried out my research as a blogger and would-be influencer, I found that fact increasingly difficult to stomach. It tainted my perspective on social media. It made me feel cynical and depressed.

Of course, I could have avoided that affective trap by maintaining a critical distance between myself and my subject. I could have slotted myself down as an observer, not a participant. Minh-Ha Pham's (2015) brilliant analysis of Asian American fashion bloggers takes that tack, as does Brooke Erin Duffy's (2017). But then I never would have known the conflict and ambivalence that underlies so much that takes place on social media today. I never would have known about the complex emotional structures underlying the picture-perfect façade of outfit-of-the-day posts. Influencers do not discuss it. It is not part of their brand. To be an influence peddler is to be a manager of personal emotion. It is to engage in affective labor, blocking out negative emotions while cultivating positive ones and directing them toward specific brands and products. I was never particularly successful at that labor. My ambivalence was always my most pronounced emotion. I could never erect an effective façade.

So that is why I am sitting here now, staring at my screen, fantasizing about what my life would be like without social media. That is why I periodically find my fingers wandering toward the "delete my account" button on Facebook, Twitter, and Instagram. I am tired of emotional investment in social media. I am tired of caring about how many likes I receive or how many people have recently unfollowed me. The "free labor" (Terranova 2013) of social media no longer feels so free. My hope, as a social media researcher, is to more and more precisely pinpoint the nature of this social media bondage—and then, when I have done so, to break it.

REFERENCES

Abidin, Crystal. 2016. "'Aren't These Just Young, Rich Women Doing Vain Things Online?': Influencer Selfies as Subversive Frivolity." *Society Media + Society* 2 (2): 1–17. doi:10.1177/2056305116641342.

Banet-Weiser, Sarah. 2012. *Authentic™: The Politics of Ambivalence in a Brand Culture.* New York: NYU Press.

Behar, Ruth. 1996. *The Vulnerable Observer: Anthropology That Breaks Your Heart.* Boston: Beacon.

Biehl, João, and Peter Locke. 2010. "Deleuze and the Anthropology of Becoming." *Current Anthropology* 51 (3): 317–351. doi:10.1086/651466.

Boellstorff, Tom. 2008. *Coming of Age in Second Life: An Anthropologist Explores the Virtually Human.* Princeton, NJ: Princeton University Press.

Bonilla, Yarimar, and Jonathan Rosa. 2015. "#Ferguson: Digital Protest, Hashtag Ethnography, and the Racial Politics of Social Media in the United States." *American Ethnologist* 42 (1): 4–17. doi:10.1111/amet.12112.

Bourdieu, Pierre. 1980. *The Logic of Practice.* Stanford, CA: Stanford University Press.

Clifford, James, and George E. Marcus. 1986. *Writing Culture: The Poetics and Politics of Ethnography.* Berkeley: University of California Press.

Dean, Jodi. 2010. *Blog Theory: Feedback and Capture in the Circuits of Drive.* Cambridge, UK: Polity.

Döveling, Katrin, Anu Harju, and Denise Sommer. 2018. "From Mediatized Emotion to Digital Affect Cultures: New Technologies and Global Flows of Emotion." *Social Media + Society* 4 (1): 1–11. doi:10.1177/2056305117743141.

Duffy, Brooke Erin. 2017. *(Not) Getting Paid to Do What You Love: Gender, Social Media, and Aspirational Work.* New Haven, CT: Yale University Press.

Findlay, Rosie. 2017. *Personal Style Blogs: Appearances That Fascinate.* Bristol, UK: Intellect.

Hayano, David M. 1979. "Auto-Ethnography: Paradigms, Problems, and Prospects." *Human Organization* 38 (1): 99–104.

Heider, Karl. 1975. "What Do People Do? Dani Auto-Ethnography." *Journal of Anthropological Research* 31:3–17.

Hine, Christine M. 2015. *Ethnography for the Internet: Embedded, Embodied and Everyday.* London: Bloomsbury.

Jones, Stacy Holman. 2016. "Living Bodies of Thought: The 'Critical' in Critical Autoethnography." *Qualitative Inquiry* 22 (4): 228–237. doi:10.1177/1077800415622509.

Luvaas, Brent. 2013. "Indonesian Fashion Blogs: On the Promotional Subject of Personal Style." *Fashion Theory* 17 (1): 55–76. doi:10.2752/175174113X13502904240749.

———. 2019. "Unbecoming: The Aftereffects of Autoethnography." *Ethnography* 20 (2): 245–262. doi:10.1177/1466138117742674.

Marwick, Alice. 2013. *Status Update: Celebrity, Publicity, and Branding in the Social Media Age.* New Haven, CT: Yale University Press.

Nardi, Bonnie. 2010. *My Life as a Nightelf Priest: An Anthropological Account of World of Warcraft.* Ann Arbor: University of Michigan Press.

Pham, Minh-Ha T. 2015. *Asians Wear Clothes on the Internet: Race, Gender, and the Work of Personal Style Blogging.* Durham, NC: Duke University Press.

Pink, Sarah, Heather Horst, John Postil, Larissa Hjorth, Tania Lewis and Jo Tacchi. 2016. *Digital Ethnography: Principles and Practice.* London: Sage.

Sadre-Orafai, Stephanie. 2008. "Developing Images: Race, Language, and Perception in Fashion-Model Casting." In *Fashion as Photograph: Viewing and Reviewing Images of Fashion,* edited by Eugénie Shinkle, 141–153. London: I. B. Tauris.

Stewart, Kathleen. 2007. *Ordinary Affects.* Durham, NC: Duke University Press.

Strathern, Marilyn. 1987. "The Limits of Auto-Anthropology." In *Anthropology at Home,* edited by Anthony Jackson, 16–37. London: Tavistock.

Terranova, Tiziana. 2013. "Free Labor." In *Digital Labor: The Internet as Playground and Factory,* edited by Trebor Scholz, 33–57. New York: Taylor and Francis.

Turkle, Sherry. 2011. *Alone Together: Why We Expect More from Technology and Less from Each Other.* New York: Basic Books.

Williams, Raymond. 1977. *Marxism and Literature.* Oxford: Oxford University Press.

4

A Semio-discursive Analysis of
Spanish-Speaking BookTubers

CARLOS A. SCOLARI, DAMIÁN FRATICELLI,
AND JOSÉ M. TOMASENA

In José van Dijck's classic *The Culture of Connectivity* (2013), the author introduces a first distinction between various types of social media. From her perspective, "social network sites" (SNSs) primarily "promote interpersonal contact, whether between individuals or groups; they forge personal, professional, or geographical connections and encourage weak ties" (8). Facebook, Twitter, LinkedIn, Google+, and Foursquare were considered good examples of SNSs. A second category is sites for "user-generated content" (UGC); these social media "support creativity, foreground cultural activity, and promote the exchange of amateur or professional content" (8). Well-known UGC sites are YouTube, Flickr, and Wikipedia. Van Dijck also mentions other types of social media, for example, trading and marketing sites (TMSs) like Amazon or eBay, or play and game sites (PGS) like *FarmVille*, *CityVille*, or *Angry Birds*.

This classification is not perfect. As van Dijck puts it, there are "no sharp boundaries between various platform categories because carving out and appropriating one or more specific niches is part of the continuous battle to dominate a segment of online sociality" (2013, 8). As the entire ecosystem of interconnected platforms and applications has been in flux and will remain volatile for some time to come, it is not easy to develop formal classifications. For example, social media like Instagram could be considered both an SNS and a UGC platform simultaneously. In any case, this taxonomy is useful for positioning YouTube in the context of the new media ecology. In the specific case of YouTube, according to van Dijck, the site, while primed to generate creative content by users, can also be considered a social network site because communities share specific postings (for example, anime videos) (2013, 9). Despite Google's keen attempts to turn YouTube into an SNS, it has remained primarily a site for UGC, prompting the search company to start its own social networking service, Google+, which failed and is now defunct.

According to YouTube (n.d.), more than two billion logged-in users visit YouTube every single month, and viewers spend over a billion hours a day watching YouTube. As of mid-2020, YouTube is the second most visited website in the world after Google. YouTube is not just a formidable volcano of viral videos and the largest archive of audiovisual contents: it is also the place where new media actors emerge, become popular, and share their contents around the world. What started as a bedroom play with the webcam has become one of the most explosive business and branding phenomena of the online culture, fostering new forms of celebrity and also an emerging creative industry outside of legacy media.

As YouTube is a particularly unstable study object marked by dynamic changes and a diversity of content, formats, and genres, it is not always easy to make sense of it (Burgess and Green 2009, 6). Although many YouTubers propose general entertainment contents, others share very specific contents regarding video games, makeup, technology, fashion, or books. Stuart Cunningham and David Craig (2017) have stated that the most successful type of videos on YouTube—gameplay, do-it-yourself (DIY), beauty, and personality vlogs—differ from established television and constitute a new space for interactive, audience-centered media that is constantly appealing to authenticity and community. Beyond YouTube and across multiple social media platforms, they have defined this new screen ecology of platforms, content, creators, and cultural and entrepreneurial practice as social media entertainment (SME).

BookTubers

Constituting a distinctive subvertical of content on YouTube, "BookTubers" are users who share videos on YouTube about their reading preferences. As other YouTubers, BookTubers speak directly to the camera, often in their room or in a closed space, and they refer directly to their audience, sometimes responding to audience members through comments or by email or other social media such as Twitter, Facebook, Instagram, or Goodreads. It is very difficult to determine exactly when YouTube videos began to review books, but there is evidence that Elizabeth Vallish was one of the first (TheRaggysworld 2009). She is a young woman from Georgia, United States, and in December 2009, she published in her channel a review of *Looking for Alaska*, a novel by John Green—half of the Vlogbrothers, who has used his social capital as a known YouTuber to promote his own books and film adaptations.

The term "BookTube" appeared for the first time in September 2011 in the title of one of Vallish's videos. At the beginning of 2010, there were also some channels that reviewed books in Spanish, such as the Mexican Abril G. Karera and the Spanish SdeLibros, Fly like a butterfly, Javier Ruescas, and Libros por Leer. During 2011–2012, the phenomenon exploded: lots of channels were opened, some textual tags emerged and subgenres began to be invented. At the same time, a sense of identity and community grew up, while a metaconversation between participants who recognized themselves as BookTubers started.

Early BookTuber research includes Karen Sorensen and Andrew Mara (2013), who studied BookTubers as a networked knowledge community. Other scholars from Latin America have studied BookTubers as an expression of participatory cultures (Souza Teixeira and Abraão Cos 2016; Vizibeli 2016; Mendonça et al. 2017; Jeffman 2017; Sued 2017; González and Lomelí 2018). Christian Ehret, Jacy Boegel, and Roya Manuel-Nekouei (2018) analyzed how "participatory pressures" affect BookTube's aesthetics and, at the same time, how they contribute to BookTubers' development of individual styles. There is also ongoing research into the way teenagers and young adults are developing reading skills through their BookTube consumption (Lluch 2017; Rovira-Collado 2017; Torralba Miralles 2018).

The data and reflections presented in this chapter are part of broader research focused on the emergence of the new actors, practices, and relationships in the media ecology. In this case, the first objective was to analyze the emergence of Spanish-language BookTubers and their progressive professionalization in the context of the new media ecology. In addition, the chapter addresses the textual production of Spanish-speaking BookTubers. In this context, the second objective was to present a semio-discursive analytical model and apply it to BookTubers' audiovisual productions.

BookTubers in the New Media Ecology

This study is based on a series of categories developed for analyzing new media and their related cultural practices, from Pierre Bourdieu's (1996) concepts of "field" and "capital" to van Dijck's (2013) ecological vision of platforms and social networking sites or Carlos Scolari's (2013, 2015, 2018) evolutionary interpretation of the emergence of new media actors in the context of sociotechnical networks. To understand the power relations that are established between the BookTubers and other actors of the publishing industry, the concepts of "field" and "capital" are applied, especially in relation to the literary field, understood as a social space where different agents who have a common sense of the practice deploy different types of capital—such as economic, social, and symbolic—to dominate a common space (Bourdieu 1996).

The construction of "communities" is a key element of social media like YouTube. According to Jean Burgess and Joshua Green, "Some YouTube content creators understand and discursively represent themselves as 'YouTubers,' and as part of a YouTube *community*. For these users, YouTube works not only as a content delivery platform, but also as a social media platform" (2018, 94). In an analysis of beauty bloggers and YouTubers, Valerie Gannon and Andrea Prothero (2018) discuss the concept of "community of practice." These communities—defined as groups "linked by a concern, problems or a passion for a topic, and whose knowledge and expertise is deepened by mutual interaction" (Gannon and Prothero 2018, 593)—share two elements: a sense of community or belonging and shared social relationships and actions.

From a complementary perspective, van Dijck considers YouTube and similar platforms, such as Facebook, as "microsystems" that, combined, constitute the "ecosystem of connective media": "Each microsystem is sensitive to changes in other parts of the ecosystem: if Facebook changes its interface settings, Google reacts by tweaking its artillery of platforms; if participation in Wikipedia should wane, Google's algorithmic remedies could work wonders. It is important to map convolutions in this first format stage of connective media's growth because it may teach us about current and future distribution of powers" (2013, 21).

Van Dijck's approach combines perspectives taken from actor-network theory (ANT) and political economy to develop an analytical model that considers platforms as both techno-cultural constructions (uses, contents, and technologies) and socioeconomic structures (property, governance, and business models). "By scrutinizing the construction of platforms over the past decade, it should be possible to attain a comprehensive view of how online sociality has evolved in this time. The ecosystem of connective media . . . is not simply the sum of individual microsystems, but rather a dynamic infrastructure that shapes and is shaped by culture at large" (van Dijck 2013, 43–44).

Regarding the media evolutionary approach, the emergence of new media actors is one of the key moments for understanding the tensions and transformations of the media ecology. During the emergence phase, a new media appears in the media ecology. The emergence of a new communication technology—for example, cinema, television, or mobile devices—entails a series of challenges that need to be met in the only way possible: trial and error. In the early 1990s, there were no web designers, in the same way that in 1915 nobody knew how to produce a radio program. In the emergence phase, there are no instruction manuals that explain what the medium is or institutions that teach how it works (Scolari 2013, 1423). In this case, the development of a new communication technology (YouTube) has accelerated the emergence of new media actors (YouTubers and their specialized offspring BookTubers). The analysis from this ecological perspective should focus on the relationships between different actors (individual BookTubers, bookstores, publishers, authors, etc.) and the processes they are involved in.

A Semio-discursive Approach to BookTubers

Our semio-discursive analysis of audiovisual contents has a long tradition in media studies. More than thirty years ago, Eliseo Verón analyzed the enunciational characteristics of news programs. In the beginning of television, the host was just a face, a "speaker" in the double sense of the word (a person who gives a speech and, at the same time, an almost neutral technical device). Later, the TV host acquired a body, and the set found an architect: "The construction of the significant body of the TV host and the increase of the space of the set were two inseparable processes: the first needed the second to unfold. The *contact space* [espacio de contacto] was born, and with it, the axis around which all discourse would come to be built to find its credibility: the axis of the gaze, the eyes-into-the-eyes" (Verón 2001, 21; authors' translation).

Regarding the verbal discourse, the TV host evolved from a direct enunciation ("Today Bagdad suffered another terrorist attack") to more complex enunciational structures based on complicity with the viewer ("Let's see what our correspondent in Bagdad tells us about the terrorist attack"). In other words, the enunciator creates a symmetry with the viewers (both of them do not know what has happened). "Making symmetric their relationship, the enunciator constructs her credibility" (Verón 2001, 23). In this context, it could be said that the TV host's enunciation became more relevant than the statement about the facts.

This is the kind of approach that will be applied to BookTubers in the following pages: an analysis focused on the discursive and enunciational aspects of the videos. We will consider discursive differences between traditional generalist YouTubers and BookTubers, their enunciation strategies, and the enunciative contracts they are proposing to their viewers.

We first introduce analytical categories: enunciation, reading contract, and genre are essential. BookTubers are, first of all, video enunciators. To analyze their enunciation, Verón's concept of the "reading contract" will be used. Verón (1985) proposed the notion of a "reading contract" when he conceptualized the relationship between newspapers and their readers. This relationship is established between an enunciator (or addresser) and an enunciatee (or addressee). The addressee can then accept or refuse the contract proposed by the addresser. The notion of "contract" has been applied in the study of various media; in this case, the research analyzes how BookTubers (as enunciators) propose a relationship to their viewers (as enunciatees) through their discourse. This analytical model has already been tested in previous research on YouTubers as new media actors in the media ecology (Scolari and Fraticelli 2017).

This study follows Mikhail Bakhtin's (1986) classic definition for "genre." If language is realized in the form of individual concrete utterances, three aspects—thematic content, style, and compositional structure—are "inseparably linked to the whole of the utterance and are equally determined by the specific nature of the particular sphere of communication." Although each separate utterance is individual, each sphere in which language is used "develops its own relatively stable types of these utterances" (1986, 60). Bakhtin called these relatively stable types of utterances "genres." And, as a type, they make possible a horizon of expectations about communicational exchange. This notion will be extremely useful for determining how BookTubers organize their discursive production.

TABLE 4.1. Top Ten BookTuber Channels (by Number of Video Views)

Channel, creation date, and country	Number of subscribers	Video views	Number of videos
Clau Reads Books, August 23, 2006, Mexico	494,000	40,663,300	324
Laspalabrasdefa, August 1, 2008, Mexico	349,000	24,752,700	241
JavierRuescas, June 1, 2010, Spain	302,000	24,505,900	441
Josu Diamond, June 12, 2010, Spain	212,000	15,593,000	616
El coleccionista de Mundos, September 1, 2012, Spain	256,000	12,856,000	234
Andreo Rowling, October 14, 2012, Spain	166,000	12,293,000	327
Fly like a butterfly, March 25, 2010, Spain	181,000	10,538,100	274
Mayayamonte, June 5, 2011, Spain	122,000	10,204,000	486
AbriendoLibros, November 2, 2012, Mexico	232,000	7,569,500	198
Nube de Palabras, January 8, 2012, Spain	84,600	4,243,300	344

Note: The list was built considering the BookTubers with channels that are most viewed, as this makes it possible to study the major trends in their audiovisual constructions and how they are connected with a wider audience. The research team used the YouTube Data Tools (Rieder 2015) to collect data through YouTube's V.3 API on May 7, 2020.

BookTubers and the Publishing Industry

Returning to the concepts of "field" and "capital," using Bourdieu (1996), BookTubers structurally belong to two different fields. On the one hand, because their popularity does not reach the level necessary to obtain significant economic benefits through advertising (clicks) or sponsorship, as gamers and fashion and travel vloggers do, they occupy a subordinate place in the ecosystem of YouTube creators. On the other hand, they occupy a prominent place in the literary field, thanks to their ability to connect with the young audiences that the publishing industry cannot reach, which allows them to obtain benefits in exchange for making visible the products that the industry wants to sell.

YouTube as a platform is more than just a system for uploading and sharing videos. As part of Google/Alphabet Inc., YouTube combines a series of sociotechnical functions, such as a search engine, video relationship algorithms, subscription mechanisms, measurements (analytics), content identification protected by copyright, ad sales (AdSense), and social networking functionalities (comment, like, share). In this context, "attention is measured by the very systems that also produce and distribute content, organize and rank a video's display, connect ads to content, and attune the algorithms that connect content to advertisers" (van Dijck 2013, 125). Hector Postigo (2016) has shown how these affordances have been designed to align users' creations according to popularity criteria and, therefore, to increase the profits of the company through the creativity of the users.

Part of YouTube's success has been the creation of a partnership program, which allows popular creators to receive part of the advertising revenue that the platform gets from advertisers. Some of these YouTubers have achieved great popularity and have become microcelebrities (Marwick 2013; García-Rapp 2016, 2017; Raun 2018). However, the most popular BookTubers in the Spanish language do not reach popularity levels high enough to receive much money through pay per click or third-party sponsorships through the mediation of a multichannel network.

The literary field, like other fields of cultural production, as Bourdieu puts it, is distinguished by having a system of inverted values: selfless creation—art for art's sake—is the supreme value, and commercial exchange is seen as suspicious or a betrayal. In the traditional hierarchy of the field, the poet, who enjoyed much symbolic prestige but little economic success (his or her books hardly sell), occupied a place of privilege; the poet was followed by the novelist, who combined a bit of both worlds; and in last place was the writer of "entertainment"—a scriptwriter, a playwright, a best-seller writer—who can earn a lot of money but does not have the status of a "true" artist. Sometimes, he or she does not even receive credit as an author.

This structural division of the field, coupled with the polarization of editorial production in a few business conglomerates with high capital concentration and multiple small independent labels, helps us to understand the double reception that the BookTubers have had in the field. The "purist" pole despises them for not having academic credentials, for speaking from personal taste and not from "argumentation," and for talking about content considered of "low quality," such as young-adult literature, horror, or science fiction. From this perspective, BookTubers would be the confirmation of the dangerous cultural drift that leads us to the trivialization of culture, the celebrity of personality, and the commercialization of social relations promoted by technological capitalism. The "commercial" pole of the field, formed by publishers of children's and young-adult books (especially those that are big enough to have a marketing department), book fairs, and self-published authors, desperately try to establish alliances with BookTubers to promote their products. For this pole, BookTubers are valued for their ability to attract younger readers, and they are exalted as an example of "young people who read." The publishing industry tries to establish cooperation alliances with BookTubers to achieve their own marketing objectives.

Alliances and Relationships

The following are the more significant actors and relationships within the ecology of which BookTubers are part.

Publishers

Most BookTubers have been contacted by the communication/marketing team of at least one publishing house, which invites BookTubers to special events and sends them free books for them to review on their YouTube channels or to be given away through their Instagram/Twitter accounts. Through these contests, BookTubers gain social capital, while publishers benefit from the exposure given to their new titles. In some cases, publishers send BookTubers a list of titles from which they can choose; in others, BookTubers receive surprise boxes with personalized messages and gifts. However, outside these nonmonetary exchanges, we found little evidence of sponsorships, monetary fees, or paid collaborations. Another dimension of the relationship between BookTubers and publishers is BookTubers' work as trend researchers, because they have a particular sensitivity for determining new popular trends: they read books that have not been published in the local market, are aware of new TV series and movies, and have a very rich literary and cultural agenda (Krom 2018). Some BookTubers work as proofreaders for publishing houses, evaluating unpublished manuscripts as well as English books that are being considered for translation.

Authors

Another relationship that BookTubers establish is directly with authors. This relationship can adopt different dynamics depending on the power relationships that are established: when the author is admired, it can be very significant in emotional terms not only for the BookTuber as a fan but also for the author, who can appreciate how his or her books are so important to others. In some cases, this relationship can become personal. But when the power balance is reversed, for instance, in the case of self-published authors, who are the most deprived agents in the field and are desperately looking for a review, some requests almost become harassment.

Book Fairs

The presence of a known BookTuber at an event can attract crowds of young people and fill rooms. Important book fairs such as those of Buenos Aires, Lima, Bogotá, and Guadalajara have started to include BookTubers in their programs. Every year, Guadalajara's International Book Fair, the largest for the Spanish language, organizes a video-review contest called #Somos-Booktubers, and the winner is chosen in two rounds: the first, through the number of views and likes on YouTube; the second, through a specialized jury. Some BookTubers are also invited as speakers at public libraries, schools, and bookstores. In these kinds of collaborations, the organizers cover travel expenses and, depending on the case, pay speaker fees.

Booksellers and Retailers

BookTubers relate to online book retailers, like Amazon or Book Depository, through affiliated links posted in the description section of their videos. This has been seen as a form or "commodification of reading," since BookTubing becomes "intricately linked with consuming" (Albrecht 2017, 33). Another case is the use of the image of popular BookTubers as part of advertisement campaigns to endorse a selection of small bookstores.

BookTubers as Authors

Perhaps the most sophisticated way to commoditize BookTubers' social capital is turning them into authors for audiences. The most popular BookTubers have started to publish books for well-established publishing houses. With this move, publishers acquire titles that already have a network of loyal fans and also develop an organic promotional campaign through the BookTuber's channel, social media platforms, and other online presence. This process is part of the larger editorial trend to publish books signed by celebrities (TV presenters, politicians, artists, and so on) and, recently, famous YouTubers, like the fashion vlogger Yuya, comedians like YosoyGerman or Chumel Torres from El pulso de la república, and gamers and entertainers like Veggeta777 and Willyrex, El Rubius and DalasReview. As John Thompson explains in his study of commercial publishing, the value of a book increases depending on an author's "platform," which is defined as "the position from which an author speaks—a combination of their credentials, visibility and promotability, specially through the media" (2013, 87).

Discursive Analysis

With the aim of differentiating BookTubers from YouTubers in the operations they carry out when they produce their videos, this research takes advantage of an analytic model of the discursive dimension of these audiovisual productions (Scolari and Fraticelli 2017). Throughout our analysis, the similarities and differences between the two discourses will be indicated.

Individuation

The possibility that any individual can open an account and identify it with their own name is a defining characteristic of the contemporary media system. Mario Carlón (2017) has indicated that this grammar of production and recognition is similar to the autobiographical genre described by Philippe Lejeune ([1975] 1991). According to Lejeune, two communicational pacts are articulated in an autobiography: the referential and the biographical. The referential supposes that what appears in the text corresponds to the extratextual reality. The biographical pact involves the identity between the main character, the narrator, and the author—in this case between the character that appears in the video, the enunciator, and the owner of the account. BookTubers stand as enunciators in this communication pact even more than YouTubers do, because, although BookTubers can occasionally play fictional characters, it is assumed that they show a correlation with reality.

Amateurism

BookTubers often appear as amateurs both in the realization of their videos and in the evaluations of their readings. They are not literary scholars or expert critics. BookTubers talk about books according to their experiences and emotions, which by definition are subjective and are not submitted to verification. The validity of their statements is rooted in its emotionality; no institution legitimizes their words. This predominance of emotion also occurs in YouTubers in the same way as phatic expressions (Jakobson 1960). The enunciation proposes continuous contact with the spectator while looking straight into the camera. This point of view operates in a similar way to that of the television anchorman: he or she looks into the eyes of each viewer, maintaining the link with the viewer and generating a tension between the public character of the exchange and the interindividual visual contact (Verón 1983; Casetti and Di Chio 1998).

Humor

In BookTubers' discourse, as in other YouTubers', the laughable occupies a significant place, although their ways of generating it are different. For YouTubers, the comic intention prevails. They propose to laugh at the antics and characters they play. For BookTubers, the humor predominates: they laugh more at themselves for suffering painful situations related to being book lovers, such as being considered geeks or suffering the wait for a new volume of their favorite saga. These situations are shared by the collective audience, which is corroborated in comments made, such as, "I can't take it any longer! I need to read it too!"

Book Fetishization

BookTubers engage in the thematic delimitation of the semantic field of the book. José Tomasena (2016) points out their main topics. The first topic is "the book as a fetish." In the era of the dematerialization of texts, BookTubers love the physical book: they smell its pages, caress the covers with relish, and proudly display their libraries full of volumes. BookTubers continue the traditional practice of accumulating books, but from the position of the collector who seeks all the copies of a saga, collection, author, and the like, approaching, in this sense, the culture of fandom described by Henry Jenkins (1992, 2006). Another topic is that "reading is a love affair." This topic integrates two recurrent motifs: "the book as a magical object" and "writing as a gift." In the BookTubers' discourse, books have an active role in reading. A book can "catch" readers and force them to read it until the end in a single sitting. Books are good when they can make readers travel to another world against their will. That relationship is relative; a well-written book does not have to please everyone. There are videos in which BookTubers confess the books that "everyone likes" that they in fact do not like (Fly like a butterfly 2017). This ability to fall in love is explained by the characteristics of the writing, which is presented as an arduous job that needs time to develop rather than inspiration. But here again the "magical" component appears, because there are certain authors who have the power (and others who do not) to captivate readers. This gift is not linked to the writing work but to a certain stylistic harmony with the BookTuber's taste. In turn, BookTubers yearn to possess that skill. Most of them want to become writers, and many have achieved that status. Publishing a book is a common desire of BookTubers that is shared with their audience. There is even a specific group of videos in which BookTubers share their writing and publishing experiences (Rowling 2018).

Aesthetics

Finally, it is important to analyze the distinction between high and low culture that is also present in BookTubers' discourse. At first glance, BookTubers seem to escape that traditional opposition. Their reading compass is pleasure. Hence, they have no qualms about dedicating most of their videos to mainstream youth literature, which does not mean that classics like J. D. Salinger's *The Catcher in the Rye* (El coleccionista de Mundos 2017) or Don Juan Manuel's *Tales of Count Lucanor* (LasPalabrasDeFa 2013) do not appear. There is, however, a belief that certain books should be read even if they are boring. These are the "obligatory" readings. As Tomasena (2016) observes, not reading them involves accusations of guilt, shame, and challenge ("I read it to get rid of it") or reinforcement of cultural assumptions about "good taste" ("I read the *Odyssey*, and I swear I liked it").

Genres

The following are the genres typically produced by BookTubers.

Reviews

The genre of the review has been transposed from the mass media to YouTube. In this passage, the most significant change is in the amateur enunciation and its subsequent loss of institutional legitimacy. In the reviews and criticisms of the traditional media, the enunciators acquire an asymmetric status with respect to the enunciatees because the former speak through the mediation of an established institution (for example, magazines or newspapers) and show a knowledge about the history of literary styles. In the case of BookTubers, these components are not required to validate their statements: they are presented as an unquestionable matter of taste. Their legitimacy lies in recognizing their statements as such and not pretending to be more than that (Diamond 2017).

Wrap-Up

Wrap-up videos integrate short reviews of the books that the BookTuber has read during a certain period of time (Nube de Palabras 2018).

Class

Unlike YouTubers, BookTubers have introduced a didactic enunciation that develops a topic about which they hold an institutionally legitimated knowledge. Although some YouTubers also have a didactic enunciation, for example, tutorials, their knowledge comes from their own experience. In BookTubers' didactic enunciations, they analyze novels using concepts from linguistics and literary studies (LasPalabrasDeFa 2015).

Bookshelf Tour

Bookshelf tours are videos in which BookTubers display the books on their bookshelves and in which they can make brief comments about them, mostly linked to their reading experience (Mayrayamonte 2016).

Book Haul

Book haul videos involve the exhibition of books that a BookTuber has purchased or that have been sent by a publisher. The BookTuber briefly reviews the book or expresses his or her expectations (if he or she has not read it yet). Audience members, through comments, give opinions about the books if they have already read them (Nube de Palabras 2017).

Booktags

Booktag videos answer questions asked by other BookTubers. The enunciator of the video has been invited to answer questions by means of *labels* and, in turn, labels other BookTubers to do the same. In this way, a dialogue between videos is created, inviting viewers to compare the answers. Usually the questions ask about biographical and intimate issues related to reading (AbriendoLibros 2014).

Miscellaneous

Finally, the research team found genres that are also produced by vloggers from other YouTube niches, such as unboxing, ranking, challenge, interview, tutorial, vlog, and what could be defined as "entertainment genres." This last category includes a wide variety of videos that propose a ludic link to the stories, characters, and transpositions of the novels read by the BookTuber and the audience, for example, the "shippers" of Javier Ruescas, short stories in which dissimilar fictional characters coexist, such as the story of the marriage between Bella Swan, the protagonist of *Twilight*, and Captain Hook, the villain from *Peter Pan* (JavierRuescas 2016).

Reader Positions

We identified four recurrent enunciations found in the textual corpus under examination. A single BookTuber can assume these enunciations to a greater or lesser degree in order to define the style of his or her production.

Neophyte Informant Reader

The neophyte informant reader enunciation position develops a tension of asymmetrical/symmetrical relationships between the BookTuber and the audience. It is asymmetrical because the enunciator informs about publishing novelties, the books he or she has read, transpositions, visited bookstores, interviewed writers, and so on, but the BookTuber talks from a place without specialized knowledge, instead using as a frame of interpretation the emotions and experiences that are shared with the enunciatee. In this sense, it is an enunciative contract that, although it has features of journalistic discourse, is closer to the recommendations made among friends. The main genres in which BookTubers develop this enunciation position are reviews and wrap-ups. All BookTubers assume the enunciation of the neophyte informant reader; however, it predominates in channels like Clau Reads Books and AbriendoLibros.

Collector Reader

The collector reader enunciation position focuses on thematizing the book as a cult object and fictions to be accumulated and collected. The relationship between the BookTuber and the audience is symmetrical, as they are both identified in a shared devotion. The genres of this enunciative contract are the bookshelf tour and the book haul. This enunciation is present in all channels.

Playful Reader

The playful reader enunciation position is built on a shared knowledge. The BookTuber is positioned as a joker who plays with the fictions, creating jokes, new stories, and so on. The enunciatee knows about the fictions alluded to and laughs with the BookTuber about these funny and sometimes ridiculous statements. It is an enunciative contract that also reaffirms a shared enjoyment, but unlike with the collector reader, the book is desacralized by promoting the active role of reading as a generator of new texts. The genres of this enunciative position are the challenge and the so-called genres of entertainment. The JavierRuescas channel is the clearest case of this enunciation.

Aspiring to Expert Reader

In the didactic enunciation of aspiring to expert reader, the BookTuber defines terms, analyzes stories, and teaches how the stories should be read. The source of legitimation of their judgments comes neither from taste nor from their own experience, as in the neophyte informant reader, but from institutionally validated knowledge (i.e., from linguistics or literary analysis). The enunciator does not take on a fully professional position but is on the way to having one, like a student. The enunciator is constructed as someone who has read the mentioned work but did not get the true meaning. In this sense, it is the only enunciative contract that postulates universal judgments. Audience members usually respond to this enunciation by assuming their own supposed poor reading: "After watching your video explaining some metaphors, symbols, etc., I realized that I did not understand anything, absolutely anything about the book and that I urgently need to read it again." The aspiring expert reader is the contract least used by BookTubers. Its genre is usually that of the class, although it can also appear in the review. The Words of F and Mayrayamontes are two BookTuber channels that use it.

Conclusions

BookTubers are not exploited by corporations, but, at the same time, they are not the best example of cultural democratization. BookTubers emerge from a complex set of negotiations with the "commercial" pole of the book publishing industry, while the "literary" pole despises them. In this context, the discursive analysis made it possible to circumscribe the operations that distinguish BookTubers from YouTubers as well as the ones they share. They both have in common the enunciation of the amateur based on an individuation that postulates a correlation between the individual who stars in the video, the enunciator, and the owner of the account. Both also produce funny videos, although in BookTuber videos, there is a predominance of humor over the comic: they propose to their audiences to laugh at themselves for the setbacks they endure due to their love of books and reading.

The discursive property that distinguishes BookTubers from YouTubers is their thematic dimension. BookTuber videos revolve around the world of books (authors, editorials, readings, writings, editorial novelties, and so forth). Many genres originally created by YouTubers, like the bookshelf tour and book haul, have been transformed and adapted by BookTubers. But BookTubers have also created brand-new genres like the review and the class.

Finally, this discursive analysis made it possible to identify four enunciative positions taken on by BookTubers and to organize the contracts proposed to their followers: neophyte informant reader, collector reader, playful reader, and aspiring expert reader.

REFERENCES

AbriendoLibros. 2014. "Taylor Swift Book Tag | Oh, Oh." YouTube video, November 24, 2014. www.youtube.com/watch?v=eO3DQBhUvks.

Albrecht, Katharina. 2017. *Positioning BookTube in the Publishing World: An Examination of Online Book Reviewing through the Field Theory*. Leiden: University of Leiden Press.

Bakhtin, Mikhail. 1986. *Speech Genres and Other Late Essays.* Austin: University of Texas Press.

Bourdieu, Pierre. 1996. *The Rules of Art: Genesis and Structure of the Literary Field.* Stanford, CA: Stanford University Press.

Burgess, Jean, and Joshua Green. 2009. *YouTube: Online Video and Participatory Culture.* Cambridge, UK: Polity.

———. 2018. *YouTube: Online Video and Participatory Culture.* 2nd ed. Cambridge, UK: Polity.

Carlón, Mario. 2017. "Segunda apropiación contemporánea de la teoría de la comunicación de Eliseo Verón: La dimensión espacial." In *A circulação discursiva: Entre produção e reconhecimento,* edited by Paulo Castro, 22–48. Maceió: Edufal.

Casetti, Francesco, and Federico Di Chio. 1998. *Analisi della televisione: Strumenti, metodi e pratiche di ricerca.* Milan: Bompiani.

Cunningham, Stuart, and David Craig. 2017. "Being 'Really Real' on YouTube: Authenticity, Community and Brand Culture in Social Media Entertainment." *Media International Australia* 164 (1): 71–81. doi:10.1177/1329878X17709098.

Diamond, Josu. 2017. "Libros Necesarios | Josu Diamond." YouTube video, November 2, 2017. www.youtube.com/watch?v=-5vM5X76EwQ.

Ehret, Christian, Jacy Boegel, and Roya Manuel-Nekouei. 2018. "The Role of Affect in Adolescents' Online Literacies: Participatory Pressures in BookTube Culture." *Journal of Adolescent & Adult Literacy* 62 (2):151–161. doi:10.1002/jaal.881.

El coleccionista de Mundos. 2017. "'El guardián entre el centeno' de J. D. Salinger | Clásicos." YouTube video, July 7, 2017. www.youtube.com/watch?v=lzDH91iFstY.

Fly like a butterfly. 2017. "Libros famosos que no he Leído y/o he abandonado." YouTube video, March 5, 2017. www.youtube.com/watch?v=aRo_xGRdJmA.

Fraticelli, Damián. 2015. "Lo risible en los programas cómicos: Una tipología del chiste, la chanza, lo cómico y el humor televisivos." *Versión: Estudios de Comunicación y Política* 35:75–84.

Gannon, Valerie, and Andrea Prothero. 2018. "Beauty Bloggers and YouTubers as a Community of Practice." *Journal of Marketing Management* 34 (7–8): 592–619. doi:1 0.1080/0267257X.2018.1482941.

García-Rapp, Florencia. 2016. "The Digital Media Phenomenon of YouTube Beauty Gurus: The Case of Bubzbeauty." *International Journal of Web Based Communities* 12 (4): 360–375. doi:10.1504/IJWBC.2016.080810.

———. 2017. "Popularity Markers on YouTube's Attention Economy: The Case of Bubzbeauty." *Celebrity Studies* 8 (2): 228–245. doi:10.1080/19392397.2016.1242430.

González, Carla, and Claudia Lomelí. 2018. "Análisis de la relación que establecen las audiencias con los Booktubers." *Virtualis* 8 (16): 99–123.

Jakobson, Roman. 1960. "Closing Statement: Linguistics and Poetics." In *Style in Language,* edited by Thomas Sebeok, 350–377. Cambridge, MA: MIT Press.

JavierRuescas. 2016. "Shippeo de Personajes Literarios con Andrea Compton | Javier Ruescas #Ad." YouTube video, May 25, 2016. www.youtube.com/watch?v=vHZmmcjo5Po&t=206s.

Jeffman, Tauna. 2017. *BookTubers: Performances e conversações em torno do livro e da leitura na comunidade booktube*. São Leopoldo, Brazil: Universidade do Vale do Rio dos Sinos.

Jenkins, Henry. 1992. *Textual Poachers: Television Fans and Participatory Culture*. New York: Routledge.

———. 2006. *Fans, Bloggers, and Gamers: Exploring Participatory Culture*. New York: NYU Press.

Krom, Andrés. 2018. "Espíritu adolescente: Los Booktubers se vuelven aliados de los editores." *La Nación*, April 4, 2018. www.lanacion.com.ar.

LasPalabrasDeFa. 2013. "Mi explicación (mal hecha) de El Conde Lucanor—Don Juan Manuel | LasPalabrasDeFa." YouTube video, December 15, 2013. www.youtube.com/watch?v=1sIiJvyunEs.

———. 2015. "¿Libro Romántico o Libro de Romance? | LasPalabrasDeFa." YouTube video, February 12, 2015. www.youtube.com/watch?v=N_OBIR2L3dY.

Lejeune, Philippe. (1975) 1991. *El pacto autobiográfico*. Barcelona: Anthropos.

Lluch, Gemma. 2017. "Los jóvenes y adolescentes comparten la lectura." In *¿Cómo leemos en la sociedad digital? Lectores, Booktubers y prosumidores*, edited by Francisco Cruces, 30–52. Madrid: Fundación Telefónica.

Marwick, Alice. 2013. *Status Update: Celebrity, Publicity, and Branding in the Social Media Age*. New Haven, CT: Yale University Press.

Mayrayamonte. 2016. "Bookshelf Tour 2016 | Parte 1." YouTube video, January 22, 2016. www.youtube.com/watch?v=vU_VbYSsHMo.

Mendonça, Guilherme, Mauricio Menon, Marilu Oliveira, and Evandro Catelão. 2017. "A curadoria da literatura na educação básica: Aproximações entre os booktubers e docentes." *Texto Digital* 13 (1): 201–221. doi:10.5007/1807-9288.2016v13n1p201.

Nube de Palabras. 2017. "Book Haul | Octubre 2017." YouTube video, November 5, 2017. www.youtube.com/watch?v=qpWYGUPdmPU.

———. 2018. "Primer Wrap Up de 2018 | Lecturas enero 2018." YouTube video, February 10, 2018. www.youtube.com/watch?v=cmKENfqGnM0.

Postigo, Hector. 2016. "The Socio-Technical Architecture of Digital Labor: Converting Play into YouTube Money." *New Media & Society* 18 (2): 332–349. doi:10.1177/1461444814541527.

Raun, Tobias. 2018. "Capitalizing Intimacy: New Subcultural forms of Micro-Celebrity Strategies and Affective Labour on YouTube." *Convergence* 24 (1): 99–113. doi:10.1177/1354856517736983.

Rieder, Bernhard. 2015. "Introducing the YouTube Data Tools." *Politics of Systems* (blog), May 4, 2015. http://thepoliticsofsystems.net.

Rovira-Collado, José. 2017. "Booktrailer y Booktuber como herramientas LIJ 2.0 oara el desarrollo del hábito lector." *Investigaciones Sobre Lectura* 7:55–72.

Rowling, Andreo. 2018. "¿Cómo Publicar un Libro? | Consejos, Experiencia, Preguntas Frecuentes." YouTube video, June 24, 2018. www.youtube.com/watch?v=BZI7Bbsf-NQ&t=212s.

Scolari, Carlos A. 2013. "Media Evolution: Emergence, Dominance, Survival and Extinction in the Media Ecology." *International Journal of Communication* 7:1418–1441.

———. 2015. *Ecología de los medios*. Barcelona: Gedisa.

———. 2018. *Las leyes de la interfaz*. Barcelona: Gedisa.

Scolari, Carlos A., and Damián Fraticelli. 2017. "The Case of the Top Spanish YouTubers: Emerging Media Subjects and Discourse Practices in the New Media Ecology." *Convergence* 25 (3): 496–515. doi:10.1177/1354856517721807.

Sorensen, Karen, and Andrew Mara. 2013. "BookTubers as a Networked Knowledge Community." In *Emerging Pedagogies in the Networked Knowledge Society: Practices Integrating Social Media and Globalization*, edited by Marohang Limbu and Binod Gurung, 87–99. Hershey, PA: IGI Global.

Souza Teixeira, Claudia, and Andressa Abraão Costa. 2016. "BookTubers Movement: Emerging Practices of Reading Mediation." *Texto Livre: Linguagem e Tecnologia* 9 (2):13–31. doi:10.17851/1983-3652.9.2.13-31.

Sued, Gabriela. 2017. "Formas distantes de ver Youtube: Una exploración por la comunidad Booktube." *Virtualis* 7 (14): 90–112.

TheRaggysworld. 2014. "BookTube History (Anthropology Research Update)." YouTube video, August 8, 2014. www.youtube.com/watch?v=vF4Fqt7L_KE.

Thompson, John B. 2013. *Merchants of Culture: The Publishing Business in the Twenty-First Century*. Oxford, UK: Wiley.

Tomasena, José M. 2016. "Los videoblogueros literarios (Booktubers): Entre la cultura participativa y la cultura de la conectividad." Master's thesis, Social Communication, Universitat Pompeu Fabra, Barcelona.

Torralba Miralles, Gloria. 2018. "Los futuros maestros se convierten en Booktubers: Una práctica de fomento lector en el grado en maestro de educación primaria." *Lenguaje y Textos* 47 (2018). https://riunet.upv.es.

van Dijck, José. 2013. *The Culture of Connectivity*. Oxford: Oxford University Press.

Verón, Eliseo. 1983. "Il est là, je le vois, il me parle." *Communications Enonciation et Cinema* 38:27–49.

———. 1985. "Contrat de lecture: Une nouvelle méthode pour les etudes de positionnement prend en charge les médias." In *Les medias: Experiences, recherches actuelles, aplications*, edited by Emile Toutai, 203–230. Paris: IREP (Institut de Recherches et d'Etudes Publicitaires).

———. 2001. *El cuerpo de las imágenes*. Bogotá: Norma.

Vizibeli, Danilo. 2016. "Contrasts between the Specialized and Unprofessional Literature Critics: The Booktubers and the Discourses about the Book and the Reading." *Texto Livre: Linguagem e Tecnologia* 9 (2): 1–12. doi:10.17851/1983-3652.9.2.1-12.

YouTube. n.d. "YouTube for the Press." Accessed August 14, 2020. www.youtube.com.

5

Critical Media Industry Studies

The Case of Chinese Livestreaming

DAVID CRAIG, STUART CUNNINGHAM, AND JUNYI LV

In the first critical monograph about the emerging livestreaming industry, T. L. Taylor notes that "livestreaming is part of a larger transformation happening within the media industries" (2018, 10). Taylor's focus lies primarily on the vertical of content known as gameplay and commercializing gameplayers, or game commentators, found on Amazon-owned Twitch, which has dominated the global livestreaming platform market, with one notable exception. China's state protected and sponsored, but also heavily surveilled, livestreaming industry is characterized by a rapidly evolving landscape of platforms with genre variety and a scale of participation and revenue generation orders of magnitude greater than Western formats. More than a media phenomenon, China's livestreaming industry has come to play an acknowledged role in China's remarkable economic and cultural transformation.

In this chapter, we position livestreaming as part of two parallel creative industries, China's *wanghong* and social media entertainment (SME) (Cunningham and Craig 2019). Our conceptual framework draws on critical media industry studies (CMIS; see Havens, Lotz, and Tinic 2009; Herbert, Lotz, and Punathambekar 2020), a middle-range approach that seeks to account for both structure *and* agency, power *and* resistance in media industries. Our major findings are that highly advanced e-commerce integration on platforms has underpinned the economic sustainability of Chinese *wanghong* and livestreamers in particular but that this enhanced sustainability must be weighed against the ever present possibility of state action in pursuit of upholding "social morality."

Chinese Livestreaming

Livestreaming refers to broadcast video-streaming services provided by web-based platforms and mobile applications that feature synchronous and cross-modal (video, text, and image) interactivity. Amazon-owned Twitch has dominated the global market outside of China, although rivals continue to enter the market, including Microsoft-owned Mixer (Willens 2019). Other live platform initiatives have been early, but mostly fleeting, aspirants (UStream, Livestream, Periscope, Meerkat), while live features launched off larger preexisting platforms have proven extremely controversial. The chronic and rampant, obscene and criminal acts broadcast across Facebook Live and YouTube Live and their inability to contain such massive social infractions has featured centrally in the larger "techlash" against Silicon Valley (Smith 2018).

Across these platforms, alongside users and hobbyists, commercializing livestreamers convert their onscreen practice and interactivity with their followers into a variety of revenue streams, including subscriptions, advertising, tip jars, and licensing. The leading streamers are "gameplayers" or "videogame commentators" (Postigo 2014), and top-tier gameplayers like Ninja secure tens of millions of followers and have become the focus of bidding wars from rival gameplay livestreaming platforms for their channels and loyal fan communities (Hernandez 2019). While other nongame content genres ("verticals") have emerged, like cooking, painting, karaoke, and "social eating" (Recktenwald 2017), the Western live space is overwhelmingly dominated by gameplay.

In China, where Western platforms are banned and an alternative tech industry and platform landscape has emerged, the livestreaming industry has been "booming" (Lavin 2018) for some time. At its peak, in 2016–2017, there were over two hundred livestreaming platforms and apps in China featuring diverse content, from general entertainment to gaming, dating, and e-commerce (Hallanan 2018). Like Western livestreaming platforms, these platforms feature millions of users, not only livestreaming but generating revenue, with some making millions of dollars (Daxau Consulting 2017). Leading Chinese gameplayers are among those securing top revenue while advancing China's game and e-sports market, which, by 2017, exceeded the total US population (Soo 2017). Unlike the West, China's livestreaming industry has nurtured highly lucrative, as well as culturally provocative, nongame verticals. The Chinese-media scholar Aynne Kokas characterized it as "an entire industry of virtual girlfriends" (quoted in Kaiman and Meyers 2017). Business and social journalists wonder at women "singing and slurping soup" (Weller 2017) and China's "stream queens" getting rich by airing their lives online (Birtles 2016).

The livestreaming industry has benefited from the integration of e-commerce features. Beauty streamers capitalize on the advanced integration of Chinese e-commerce platforms like Taobao and mobile payments systems like WeChat Pay. When the leading livestreamer Zhang Dayi rang the bell at NASDAQ in 2019, he had a net worth of US$85 million (Anman 2019). Li Jiaqi, known as the "lipstick king," is a twenty-seven-year-old male beauty livestreamer who earned US$29 million in 2019 (Huang 2020). Weiya, one of the top female livestreamers on Taobao, has eighteen million followers and sold US$424 million of merchandise in 2019 during the annual shopping promotion day held on November 11 and known as "Double-Eleven" (The Egg, n.d.). Her *wanghong* brand is hugely expansive, featuring consumer goods such as cosmetics and agricultural products, durable goods such as luxury automobiles and apartments, and even a rocket-launching service worth US$5.6 million (Wang 2020).

The COVID-19 crisis proved an accelerator for the livestreaming industry. After the coronavirus outbreak in China, the National Bureau of Statistics commented that livestreaming-e-commerce would perform even better in the future (CCTV.com 2020). Press accounts describe how livestreaming e-commerce "helped Chinese farmers survive the pandemic" (Hao 2020) and how *wanghong* streamers "help brands stay engaged and competitive" (Chu 2020) and "prove a lifeline for China's small retailers" (Ouyang 2020).

The influence of the industry has been met by a "carrot-and-stick" array of interventions by the state. While the Chinese state has broadly facilitated livestreaming as an economic system, officials have also instigated a series of crackdowns and warnings directed toward livestreamers, platforms, and applications. In mid-2016, the State Administration of Press, Publication, Radio, Film, and Television (SARFFT) banned female livestreamers from "erotic banana-eating" (Phillips 2016). The ministry shut down ten online platforms and around 30,000 livestreaming accounts, aiming to weed out content that is "vulgar, obscene, violent, superstitious, concerns gambling, or harms the psychological health of underage people" (Lai 2017). These bans continued into 2017 and accelerated when SARFFT shuttered 73 platforms, 1,870 livestreamers received lifetime bans (Xinhua 2018), and over 400 livestreaming platforms experienced a crackdown because of "violence, pornography, gambling, superstition, and other values harmful to public morality" (P. Yang 2018). Some of these directives may be motivated by economic protectionist strategies toward China's tech sector as much as by rising cultural anxieties. In order for Chinese fans to watch their favorite Chinese gameplayers at a Western e-sports event, they downloaded Amazon-owned Twitch. The app became the third most popular in China, until it was abruptly shut down and removed from Apple's Chinese App Store (Hall 2018).

Signaling ongoing governance concerns as well as the fragmented nature of state policy, Chinese Communist Party–related groups are championing new forms of oversight and censorship. In 2019, the All-China Youth Federation submitted a proposal to the party for a law that would forbid children under eighteen (who constitute upward of 45 percent of livestreamers) from engaging in the activity (Koetze 2019). Some platforms, like Douyin or Kuaishou, have already developed a youth-friendly or "parents' control" version such that only certain types of content or functions can be used (*China Youth Daily* 2019).

SME, *Wanghong*, and CMIS

We understand both Western-based and Chinese livestreaming industries as components of the emerging social media entertainment and *wanghong* industries (Cunningham and Craig 2019). SME operates globally outside of China and primarily on Western-based platforms, whereas *wanghong* refers to China's alternative social media entertainment industry operating primarily within its own borders. Both industries are a dynamic ecology of social media platforms, cultural producers and entrepreneurs, and intermediary firms, operating in parallel with, and challenging, the economic and cultural power of traditional media and advertising industries. These industries have been built on the features, services, and affordances of social media platforms: SME is practiced on YouTube, Twitter, Facebook, Instagram, or Twitch; the Chinese platform landscape includes *wanghong* on Youku, Weibo, Kuaishou, Douyin (TikTok), and Douyu. In contrast to video-streaming "portals" for "internet-distributed television" (Lotz 2017), like Netflix, Hulu, and Amazon, these platforms combine varying modalities (recorded and live, short and long video, images, text, or audio) with social networking interactivity that allows for messaging, commenting, sharing, and liking.

Across these platforms, creators constitute a new wave of cultural producers and entrepreneurs building cultural and commercial value. In SME, alternative terms include *YouTubers, vloggers, influencers, gameplayers*, or *livestreamers*; in China, *KOLs* (key opinion leaders), *wanghong, zhubo*, and other terms. The term *wanghong* translates as "internet famous" and refers to microcelebrities (Tse et al. 2018). As Elaine Jing Zhao notes in her chapter in this volume, *wanghong* is a polysemic term not only because it embodies a diverse range of creators popular on the internet, with various possibilities for commercialization and different levels of sustainability, but also because it is celebrated and stigmatized at once. *Wanghong* is now routinely used to describe the contours and dimensions of this entire industry, as we do here.

Our theoretical framework draws on critical media industry studies (CMIS) (Havens, Lotz, and Tinic 2009), a theory of the middle range that seeks to account for both structure *and* agency, power *and* resistance in media industries. Timothy Havens, Amanda Lotz, and Serra Tinic argue that, among the classic trio of industry, text, and audience, the vast majority of critical media scholarship has favored the latter two areas. Ultimately, the intent in this approach is to make the media and communication field more coherent. This requires bringing the concerns and focus of macrolevel political economy and cultural studies closer together. To do this, however, it is necessary to critique both. CMIS pays close attention to the political, economic, and social dimensions of popular culture and its production practices. What political economy and cultural studies often see as mass culture fatally compromised by commercialism, CMIS regards as a major focus for representation and contestation, often around marginalized and emerging groups. "Ignoring the logic of representational practices in entertainment production works to reinforce the relative invisibility or misrepresentation of those who often have the least power in the public sphere" (Havens, Lotz, and Tinic 2009, 250).

Cultural studies inform CMIS's focus on "the complex and ambivalent operations of power as exercised through the struggle for hegemony" (Havens, Lotz, and Tinic 2009, 235). But serious, sustained attention to the industrial processes of digitization and globalization differentiates CMIS from cultural studies. On the other hand, the tendency in political economy to focus on news media means that CMIS often differentiates in its focus on entertainment—where pursuing the implications of power and influence ought to be much more nuanced:

> If and when popular culture is considered within a political-economic analysis, there is a reductionist tendency to treat it as yet another form of commodified culture operating only according to the interests of capital. There is little room to consider the moments of creativity and struggles over representational practices from that vantage point. That said, similar to political economy, and in contrast to other forms of media industry analysis, we are fundamentally concerned with questions of power; although we perhaps draw from a different range of thinkers in order to explain what we identify as the "complex, ambivalent, and contested" behavior . . . which occurs in these industries. (Havens, Lotz, and Tinic 2009, 236)

Havens, Lotz, and Tinic's call for attention to "quotidian practices and competing goals" (2009, 236) is crucial, with its sustained attention to everyday agents and clashes of business culture and state strategy. Methodologically, we also align with their emphasis on midlevel fieldwork in industry, including, given the emergent nature of SME, the knowledge of the realities of new media practice acquired through interviews. Our research is based on mixed methods, including content and discourse analysis of Chinese-language media accounts, industry reports, and media content, and fieldwork interviews conducted in Beijing, Shanghai, and Guangzhou with platform executives, livestreamers, and intermediary firms and professionals from 2016 to 2019. Most platform executives were contacted first on social media platforms such as Linkedin and Weibo. Livestreamers were introduced by platform executives and by our connections through alumni and events at USC Annenberg and Shanghai Jiao Tong University.

However, we are well aware of the need not to try to push social media entertainment (and livestreaming as a subcomponent of it) back into a box called "media industries" as they are traditionally understood. SME needs to be understood as *communication* as much as *content* media and as exhibiting and exploiting the technological and commercial affordances of platforms captured within the emerging fields of platform studies and social media studies (Papacharissi 2015; Bucher and Helmond 2018). But the big differences—at least for media studies—between legacy media and social media entertainment lie not only in such affordances of what Nick Srnicek (2016) calls "platform capitalism" but also, just as importantly, in the agency and identity of creators who work in this industry.

These foci also differentiate our work from production studies (Caldwell 2008; Mayer, Banks and Caldwell 2010) and introduces key twists in the narrative of labor precarity that dominates this subdiscipline. SME creators, and *wanghong* as the Chinese contingent of them, are largely composed of those who started out as amateurs, and the industry does not have anything like the division of labor seen in established media.

This chapter therefore adopts a creator-centric optic to illustrate the interdependencies among industrial, social, technological and economic, and political vectors in Chinese livestreaming, exemplifying CMIS's attempt to keep structure and agency, power and resistance in creative tension while being attentive to the layered, or multiscalar, flexibility of focus of media industry studies (Herbert, Lotz, and Punathambekar 2020). The *industry* optic is seen through the way Chinese livestreaming gameplayers operate as central actors within the Chinese video-game market, comprising China's more integrated games, e-sports, livestreaming, and *wanghong* industries. This cross-industry integration and leverage evinces the depth and innovation of China's digital creative industries. Analysis of the *social* dynamics of livestreaming focuses on the fact that, while gameplayers are overwhelmingly male in a highly gender-ordered industry, entrepreneurial female livestreamers have been empowered by state-sponsored cultural shifts in economic migration and engage in gendered performativity across platforms that see "pretty girls" appealing to the emotional needs of "lonely leftover men." World-leading *technological and economic* innovation is exemplified in e-commerce integrations. In response to a rapidly scaling Chinese middle-class consumption culture, Chinese livestreamers find success by advancing marketing imperatives directing consumers to cross-integrated platforms to engage in what has been called "live commerce" (Kim 2018) or the "social+" strategic business model (Yu 2019; Soo 2018). However, *politically*, Chinese livestreaming is deeply problematic; platforms and streamers have been the repeated target of state intervention, regulation, censorship, and outright bans.

Industrial Vector: Pay for Gameplay

The success of China's gameplay platforms and gameplayers has been fueled by the coevolution of China's globally dominant video-game and e-sports industries. In 2019, Chinese gamers outnumbered the total US population, and estimates are that China's game market will be worth US$41.5 billion and e-sports market will be worth US$9.5 billion by 2023 (Takahashi 2019). This success is also the consequence of the Chinese state-supported tech industry, composed of the national "champions" known as the "BATs" (Baidu, Alibaba, and Tencent). These firms have become central drivers of the Chinese digital economy, fostering the accelerated growth of the platform ecology and emerging cultural industries. In addition to numerous streaming video, social media, messaging, e-commerce, and livestreaming platforms, Tencent became the world's largest game company in 2018 (Takahasi 2018).

The strength and innovativeness of Chinese digital culture is clear from the extent to which gameplay is vital to the growth and competition across three industries: game publishers, e-sports tournaments, and livestreaming platforms. The integrations established among these three industries have been more seamless and more effective than in the West. According to Newzoo, the top gameplayer in 2018, XuXuBaoBao on Douyu, can reach earnings of over US$10 million per year (Toubang. tv 2019). Gameplayers secure revenue through diverse streams. Liu Shuo (2017), an executive at QuanminTV, a gameplay and e-sports platform, made clear in an interview that, because of the level of cross-industry integration and gameplayer embeddedness, gameplayers typically receive a base salary plus gifts. Premier players can dictate the terms of their salary and percentage of gifts. The contrast between the sustainability of Chinese gameplay and that in the West could not be starker.

Platform diversification is the consequence of a competitive platform landscape but also the competition for premier gameplayers. An executive at Huya noted, "Since 2016, we added content other than game livestreaming because signing game livestreamers can be very expensive. Livestreamers can jump among different platforms and take their fans with them" (Anonymous 2017). Xu Songsong at Qixiu, a livestreaming platform owned by iQiyi, explained further: "A game livestreamer is so expensive for platforms because his or her fans are valuable. A head game livestreamer can have one or two million in their online audience. For platforms, such a large number in the online audience is ideal to advertise. But the fans will follow the livestreamers if they move to different platforms. It is a challenging battle for platforms to avoid losing players and their audiences" (Xu 2017).

Social Vector: "Pretty Girls and Lonely Guys"

Our analysis of the most relevant Chinese trade and popular coverage, as well as 150 of the most relevant instances of Chinese academic writing, suggests that livestreaming is highly problematic. Scholars talk of "vulgar and sexual content" (Wang J. 2016) and "being vulgar, going low" (Yang S. 2016). Ge Zhang and Larissa Hjorth frame Chinese female gameplayers, or *nüzhubo*, as engaging in gender performativity, demonstrating entrepreneurial agency while subverting "traditional performative norms" around gender (2017, 17). While these accounts focus on critique of gendered representation, there is a need to consider the underlying history that has given rise to the conditions that have incubated these practices.

China's one-child policy—now modified to some extent—has contributed to a vast gender imbalance, estimated to be near seventy million more men than women in 2020, with millions of "lonely leftover men" (Sun 2017). China's shift from a rural agrarian and low-cost export-oriented manufacturing base to a more consumer-oriented, service-based economy has contributed to mass migration from rural to urban centers, often government sponsored (Johnson 2013). What Babs Grossman (2012) calls the "feminized service sector" has further contributed to gender imbalance, as young women move to cities to pursue training and opportunities while rural men remain to maintain family-run enterprises in agriculture and small-scale manufacture.

The consequence of these conditions has left millions of Chinese men partnerless with little opportunities for family formation and romance. Rural Chinese men rely on smartphones for basic communication, but these also provide entertainment and interactivity that was previously limited, inaccessible, or unaffordable. Their phones provide access to hundreds of applications, which now include any number of livestreaming applications and, in turn, "virtual girlfriends." As the Beijing Normal University scholar and livestreamer Zhang Hongzhong (2017) claimed, "Chinese people are lonely due to the fast pace of urbanization. A large number of people are going into big cities, where they feel lonely. Thirty million lonely souls are floating above the sky of Beijing. Alternatively, these conditions apply in the countryside because rural Chinese have fewer entertainment options."

In field interviews, platform executives confirmed the point that Chinese migratory loneliness informs the success of gendered livestreaming. Qixiu manager Xu Songsong (2017) was clear that "Chinese people lack companionship, rarely have occasion or places to spend time, money, and energy. Watching livestreaming can partially satisfy their needs."

Entrepreneurial opportunity and agency has advanced along with a deeply gender-ordered cultural politics of labor and exploitation. Platform affordances have enabled some female livestreamers to craft their careers against the grain of inexorable eastwardness. Liu Xinling (2017), a manager at Momo, gives the example of a female livestreamer in Sichuan who is "not very pretty but funny" and who found success through livestreaming: "She works for a local supermarket as a cashier. Sometimes she livestreams in her uniform so the audience knows. She is different from other pretty girls for her authenticity. She tells jokes and does crazy and funny things so people think she is a comedian. She can make RMB 10,000 a month, which is higher than many white collar incomes locally. She does not have to move to a big city for better resources since she can live a decent life in her hometown."

The increasing demands on female livestreamers to perform in an increasingly more provocative fashion can be met with an entrepreneurial determination. Anna (2017), a livestreamer on Bigo, acknowledged that she is "fully aware of what kind of livestreamer" she wants to become, while also expressing frustration that other female streamers do not enjoy showing their body but simply perform for the money. She described her manager encouraging her to "tease" her male followers, saying, "There are so many *wanghong*. How else can you get virtual gifts?" As Anna defiantly declared: "I did not come to this job to do this. . . . I was upset and walked away. I told his manager that it was not acceptable. Then the manager above us told me, 'Don't worry. Just ignore it.' So I did. But there are still people like that, unfortunately. . . . This is how they think they are going to attract people. . . . Girls who are sixteen or seventeen, educated to believe that they can make lots of money this way."

Provocative livestreaming may be a viable strategy for securing attention early in a female livestreamer's career but rarely proves sustainable. A Huya manager explained that sexually explicit content may feature at the beginning but eventually "dies down" due to censorship and audience boredom (Anonymous 2017). These concerns may also be a symptom of a maturing industry. As Huo Nifang (2017), the COO of Papi Jiang, the most famous creator in China, explained as she distinguished Miss Papi's operation from livestreaming, "Livestreaming is messy now. It has supervision and management, but it feels that the industry is mostly about sexually explicit content. Livestreaming is a very good concept, but the field does not have good content now. Some *wanghong* are making money, but the whole industry goes to a direction that I do not feel right. So we have not entered into this field."

Technological and Economic Vector: "Social+"

Wanghong pursue a lucrative practice of integrating their streaming with an e-commerce strategy to promote other brands and products as well as to launch and produce their own. These practices have been coined "live commerce" (Kim 2018) and a "social+" business model (Soo 2018) to capture how *wanghong* integrate the features and affordances of social networking platforms with e-commerce and mobile payments systems alongside their content practices and forms of interactivity. This model has impacted the retail value chain, most notably advertising and distribution. As the investment consultant Tim Shirata (2017) explained,

"WeChat's livestream platform includes integrated e-commerce built into the app itself. It's as if a Facebook live feed from your favorite celebrity discussing some product they love had an e-commerce shopping cart right next to the video." Livestreamers launch online stores through Alibaba's Taobao and T-mall e-commerce platforms (a cross between Amazon and eBay), where fans can purchase snacks, computer keyboards, and other products with a percentage of the purchase going to the livestreamer. According to our interview with Catherine Zhang (2019), a leading *wanghong* industry professional, ongoing iterations of these platform features not only reduce transaction costs but improve returns for *wanghong*.

While we have seen the extent to which Chinese authorities will go to exercise control regarding social and sexual matters, the US government's regulatory posture toward disclosure and transparency of commercialized activity on platforms is much sterner than China's commercial laissez faire. Whereas "times are about to get tough for [US] influencers . . . with the Federal Trade Commission (FTC) watching very closely how social media personalities disclose their relationship with brands and more stringent enforcement possibly in the works, [there are] *no such problems in China*" (Shirata 2017). In China, commercial practices driven by livestreaming have been relatively uninhibited by regulatory oversight with regard to brand integration disclosure. However, in late 2017, the state issued the PRC E-Commerce Law, described as "an attempt to gain greater control over online consumer markets" (Dickinson 2017). All online retailers must register with the state, and this oversight is intended to thwart smuggling and counterfeiters, while also protecting intellectual property (Banerjea 2018).

Across platforms, the hypercommercialization of live commerce—perhaps part of China's equivalent of the US Gilded Age—has to be managed carefully by creator and platform alike. Along with press accounts, field interviews regularly surfaced complaints about livestreamers engaging in too much product placement and advertising. Platforms have exerted limited control over their livestreamers, reflecting the power dynamics of platforms and streamers. Liang Yiping (2017) at YY E-sports commented, "YY livestreamers make money by virtual gifts mostly. They also do product placement, whether selling dried pork floss (rousong) cakes or computer keyboards. Some of them also own

WeChat stores or Taobao Stores. But we do control their ads or product placement because these may affect their performance. It is not good to users if they just advertise all day long."

The success of the "social+" strategy has positioned the *wanghong* industry as a potential rival to the SME industry in shared markets. Further expansion of Chinese live commerce is predicated on the ability of Chinese platforms to "go out" beyond the firewall, alongside changes in consumption patterns in countries where legacy retail and advertising industries remain in place. While Zhang Dayi aspires to expand her live commerce business across Asia, "one obstacle she identified is that the e-commerce infrastructure and online buying habits of the populace is different in these countries from the way they are in China" (Pan 2017). China's sophisticated e-commerce integration portfolios will aid its soft as well as harder power strategies that are emerging in its Belt and Road Initiative.

Political Vector: Censorship and "Edge Ball" Content

Creators' precarity in Western systems is largely driven by the experimental and volatile nature of the SME market for brands and advertisers, together with the endlessly iterative algorithmic tinkering engaged in by platforms, with often little thought given to creators' sustainability. On the other hand, in China, the precarity of the *wanghong* industry is due to its problematic social status, which puts it squarely in the political crosshairs. For Pierre Bourdieu, *précarité* mapped the difference between laborers "with permanent jobs and those with casual ones" (Alberti et al. 2018, 448). In China, authorities' policies and decisions significantly influence how "permanent" livestreamers' work can be. If it were simply a matter of market and platform functioning to meet demand, Chinese livestreaming would be an outstanding success. Instead, we have a replay of "edge ball"—borderline acceptable online expression—which has been a feature of Chinese popular cultural practice for decades (Keane 1998).

As we have noted, crackdowns on livestreaming practices continue at an accelerating pace. These policy interventions have shifted partial oversight to the platforms, and the effects on company practice is now manifest, as moral surveillance is accomplished through machine learning. All the platforms whose representatives we interviewed have divisions dedicated to supervision and censorship. Once livestreamers are discovered to have erotic or sexually explicit behaviors, their accounts are shut down by the platform. In an interview with an executive at Huya, a leading livestreaming platform, the executive acknowledged that "compared with recorded video content, livestreaming content is more difficult to censor since things happen so fast" (Anonymous 2017). Platform executives repeated the phrase "be obedient to government" (tinghua).

Platforms have developed diverse strategies that combine human and automated curation. According to He Jinkai (2017), a marketing manager at Yi Live, of the two thousand employees at the firm, half are involved in online supervision. In contrast, according to Liang Yiping (2017) at YY E-sports, "YY does not have many staff for supervision. Most of the supervising work is done by software. Real people are just a complement for the content that cannot be identified by machines." Platform executives confirmed that their censorship teams often number in the thousands and are located across the country, flagging concerns around pornography, gambling, drugs, and "edge ball" content.

The cultural politics of the Chinese state are not necessarily in conflict or misaligned with the values of streamers or their fan communities. The livestreamer Liu Xinling (2017) emphasized that she understands the position of the government. Compared to preemptive state-based guidance and direction, self- and community censorship are preferable. Even those individual livestreamers who have been targeted by the state may be acquiescent. As Bobby Kiki (a pseudonym; 2017) said, "I started to do livestreaming on some new platforms, and one of them is Huoshan [Volcano]. My account was shut down, so I asked the platform what happened. They said my skirt shows my thighs. When I stand up, the skirt shows a bit of my legs, and it is not allowed." But she also added, "My family members [i.e., fans] are strict. They do not want me to wear sexually explicit clothes. I need their permission before shooting advertisements or appearing in reality shows." She continues to operate as a livestreamer on other platforms.

Conclusion

Any examination of cultural production and cultural politics on Chinese platforms must take into account the distinctly different relations in China between state, market, technological innovation, and society. We have argued that critical media industry studies is an appropriate explanatory framework to examine cultural and economic opportunities on the part of individual and small business agents in this dynamic macro-political and technological context, and we have situated our approach in relation to cultural studies, production studies, platform studies, and social media studies. Our major findings are that highly advanced e-commerce integration on platforms has underpinned the economic sustainability of Chinese *wanghong*, and of livestreamers in particular, but that this enhanced economic sustainability must be weighed against the ever-present possibility of state action in pursuit of upholding "social morality."

As Guobin Yang (2014) has cautioned, scholars need to consider the distinctive Chinese ideals and practices that have shaped the Chinese internet. Such cautions should include that we need to recognize that state action may appear contradictory but is in fact strategic, involving simultaneously market framing and management, incubation and support for world-leading technological innovation, as well as strict moral censorship of these rapidly evolving social media entertainment industries that provide Chinese netizens with voice, meaning-making, and potentially sustainable—and, for some, lucrative—careers.

REFERENCES

Alberti, Gabriella, Ioulia Bessa, Kate Hardy, Vera Trappmann, and Charles Umney. 2018. "In, Against and Beyond Precarity: Work in Insecure Times." *Work, Employment and Society* 32 (3): 447–457. doi:10.1177/0950017018762088.

Anman. 2019. "Shenjia 6 ge yi! 31sui nvwanghong kaitaobaodian yezai meiguo shangshile" [Net Worth RMB 600 Million! 31-Year-Old Female *Wanghong* Opened Taobao Store and Went Public at NASDAQ]. *China Fund News*, April 4, 2019. https://news.futunn.com.

Anna. 2017. Livestreamer and former employee of Bigo Live. Interview with Junyi Lv, China, June 19, 2017.

Anonymous. 2017. Management executive at Huya. Interview with Junyi Lv, China, June 20, 2017.

Banerjea, Sejuti. 2018. "Why U.S. Brands Need to Play by Alibaba's Rules in China." Nasdaq, April 24, 2018. www.nasdaq.com.

Birtles, Bill. 2016. "Chinese Social Media 'Stream Queens' Getting Rich by Broadcasting Their Lives Online." *ABC News*, July 27, 2016. www.abc.net.au.

Bobby Kiki. 2017. Livestreamer, YouKu-Laifeng and Houshan. Interview with Junyi Lv, China, June 13, 2017.

Bucher, Taina, and Anne Helmond. 2018. "The Affordances of Social Media Platforms." In *The Sage Handbook of Social Media*, edited by Jean Burgess, Alice Marwick and Thomas Poell, 233–253. London: Sage.

Caldwell, John. 2008. *Production Culture: Industrial Reflexivity and Critical Practice in Film and Television*. Durham, NC: Duke University Press.

CCTV.com. 2020. "Guojia tongjiju xinwen fayanren tan zhibo daihuo: xiaofei qianli shifang xinxing xiaofei hui biaoxian gengjia qiangjin" [The Spokesperson of National Bureau of Statistics of China Talks about Livestreaming E-commerce: The Potential of Consumption Releases; New Forms of Consumption Will Perform Even Better]. April 17, 2020. https://m.news.cctv.com.

China Youth Daily. 2019. "Zhege hangye jinzhi weichengnianren 'shezu'? Wangyou yizhi shuohao" [Forbid People under 18 Livestreaming? Netizens All Said Good]. March 9, 2019. https://mp.weixin.qq.com.

Chu, Frankline. 2020. "These Tactics Are Helping Chinese Retailers Survive the Coronavirus Crisis." *DigitalCommerce360*, April 23, 2020. www.digitalcommerce360.com.

Cunningham, Stuart, and David Craig. 2019. *Social Media Entertainment: The New Intersection of Hollywood and Silicon Valley*. New York: NYU Press.

Daxau Consulting. 2017. "China's Livestreaming Millionaires: Where Does the Wealth Come From?" April 13, 2017. http://daxueconsulting.com.

Dickinson, Steve. 2017. "China E-Commerce: Resistance Is Futile." *China Law Blog*, November 13, 2017. www.chinalawblog.com.

Grossman, Babs. 2012. "The Feminised Service Sector: From Micro to Macro Analysis." *Work Organisation, Labour & Globalisation* 6 (1): 63–79. doi:10.13169/workorgalaboglob.6.1.0063.

Hall, Charlie. 2018. "Twitch Suddenly Blocked in China." *Polygon*, September 21, 2018. www.polygon.com.

Hallanan, Lauren. 2018. "A Snapshot of Live Streaming Platforms in China." *KrASIA*, October 31, 2018. https://kr-asia.com.

Hao, Karen. 2020. "Live-Streaming Helped China's Farmers Survive the Pandemic: It's Here to Stay." *MIT Technology Review*, May 6. 2020. www.technologyreview.com.

Havens, Timothy, Amanda Lotz, and Serra Tinic. 2009. "Critical Media Industry Studies: A Research Approach." *Communication, Culture & Critique* 2 (2): 234–253. doi:10.1111/j.1753-9137.2009.01037.x.

He Jinkai. 2017. Director of Commercial Department, Yi Live. Interview with Junyi Lv, China, June 9, 2017.

Herbert, Daniel, Amanda Lotz, and Aswin Punathambekar. 2020. *Media Industry Studies: A Short Introduction*. Cambridge, UK: Polity.

Hernandez, Patricia. 2019. "Ninja Is Leaving Twitch, Will Start Streaming on Mixer Exclusively." *Polygon*, August 1, 2019. www.polygon.com.

Huang, Alice. 2020. "Who Is Millionaire Li Jiaqi, China's 'Lipstick King' Who Raised More than US$145 Million in Sales on Singles' Day?" *South China Morning Post*, March 9, 2020. https://scmp.com.

Huo Nifang. 2017. Chief Operating Officer, PapiTube. Interview with Junyi Lv, China, June 12, 2017.

Johnson, Ian. 2013. "China's Great Uprooting: Moving 250 Million into Cities." *New York Times*, June 15, 2013. www.nytimes.com.

Kaiman, Jonathan, and Jessica Meyers. 2017. "Chinese Authorities Put the Brakes on a Surge in Livestreaming." *Los Angeles Times*, June 24, 2017. www.latimes.com.

Keane, Michael. 1998. "Television and Moral Development in China." *Asian Studies Review* 22 (4): 475–503. doi:10.1111/1467-8403.00027.

Kim, Daniel. 2018. "Live Commerce Is Here: Is Your Company Ready to Take Advantage?" *SendBird* (blog), February 5, 2018. https://blog.sendbird.com.

Koetze, Manya. 2019. "China Youth Federation: Ban Minors from Livestreaming Platforms." *What's on Weibo*, March 9, 2019. www.whatsonweibo.com.

Lai, Catherine. 2017. "Chinese Live-Streaming Platform Punished for Broadcasting Fake 'Forbidden City' Video." *Hong Kong Free Press*, May 26, 2017. www.hongkongfp.com.

Lavin, Frank. 2018. "China's Live-Streaming Industry Is Booming—Here's How It Works." *Forbes*, June 19, 2018. www.forbes.com.

Liang Yiping. 2017. Manager of Content Development, YY Live. Interview with Junyi Lv, China, June 19, 2017.

Liu Shuo. 2017. Manager, Quanmin TV. Interview with Junyi Lv, China, June 20, 2017.

Liu Xinling. 2017. Manager of the Public Issues Department, Momo. Interview with Junyi Lv, China, June 15, 2017.

Lotz, Amanda. 2017. *Portals: A Treatise on Internet-Distributed Television*. Ann Arbor: Michigan Publishing, University of Michigan Library.

Mayer, Vicki, Miranda Banks, and John Caldwell, eds. 2010. *Production Studies: Cultural Studies of Media Industries*. New York: Routledge.

Ouyang, Iris. 2020. "Coronavirus: Live-Streaming Sales Prove a Lifeline for China's Small Retailers as Pandemic Disrupts Business Models and Consumer Behavior." *South China Morning Post*, April 25, 2020. www.scmp.com.

Pan, Yiling. 2017. "Top Web Celebrity Zhang Dayi Reveals the Key to Her Business Success." *Jing Daily*, July 19, 2017. https://jingdaily.com.

Papacharissi, Zizi. 2015. "We Have Always Been Social: Manifesto (Inaugural Issue)." *Social Media + Society* 1 (1): 1–2. doi:10.1177/2056305115581185.

Phillips, Tom. 2016. "Gone Bananas: China Bans 'Erotic' Eating of the Fruit on Live Streams." *The Guardian*, May 9, 2016. www.theguardian.com.

Postigo, Hector. 2014. "The Socio-Technical Architecture of Digital Labor Converting Play into YouTube Money." *New Media & Society* 18 (2): 1–18. doi:10.1177/1461444814541527.

Recktenwald, Daniel. 2017. "Toward a Transcription and Analysis of Livestreaming on Twitch." *Journal of Pragmatics* 115:68–81. doi:10.1016/j.pragma.2017.01.013.

Shirata, Tim. 2017. "Social Commerce, Livestreaming, and Virtual Goods: Chinese E-Commerce Innovation Pulls Ahead." *Guild Investment*, June 2, 2017. https://guild-investment.com.

Smith, Eve. 2018. "The Techlash against Amazon, Facebook and Google—And What They Can Do." *Economist*, January 20, 2018. www.economist.com.

Soo, Zen. 2017. "The Phenomenal Rise of E-Sports in China Where Gamers Outnumber the US Population." *South China Morning Post*, August 2, 2017. www.scmp.com.

———. 2018. "China's Internet Companies Adopting New 'Social+' Business Model to Succeed." *South China Morning Post*, May 12, 2018. www.scmp.com.

Srnicek, Nick. 2016. *Platform Capitalism*. Oxford, UK: Polity.

Sun, Wanning. 2017. "'My Parents Say Hurry Up and Find a Girl': China's Millions of Lonely 'Leftover Men.'" *The Guardian*, September 28, 2017. www.theguardian.com.

Takahashi, Dean. 2018. "The DeanBeat: Tencent Leads China's Domination of the Global Games Business." *Venture Beat*, April 20, 2018. https://venturebeat.com.

———. 2019. "Niko Partners: China's Game Market to Hit $41.5 Billion and 767 Million Players by 2023." *Venture Beat*, May 7, 2019. https://venturebeat.com.

Taylor, T. L. 2018. *Watch Me Play: Twitch and the Rise of Live Game Streaming*. Princeton, NJ: Princeton University Press.

The Egg. 2020. "The Power of Livestream in the Age of COVID-19." April 23, 2020. https://theegg.com.

Toubang.tv. 2019. "18nian Zhongguo quanwang youxi zhubo shouru paihangbang chulu, Douyu liuwei zhubo shangbang" [2018 China's Online Game Streamer Income Ranking Is Published: Douyu Has 6 Game Streamers on the List]. April 26, 2019. www.toubang.tv.

Tse, Tommy, Vivienne Leung, Kimmy Cheng, and Joey Chan. 2018. "A Clown, a Political Messiah or a Punching Bag? Rethinking the Performative Identity Construction of Celebrity through Social Media." *Global Media and China* 3 (3): 141–157. doi:10.1177/2059436418805540.

Wang Jiangshan. 2016. "Toushi Zhongguo wangluo zhibo dangqiande wenti yufazhan qushi" [See through the Current Problem and Future Development of Chinese Online Livestreaming]. *Journal of News Research* 7 (13): 321.

Wang Yiqing. 2020. "Doubt Livestreaming's Potential? Someone Just Sold a Rocket Online." *China Daily*, April 3, 2020. www.global.chinadaily.com.cn.

Weller, Chris. 2017. "Chinese Women Are Creating a Billion-Dollar Livestreaming Industry Based on Singing and Slurping Soup." *Business Insider*, May 1, 2017. www.businessinsider.com.

Willens, Max. 2019. "Once Dominant, Amazon-Owned Gaming Platform Twitch Has More Competition and More Problems." *Digiday*, August 14, 2019. https://digiday.com.

Xinhua. 2018. "Livestreaming Revenue Exceeds 30b Yuan in China in 2017." State Council, People's Republic of China, January 21, 2018. http://english.gov.cn.

Xu Songsong. 2017. Manager of the Content, Market, and Commercial Department, Qixiu, iQiyi. Interview with Junyi Lv, China, June 22, 2017.

Yang, Guobin. 2014. "The Return of Ideology and the Future of Chinese Internet Policy." *Critical Studies in Media Communication* 31 (2): 109–113. doi:10.1080/152950 36.2014.913803.

Yang, Peter. 2018. "A Primer on China's Livestreaming Market." *Hackernoon*, September 9, 2018. https://hackernoon.com.

Yang Shiyu. 2016. "Wangluo zhibo luanxiang beihoude sikao—Yi Douyu weili" [A Thought on the Mess of Online Livestreaming—Using Douyu as a Case]. *Xibu Guangbo Dianshi 6 (2016): 75, 79.*

Yu, Haiqing. 2019. "China's 'Social+' Approach to Soft Power." East Asia Forum, June 27, 2019. www.eastasiaforum.org.

Zhang, Catherine. 2019. *Wanghong* industry professional. Interview with David Craig, China, May 19, 2019.

Zhang, Ge, and Larissa Hjorth. 2017. "Livestreaming, Games and Politics of Gender Performance: The Case of Nüzhubo in China." *Convergence: The International Journal of Research into New Media Technologies*, November 8, 2017. doi:10.1177/1354856517738160.

Zhang Hongzhong. 2017. Dean of the School of Journalism and Communication, Beijing Normal University, and livestreamer. Interview with Junyi Lv, China, June 15, 2017.

PART II

Genres and Communities

6

Video Gameplay Commentary

Immersive Research in Participatory Culture

HECTOR POSTIGO

Everybody loves a mystery. We may not like the characters, but we love puzzling over mysteries, often returning to books or TV shows of that genre for more clues, trying our hands at sleuthing. Some students of persuasion and the chicanery of the con have observed that mysteries are a good way to focus attention (Cialdini 2008, 2016). While we're busy waiting for the next clue or the "big reveal," someone is picking our pocket or selling us a bridge in Brooklyn, cheap.

Like solving a mystery, looking for authenticity in videogame commentary (VGC) is not unlike attempting to see past a presentation of self that is not always complete or authentic. What is VGC? you might be asking. In short, it's the practice of recording one's gameplay and then afterward producing voice-over commentary to accompany it and putting the finished product on YouTube. VGC commentators can provide tips and tricks, offer a witty, funny, or serious monologue on game culture situated in the game being played, or use the game to vlog on topics that might not be at all related to the game.[1] But who were the commentators I was studying? Why were they spending so much time and resources in what appeared to be a hobby? Were they really that good at the game? Were they as mean to each other as some of their commentary showed, or were they as nice as other videos showed? Or were they trying to break into the YouTube-money business model and being great marketers?[2] I suppose I could have interviewed them, although, as Stephens-Davidowitz (2017) has argued, everybody lies, or at least embellishes the truth, particularly before an audience. So what methods should one use to know who VGC commentators really are as a creator culture? The answer is (1) a *deep (nearly monomaniacal) immersion* in the techno-culture of the creator community, (2) *observation and collection (scraping) of every detail* in all of the community's creative works, comments, tweets, and so on, and (3) *analysis*, connecting the dots between what was said, done, when, where, and how to increase video views and the social proof of showing up at the top of a Google search.

Wrestling with Definitions and Surrendering to Indeterminacy

Authenticity is messy. Research across disciplines, defining the concept in a myriad of ways, is legion. I won't belabor the debate on what it is and what sort of theoretical insights it provides as a lens, heuristic, pithy keyword, or predictive model for those of us studying the political economy of the creative industries, the web, or branding strategies.[3] Personally, I am interested in what creative communities think it is and how they perform it when they make content that features themselves and something they love to do as entertainment. They must reconcile the person they perform for the audience with the person the audience thinks they are "in the real" in a way that seems—dare I say it?—authentic. Or maybe they don't care either way, and their endgame is something else. We'll see.

For the sake of definitions, I should tell you where I'm coming from when I think of authenticity in this case. I marvel at how hard artists work at crafting their public personae to reinforce their performative personae and how that endeavor fails when a cloud server is hacked or when paparazzi get a glimpse behind the veil of poise. How much harder it must be in the age of Twitter and Instagram, a world full of people with cell-phone cameras and the web. I've wondered how that endeavor affects how they see their craft. Does it lose the luster of freedom/independence when "the show must go on," even when they just want to get a goddamn latte and get home to binge on Netflix? If the "show" doesn't go on and they appear inauthentic, they may not get the next paycheck, and they'll only hear the sound of summer crickets when next they take the stage.

Comparatively, I know people making VGC on YouTube certainly aren't managing public image to the same degree that Will Smith or Taylor Swift are, but I think commentators are held to higher standards for authenticity. Given that video-game commentators chose YouTube as their platform, when I started conducting the research, I presumed that the performative persona (playing a video game along with commenting on it) must be a convincingly real one, or else it would be hard to convince an audience that it's really "You" in the "Tube." Unlike starring in a major motion picture, playing video games in front of other people, talking trash, laughing, raging, and/or having fun is something a great deal of people do. The audience knows what it's like; therefore, for commentators, authenticity better mean equivalence between a performative and a private persona that the audience recognizes in themselves. That's a high bar.

I have to balance that standard with what the people performing may give me as a definition, which only makes it harder to define. My working assumption when observing and interviewing people is that if I ask a person with a public persona what authenticity is and if they are authentic, they'll probably tell me what I want to hear or some version of what they believe will serve them best. Either way, they'll strive to make it consistent with the various personae (private and performative) they hope to represent as perfectly aligned. Whatever definition they give won't encapsulate what it is in practice because definitions are by necessity only words. Their practices seem at times contradictory or hint at something more than authentic, defined as consistent self-presentation.

If I had to say what the definition of *authentic* is, I'd say it's a state of being and a process. In other words, authenticity is *performed*, so I can't solely rely on what is said. Getting at a more complete definition, and therefore understanding the subject position, requires a nearly obsessive immersion in practice. Herein lies an argument *for practice as epistemology*, which is the idea that only by doing what the research subject does can one know how they understand their technologies, communities, and matrix of meanings that make up their particular creator culture. To know the business of making poetry, for example, one must write poetry and put it out there to "suffer the slings and arrows of outrageous fortune" or to bask in the roar of applause. One must use the technologies, networks, and platforms to bellow out those mutterings and stutterings and wait, sometimes forever, to see who is listening.

Enter deep immersion in creator techno-culture.

What would this form of immersion mean for you if you wanted to chase down "being authentic" or the practice epistemology in VGC creator culture that I describe here? It's more than participant observation. It's "going native." In the case of creator communities like VGC, who are deeply embedded in techno-culture, it requires engagement with a bricolage of technologies in the form of hardware and software. You must hack—hack at hardware, software, play style, and even identity. Not only must one know how to use the game console, PC, web platform, the community's idiom, mores, and so on, but one should also know how to hack them, piece them together creatively, exploit their avenues for tinkering, and leverage their affordances to one's ends.

Admittedly not everyone has the patience, skill set, or means to do/learn how to do those things. Different creative communities use different technologies and skills. I'm assuming the reader would want to study a group that distributes the bulk of their creative work online and that works with digital technologies primarily—and that they're using hardware you can get at a local or online retailer and editing software that comes with your computer or phone or that you can find for free on the web.

At the time I did the research, my deep immersion required a PC, an Xbox360, a PS3, a cell phone, a CRT monitor, a Scuff modded controller, four sets of surround-sound headsets (for example, Sennheiser for PC, Turtle Beach for PS3, Tritons and/or Astros for the Xbox), a Black Magic capture card (before that a Hauppauge video-capture pass-through), terabytes of hard-drive space, and a very good internet connection. On the software side of things, I needed video games (see note 1), video editing software (Sony Vegas), UDP data-flooding software (for when lag compensation created awful disadvantages for players with fast internet connections),[4] and Creative Commons music.[5] On the knowledge-base side of things, I had to watch interminable "how-to" videos for using the gear and software, for solving technical problems or preempting them. Most of the videos (or suggestions on where to look for information) came from the YouTube VGC community I studied.

Before this section's extensive notes and technical descriptions start to make this chapter feel like "Cetology" in *Moby Dick*, I should qualify them with an insight that came from gathering technical information for how to get on board the VGC boat (seafaring reference intended). I found it peculiar that commentators would openly share tricks of the trade. VGC at the time I started studying it didn't have the audience size to merit calling it a media business phenomenon (I was studying it pre-Twitch.tv and YouTube Gaming). Nonetheless, I could tell it was going to be a significant genre, so it felt like I was watching a magician give away her tricks while still working on the sidewalk in Times Square, before making it to Carnegie Hall. That clued me into something about the performance of authenticity as it is practiced in some creator cultures and early business ventures that hope for a large audience. *Giving away content (or important information) is seen as a gift, even if the receiver doesn't need it, and the sort of generosity that comes simply from the joy of giving.* It doesn't feel transactional to the receiver. As vast marketing research literature shows, it's when someone gives us something and doesn't appear to want anything in return that we feel we're seeing something genuine and that leads the receiver to want to give back in turn by, for example, in this case, liking, subscribing, and following a commentator on Twitter. Creating a context where reciprocity is felt by the receiver is a powerful way of creating brand loyalty.

The other bit of knowledge I needed to immerse myself in the practice I was researching was learning how to play the game well. I had to play the game online with others because I needed to learn the norms, language, and ideas present in play that found their way into commentary and vice versa. The working hypothesis was that the narratives that evolve as entertaining or interesting in gameplay commentary have some connection to common experiences in public game lobbies. If commentators can tap into that through references to those narratives, they develop an insider status. Essentially, they communicate, "I am one of you." And we tend to feel allegiance to those who are like us in one way or another.

As I picked up on the various ways that the game's oddities, flaws, and successes created topics for conversation in public lobbies and in commentary, I noticed something that should have been obvious sooner. When I started this endeavor in mid-2009, I wasn't very good at the games. Once after a match in competitive play, someone I didn't know sent me a private message telling me, "Could you please turn down the suck?" As far as hate mail from the online gaming communities goes, that's comparatively light fare, but it pointed to something typical about competitive gameplay in public lobbies that I had known about but not paid attention to: competitive play can inspire rage.

Obviously untempered anger is never productive, but for the purposes of VGC, it had the potential to be both an entertaining and unifying theme in the gaming experience. As long as no one is getting hurt, people tend to find the thought of someone losing it in colorful ways funny. If it's because of something that also has happened to us, we, the audience, may briefly feel their pain, but after the flash of empathy passes, we still laugh. People may not admit it, but most who have been in a *CoD* game lobby (or any competitive video game) can identify a moment when they've been the ones raging because the game had a bug that caused them to lose a match or a random teammate just couldn't "turn down the suck." Commentators knew this, so they posted gameplay where those moments happened to them. They often got a spike in views. One commentator made it his genre of choice.[6] Designers noticed the possibility that frustration or rage might be entertaining too. The last *CoD* game I played for this research (*Modern Warfare 3*) created a two-second moment for eavesdropping during competitive play. For a couple of seconds after a player won an engagement, the winning player could listen to what the losing player might be saying into his or her mic. Of the 960 hours of gameplay and the terabytes of content I recorded over 3.75 years, eight out of ten times a clip had a two-second span of eavesdropping, there was rage on the other end of the mic, and it made me chuckle.

Reading the preceding vignette, you might be wondering if I've strayed from Ariadne's thread and started describing "observations," forgetting that I set out to describe deep immersion in the tech of the VGC techno-culture, but that's not the case. Elements of what I describe as frustrating and how they were leveraged as material both in the game and outside of it *originated in failures of technology or in-game mechanics.*

As I mentioned previously, overzealous lag compensation inspired a lot of anger and a bit of hacking within some sections of the gaming community (for further insight, see note 4). I didn't learn how to deploy workarounds to bugs (perceived or real) from a computer networking course. I learned that from the *CoD* gaming community. In other words, if I had not been as immersed as I was in getting "YouTube-worthy gameplay"[7] myself, I may never have asked around to see how others were circumventing what was clearly a networking bug in the game. If I hadn't tested it, I wouldn't have found that they were right. So does this finding show that because commentators and players were willing to do anything short of cheating to make sure they had the technological advantage for making gameplay, their talent at the game was completely staged, inauthentic? Maybe, but only in the same way that an athlete's seemingly natural talent is staged when she uses the best equipment she can get her hands on before competing. Besides the deeply technological means of creating the illusion of great gameplay, what else was there? That's where a lot of observation and data scraping came in.

Observation in Every Direction

I could not search for data on how this community of creators shaped their performative personae in one place. So observation had to be multiplatformed. That required a kind of orthogonal vision. Like Argos, I had to look in every direction at the same time: Twitter, Facebook, YouTube, Justin TV (precursor to Twitch.tv), conventions, and random bulletin boards. They used every networked medium available to them to inform themselves and to *capture, cache,* and ultimately *convert* their audience into YouTube ad dollars and other revenues streams. I call that the 3Cs of getting YouTube money: capture, cache, and convert (for more on the 3Cs, see Postigo 2014).

Capture means growing the audience, and that requires producing regular content. In the early days of the community, some commentators would post two to three videos per week. Others, with less time on their hands, would post one per week or less. They'd follow a post with messages to followers on Twitter or YouTube about the new content. That strategy wasn't particularly new in 2009, but it felt new to me because mostly it was young men and some women in their teens and early twenties showing a tremendous amount of discipline about it. Sometimes they'd message their audiences on Xbox Live or the PlayStation Network (PSN) and hosted open lobbies, drawing attention to their channels.

The data on how they grew their audience are robust. Time stamps are a great thing. For example, take what some people called "the Twitter beef." I could trace a disagreement that started on Twitter and moved to a YouTube channel's comments and watch it ping back and forth between commentators' audiences, growing in size as it went. I could also trace how the views for videos, hours and a few days following the start of the beef, grew significantly and count the change in the number of negative comments on each channel owner's comment feed. After watching and tracing a few of these, what's happening becomes clear. The "beef" had driven one commentator's fan base to the opposing commentator's channel. I wondered if users realized that by commenting on a video, even negatively, they were helping that channel owner increase his or her content's ranking. Like the world of professional wrestling on television, the "beefs" were almost always staged. After some back-and-forth, the channel owners would make up—back to business as usual.

Other sources of data for observing and discerning patterns were also fruitful. At the time, Twitter was the preferred outlet for igniting a "beef," for example. The Twitter API made it possible to scrape the Tweets, and pattern analysis made it possible to find topics that tended to instigate the staged acrimony. "Camping" seemed to be a favorite. No, not camping in the woods but camping behind a corner during competitive play and waiting for someone to rush past and then surprising them with a virtual knife to the back. That was rage-inducing. In public lobbies, it was widely loathed, but it was some commentators' bread and butter. *CoD* made that pesky play style easier. During the hundreds of hours I played in the course of nearly four years, someone would regularly complain about it or level some hate at the alleged camper. I never camped. Honest. But, as I mentioned previously, some commentators would do so as a sort of lobby-trolling or sometimes simply because it was a good strategy depending on the opposing team's skill level.

What may appear like an overwhelming amount of data can be, but because there's so much of it in different platforms and showing patterns intimating cause-and-effect relationships, validated by time stamps, what I observed through experience could be augmented by a VGC channel's comment threads, tweets, Facebook posts, and so on. Managing, processing, and analyzing the data is not easy. Python's NLTK packages can help get started on finding some patterns in a text-based dataset and hypothesizing some sentiment, but you still need a human to see if it's correct. I had a lot of data, and getting automation into the mix isn't always productive or necessary. Not everybody needs to be a data scientist and ethnographer at the same time. But, in my opinion, we ought to try that duality, just out of curiosity.

Before I close this section, I'll digress briefly to make an argument for immersive mixed methods by way of a brief contemplation of complementarity and duality in a quest for more complete epistemology. The philosopher Isaiah Berlin categorized those who engage in intellectual labor as either hedgehogs or foxes. Hedgehogs are singular in their heuristic for understanding the world. Foxes are multimodal in their epistemologies. In his famous essay, Berlin (1993) argued that Tolstoy was a fox trying to be a hedgehog and that cost him. Nietzsche years before Berlin did something similar (though not as explicitly or as focused on categorizing writers or intellectuals) in *The Birth of Tragedy* when describing an aspect of being human. Nietzsche (1994) contemplated Apollo and Dionysius as the ever-present tension between reason and passion. The physicist Niels Bohr contemplated duality and complementarity throughout his thinking on how to tackle paradoxes in quantum mechanics. He had to, since nature appeared to be both wave and particle at the same time. He and others got those ideas from the Vedas, an ancient text on spirituality, and Schopenhauer's ideas based on the same. When Bohr was knighted, he chose as part of his coat of arms the yin-yang symbol (Halpern 2016; Schopenhauer 2014). All this to say that methods that may appear mutually exclusive—when predicting patterns of future media industries or cultural production, human nature, or physics or explaining the subject position—might actually be complementary. Given the ease with which many sorts of data can be collected and the various sources from which they can be triangulated, it would seem wasteful not to use all the tools available when making assertions about how cultures take shape and change and how people feel when they take part in cultural production. Hopefully the reader is persuaded to be a fox. I turn now to connecting the dots among all the various data sources and observations.

Methods for Connecting Dots: Gut Feelings, Data Patterns, and Deviations from the Norm

To illustrate how connecting dots was done, I'll give an example from the project described herein. During deep immersion in VGC practice from mid-2009 until mid-2013, I followed ten to twenty YouTube commentators. The range in the group's number indicates that it fluctuated.

I'll pick one for this example. The one commentator in this example was the oldest of the group (late thirties) and had a spouse, children, and a profession that occupied his days. It's reasonable to infer that the bulk of the creative work for his YouTube channel was done on the weekends or after work hours and after family responsibilities had been met. His spouse was also a working professional, so they shared those responsibilities. A few months prior to actually doing so, he started thinking seriously about doing the YouTube thing full time—a big move for a person whose income provided half of the support for a family.

I seem to know a lot about this man, don't I? Some of that information was shared openly with viewers before the change in profession occurred; some was not shared until after. The fact that he was considering the move was definitely not shared until he was doing it already. But something peculiar started happening in his videos, tweets, and tone leading up to the change. First, the scheduling started to change. Time stamps started shifting from times like weekends and nights to days. Next, the length of his videos got a little longer, implying he'd spent more time playing or editing or commentating. Typically, videos hadn't exceeded seven minutes, but suddenly they were longer. His commentary was often straightforward, giving advice on how to play the game but also a bit of vlog. Leading up to the announcement, the amount of life advice he was giving increased. The language, pace of gameplay, and tone became more deliberate.

None of these changes are quantifiable, showing statistical significance, mind you. They'll be noticeable to an ethnographer who has been spending his or her days listening to and reading every word a person wrote for over three years. They'll also be noticeable to a data scientist who has a written record (tweets, videos, comments, and transcripts thereof), has sat with the data, thinking of creative ways of representing them to herself, asking them questions and deploying the most cursory word-frequency analysis looking for comparative frequency shifts over time, if one's a novice, or more complicated visualizations, if more expert.

To me, a researcher who had been closely following this commentator's growing media enterprise, the shifts instinctively stood out as deviations from the norm. Instinct said, "Something has changed about his outlook on playing." The data analysis reaffirmed it, and I then waited to see. After his announcement, he began referring to VGC as a "job," something he "had to do." I recently revisited the data using more robust methods, and they confirmed my observations again. Qualitatively, the videos were still engaging, but he was noticeably having a little less fun. I never interviewed him or asked him directly. By the time I did the analysis to confirm my observations, he was running a full-fledged media enterprise, and I would have needed to talk to his agent, which would have made my search for predictive nuance harder. However, the data spoke for themselves, so I was content. I saw the shift, predicted a change, and reconfirmed it, and I'm confident it's not hindsight bias.

Can we start predicting where people (audiences, culture, individuals) might be going because we know so much about where they're coming from? I'm certain that we can. We've all done it instinctively from time to time, spent so much time among one group that we develop a sort of muscle memory for their tone of voice. It's as if our eardrums tuned themselves to subtle emotional tones, and when that tone shifts, we notice. Often, we disregard our sensation that something is different or feel weird about it because we can't place it and it's not verifiable, but sometimes that intuition is spot on. The more data I reviewed and the more I took the time to note shifts and correlate patterns from one source to another, the more I started to think I might understand where I could find what was authentic about what I was seeing.

Authentic authenticity (as opposed to its being performed) wasn't what commentators said in one instance or another; it consisted of patterns they established over time. What made what they were doing very real and honest was that they had put so many records of their performative personae on platforms that they afforded easy collection and subsequent analysis. Patterns indicating consistencies in attitudes and behavior, or changes thereof, emerged, suggesting I was seeing something essential about who they were. Without fail, for example, the bigger[8] the channels got, the more the commentators I followed started referring to making VGC as a job. "They're being explicit," you're thinking; "that's not predictive." No, but almost always before those sorts of statements started showing up with more frequency, the channel experienced a growth spurt, and the commentator's regular output increased to accommodate it. Then it decreased a bit as the commentator seemed to be getting overrun. I would ask anyone doing similar research on other creative communities to test this observation. I propose that you can reliably predict that, at least on YouTube, there will be a certain "burnout" phase associated with rapid growth.

Instinct also plays a role inasmuch as it's the feeling you have when something is subtly off the norm. It's like having a sixth sense for data. That's a nice metaphor for it, but it's not a superpower. It's the sort of thing we do all the time as we make everyday decisions. We're always making some prediction or another about what's coming down the pike, but I don't think many of us are paying attention. In other words, *I don't think we're paying attention to how we pay attention* and how that's connected to how we make everyday predictions. Phillip Tetlock has written at length about that skillset in his work on forecasting, and economists have used the idea of "satisficing" to explain some characteristics of consumer behavior when a buyer is given a binary choice (Tetlock 2015; Gigerenzer, Hertwig, and Pachur 2015). For researchers immersing themselves so thoroughly in a practice and creator community, it may serve us to pay attention to our predictions or to try our hand at attempting them from time to time.

Whether immersion and large data troves help us be more predictive or not, the opportunity associated with having immersed oneself in the creative practices and culture as I've described here is that we can always check what we intuit from what we are hearing or reading with a record of practices and patterns that stretches over days and months, sometimes minute by minute. If they match, then we can be a little more certain that what we've heard in an interview or observed in one instance at a convention is not just aspirational or good PR but representative of something authentic (and therefore predictable).

Ultimately, what's the takeaway from being so absorbed in a creative community's practice as a methodological approach? Practice is a form of epistemology, as I noted earlier. UGC (user-generated content) production processes that transition into full-fledged media enterprises teach us a lot about platforms that typically remain opaque. In other words, the machinations of otherwise-hidden platform logics whisper through when we're forced to engage them for our own ends, not just the platform owner's desires.

Conclusion: Practice-Epistemology

I'll close this chapter with a final example from my research that shows what I mean by practice-epistemology. One of the commentators I followed was sixteen years old when he started his channel. By the time I stopped producing content (three years later), he had quit college to pursue content production on YouTube full-time. How did a sixteen-year old manage to do that? Like other early commentators, he figured out how to boost his rank on Google and/or YouTube search results when users searched for videos about one of the titles in *CoD*. He orchestrated his place in the YouTube ranking, in other words. "How?" you may be asking. By persuading his audience to rate, comment on, and subscribe to his videos and channel with giveaways.

Nowadays this might not seem like a particularly insightful discovery. And I'm not telling you anything that great researchers and journalists who've studied YouTube probably haven't told you already.[9] Even before 2010, it may have been an obvious strategy for getting increased ranking on search results, especially to those who were already doing it when Yahoo and Lycos were the search portals of choice and YouTube didn't exist. But still, I was impressed that a sixteen-year-old had been watching how the platform worked closely enough to sort that out and invest in giving merchandise away. Maybe he had help. Maybe he read a digital-marketing article or text. I don't know. Whatever way he figured it out had something to do with his engagement with the platform. The only way to really do that, I learned through my own engagement with it, is to start my own channel. Key words, music, and thumbnails of video content for search returns are particularly important. But you wouldn't know that unless you tried to start a channel and think strategically about how to build an initial following.

When engaging with the platform becomes a way of knowing what is happening when you post a video, it changes how you see your work on the platform. At first, posting videos was about having fun, maybe finding another group of video-game fans. At least that was the reason for many of the commentators and for me. Then it became transactional and a game in itself. I stopped thinking of what I was doing as "posting a video" and started thinking of it as "working" the algorithm and persuading an audience so that views and subscriber numbers would increase. One starts to ask oneself questions like, "What would make good click bait for this video?" or "Should I use my video editor to marginally speed up the playback, so the final product looks like I've got the fastest reflexes ever?" Authenticity be dammed.

Without knowing it, one starts asking oneself the questions that advertisers and media marketers ask themselves all the time. It's kind of like the experience the karate kid had when Mr. Miyagi asked him to wash and buff cars and paint fences repeatedly. Unbeknownst to him, the practice taught him karate. Maybe the comparison stretches the point a little, but many of the early commentators I started following in 2009 with less than one thousand subscribers had between six hundred thousand and one and a half million subscribers and the regular views to match by the time I stopped collecting data on the VGC genre in early 2013. Also, they didn't exactly keep their learning about how to game search results and create a steady income stream a secret. In comments or commentary, they'd let slip now and again what they were trying to do and how.

Ultimately, commentators learned how to leverage search algorithms and network effects to establish themselves as gatekeepers for future commentators. They worked together staging content, referencing in-game culture and each other to collectively capture and cache the audience. The cash side of the 3Cs mentioned earlier came from ads and partner deals once a commentator's subscriber numbers reached a critical mass. The rest is history, and the only thing I know for sure was authentic was the desire to make play work as a means for making money (most "play" puns intended; I've lost count). Whether the commentators liked it or not, a practice that started out as a passion become an exercise in rational actor behavior. Twitch now dominates the gameplay-as-entertainment genre. Authenticity there is something a little different but I think also the same. Future research will tell.

The methods and findings described here took a long time to carry out and come together—maybe more time than most people have on hand. The project's timeline and the date of this publication should indicate that it's not the sort of approach that will immediately lead to findings you can write and publish about confidently. In many ways, when engaging in immersive research of this kind on a medium, product, and community that changes rapidly, one is researching history before it happens. It's not for everyone, but it's a lot of fun.

NOTES

1. From the middle of 2009 until the first months of 2013, I studied the VGC communities on YouTube, focusing on *Call of Duty (CoD) Modern Warfare 2, CoD Black Ops*, and *CoD Modern Warfare 3*, played on Xbox or PS3.

2. For foundational research in that vein and background, see Postigo 2012, 2014, 2016, 2018; Postigo and O'Donnell 2017.

3. For an admittedly incomplete smattering of various disciplines' take on authenticity, its usefulness, or lack thereof, see Gilmore and Pine 2007; Trilling 1973; Taylor 1992; Barker and Taylor 2007; Phillips 1998; Boulding 1956; Duffy 2017; Jenkins, Ford, and Green 2013; Banet-Weiser 2012.

4. For "hardcore" gamers, playing the *CoD* series, the flawed lag compensation was rage-inducing. Many invest in a fast internet connection because it can decrease the lag time between the client and the server hosting the game. In the games I studied, since there were no central servers hosting games, a random player was chosen to host online play. The gaming community called that "host advantage," meaning that the host will be some milliseconds ahead of everyone else during play. Those who are closest to host and with fast internet connections will similarly benefit. To compensate for that, designers create artificial lag for hosts and players with short pings to host. In *Modern Warfare 3*, the system overcompensated, and players with fast connections (close to the host or a short ping) noticed. Theoretically, one way around that is to fool the match-making algorithm into thinking you have an unstable and slow connection as it finds a host. One can do that by running a script to flood one's home router with UDP data from a PC on the home network. The game's algorithm checks for UDP data reliability to establish which person in the lobby has the most stable network to pick as a host. If you flood your home network with UDP data, you're essentially subjecting your router to a DNS attack while the lobby waits for a host and the algorithm assigns the lag-compensation packages accordingly. Once the game starts, the player can then turn off the UDP data flood and play the game nearly free of debilitating lag compensation. Caveat emptor: flooding your home router with data for too long will overheat it. Most will automatically shut off. Some may not, in which case you may "fry" your router. The router address also matters when running this operation. You may flood your ISP's switch box (that is, the one with the co-ax in the basement). If you overheat that one, you'll boot everyone in the house off the internet and may incur anger from your spouse. I take no responsibility if you try this.

5. Creative Commons music is important when picking soundtracks for YouTube commentary videos. One of the videos on my YouTube channel, which I used for this project, was pulled by the YouTube copyright-enforcing algorithm because it

used Bing Crosby's "It's Beginning to Look a Lot like Christmas" as I ran around "pwning Christmas noobs," as the community liked to call them. I wanted to test if the algorithm could tease out proprietary music layered over game sounds and commentary sound. In my experience, it cannot. Only when the music is the only sound layer will it recognize the proprietary music reliably. I last tested this in 2012, so the algorithm may have improved.

6. Since this research was conducted, one channel that was particularly focused on this topic has been closed. For montages of that channel's content, see thebossmann222 2014.

7. What makes gameplay "YouTube worthy" is relative to what an audience finds entertaining or what a commentator might have set as a standard.

8. "Bigger" means that the channel grew in subscriber numbers and video views.

9. The research on this subject is legion. If I missed anyone I apologize. See Walker 2012; Rick 2012; Nalty 2010; Burgess and Green 2009, 2010; Senft 2008; O'Neill 2010; Marwick 2015; Nalty 2008; Gabel 2009; Burgess 2011.

REFERENCES

Banet-Weiser, Sarah. 2012. *Authentic™: The Politics of Ambivalence in a Brand Culture.* New York: NYU Press.

Barker, Hugh, and Yuval Taylor. 2007. *Faking It: The Quest for Authenticity in Popular Music.* New York: Norton.

Berlin, Isaiah. 1993. *The Hedgehog and the Fox: An Essay on Tolstoy's View of History.* Chicago: Ivan R. Dee.

Boulding, Kenneth E. 1956. *The Image: Knowledge in Life and Society.* Ann Arbor: University of Michigan Press.

Burgess, Jean. 2011. "User-Created Content and Everyday Cultural Practice: Lessons from YouTube." In *Television as Digital Media*, edited by Niki Strange and James Bennett, 311–331. Durham, NC: Duke University Press.

Burgess, Jean, and Joshua Green. 2009. *YouTube: Online Video and Participatory Culture.* Cambridge, UK: Polity.

———. 2010. "User-Created Content and Online Social Networks." In *The Media & Communications in Australia*, edited by Stuart Cunningham and Graeme Turner, 295–306. Crows Nest, NSW: Allen and Unwin, 2010.

Cialdini, Robert B. 2008. *Influence: Science and Practice.* 5th ed. Boston: Allyn and Bacon.

———. 2016. *Pre-Suasion: A Revolutionary Way to Influence and Persuade.* New York: Simon and Schuster.

Duffy, Brooke Erin. 2017. *(Not) Getting Paid to Do What You Love: Gender, Social Media, and Aspirational Work.* New Haven, CT: Yale University Press.

Gabe, Glenn. 2009. "YouTube Ranking Factors—YouTube SEO beyond Views, Titles, & Tags." *Tubular Insights*, April 14, 2009. https://tubularinsights.com.

Gigerenzer, Gerd, Ralph Hertwig, and Thorsten Pachur. 2015. *Heuristics: The Foundations of Adaptive Behavior.* Oxford: Oxford University Press.

Gilmore, James H., and B. Joseph Pine II. 2007. *Authenticity: What Consumers Really Want*. Boston: Harvard Business Review Press.

Halpern, Paul. 2016. *Einstein's Dice and Schrödinger's Cat: How Two Great Minds Battled Quantum Randomness to Create a Unified Theory of Physics*. New York: Basic Books.

Jenkins, Henry, Sam Ford, and Joshua Green. 2013. *Spreadable Media: Creating Value and Meaning in a Networked Culture*. New York: NYU Press.

Marwick, Alice. 2015. *Status Update: Celebrity, Publicity, and Branding in the Social Media Age*. New Haven, CT: Yale University Press.

Nalty, Kevin. 2008. "How Much Money Can You Make on YouTube?" *Will Video for Food*, April 2, 2008. http://willvideoforfood.com.

———. 2010. "Exclusive: How Much Money YouTube Partners Make." *Will Video for Food*, January 5, 2010. http://willvideoforfood.com.

Nietzsche, Friedrich. 1994. *The Birth of Tragedy: Out of the Spirit of Music*. Edited by Michael Tanner. Translated by Shaun Whiteside. London: Penguin.

O'Neill, Megan. 2010. "How Content Creators Make Money On YouTube." *AdWeek*, May 04, 2010. www.adweek.com.

Phillips, David. 1998. *Exhibiting Authenticity*. Manchester: Manchester University Press.

Postigo, Hector. 2012. "Podcast: Hector Postigo, 'Cultural Production and Social Media as Capture Platforms: How the Matrix Has You.'" *MIT Comparative Media Studies/ Writing* (blog), September 16, 2012. http://cmsw.mit.edu.

———. 2014. "Capture, Fixation and Conversation: How The Matrix Has You and Will Sell You, Part 1 of 3." *Culture Digitally* (blog), April 8, 2014. http://culturedigitally. org.

———. 2016. "The Socio-Technical Architecture of Digital Labor: Converting Play into YouTube Money." *New Media & Society* 18 (2): 332–349. https://doi. org/10.1177/1461444814541527.

———. 2018. "Can Your Platform Afford Play? How Video Gamers Invented New Entertainment Genres." Talks at Google, YouTube, May 21, 2018. www.youtube.com/ watch?v=BasVg3GvMrw.

Postigo, Hector, and Casey O'Donnell. 2017. "The Sociotechnical Architecture of Information Networks." In *The Handbook of Science and Technology Studies*, 4th ed., edited by Ulrike Felt, Rayvon Fouché, and Laurel Smith-Doerr, 583–608. Cambridge, MA: MIT Press.

Rick, Christopher. 2012. "YouTube Profitability Watch Update—2011 to Top $2.25B?" *Tubular Insights*, June 29, 2012. https://tubularinsights.com.

Schopenhauer, Arthur. 2014. *Schopenhauer: The World as Will and Representation*. Edited by Christopher Janaway. Translated by Judith Norman and Alistair Welchman. Cambridge: Cambridge University Press.

Senft, Theresa. 2008. *Camgirls: Celebrity and Community in the Age of Social Networks*. New York: Peter Lang.

Stephens-Davidowitz, Seth. 2017. *Everybody Lies*. New York: HarperCollins.

Taylor, Charles. 1992. *The Ethics of Authenticity*. Cambridge, MA: Harvard University Press.

Tetlock, Philip E. 2015. *Superforecasting*. New York: Crown/Archetype.

thebossmann222. 2014. "El Pressesador Rage Montage #6." YouTube, June 25, 2014. www.youtube.com/watch?v=xeSxTlJsOKE.

Trilling, Lionel. 1973. *Sincerity and Authenticity*. Cambridge. MA: Harvard University Press.

Walker, Rob. 2012. "On YouTube, Amateur Is the New Pro." *New York Times*, June 28, 2012. www.nytimes.com.

7

Value, Service, and Precarity among Instagram Content Creators

BROOKE ERIN DUFFY AND MEGAN SAWEY

In March 2019, the White Banana, a voguish resort located on the Philippines coast, made international headlines after one of its co-owners brazenly posted the following on its Facebook page: "We kindly would like to announce that White Banana is not interested to 'collaborate' with self-proclaimed 'influencers.' And we would like to suggest to try another way to eat, drink, or sleep for free. Or try to actually work" (Locker 2019). The post—a response to reported requests for free lodging from Instagram-enabled "freeloaders"—ratcheted up tens of thousands of likes, comments, and shares, in addition to garnering attention from the likes of the *New York Times*, CNN, and *The Independent*. Perhaps unsurprisingly, the message also sparked blowback from members of the influencer community, who expressed resentment at such a vehement devaluation of their labor. The resort amended their original post soon thereafter, clarifying that the company is "not against INFLUENCERS. Just against freeloaders." "A REAL influencer," the message continued, "is called as such by the rest, he [*sic*] does not address him/herself as an influencer. . . . There are real influencers, [but in those cases] we will contact them and pay or offer something" (White Banana Beach Club Siargao 2019). By invoking this imagined boundary between established content creators (that is, "real influencers") and parasitic wannabes (that is, "freeloaders"), the company suggested there was something distinctive about those who provide a *service* to brands—in contrast to those self-proclaimed "influencers" seeking to game the system without providing added value to brand marketers.

This chapter draws on in-depth interviews with thirteen Instagram content creators,[1] as well as insights gleaned from a multiyear study of the Instagram community (for example, Duffy 2017; Duffy and Hund 2019) in order to examine how the protocareer of influencer is, above all, a *service* that provides value to three distinct stakeholders: audiences, members of the Instagram creator community, and brand partners. In conceptualizing social media content creation as *service*, we build on recent interview- and ethnographic-based studies that examine bloggers, vloggers, and influencers as creative *laborers* (for example, Abidin 2016; Duffy 2017; Rocamora 2018; Cunningham and Craig 2019). By shifting the analytic focus from labor to service, we aim to highlight how influencers are beholden to distinctive groups that exert competing demands on their time, energy, and creative output. After exploring how service to these various groups shapes the cultural experiences and valuations of influencers, we show how these relations are ultimately structured by the platform itself; that is, Instagrammers are subject to the whims of what Stuart Cunningham and David Craig have aptly described as "platform precarity" (2019, 94). In some cases, the precarious nature of the site has attracted wider attention, such as when Instagram instituted a major change in its algorithmic ranking in 2017 or later, in 2019, when the company first tested the concealment of "likes." Consequently, though Instagram's role in a multiplatform social media economy may ebb and flow, we contend that the continued evolution of the Facebook-owned image-sharing site cannot be understood apart from the vernacular of influencer culture.

Rise of Instagram as a Space for Aspirational Content

Since Instagram's launch more than a decade ago, the platform has undergone a series of marked transformations; such changes are implicated in the platform's affordances, its placement in the wider social media ecology, and its staggering uptake by audiences and advertisers alike. Indeed, while the site's initial user base was a grassroots creative community lured by the app's tools for artistic expression—or what Megan Halpern and Lee Humphreys (2016) described as "iPhoneography"—today's sprawling network of more than one billion active monthly users includes more than twenty-five million businesses and countless participants in the so-called system of influencer marketing (Omnicore 2019). Of course, as the opening anecdote makes clear, the very term "influencer" is a fraught one, with conflicting deployment across communities of marketers (Cunningham and Craig 2019), content-creator-cum-internet-celebrities (Abidin 2016, 2018), influencer intermediaries (Stoldt et al. 2019), and social media user-audiences.[2] Those who self-identify as "influencers," moreover, are often subjected to criticism or mockery for their use of such a self-aggrandizing title. And Instagrammers are routinely dismissed as vapid, vain, or idle— denigrations that represent a lack of clarity about exactly *what* the profession of influencer entails (Abidin 2016). As Tiffany, one of our interviewees, noted to this end, "I think being an influencer gives the idea of, 'Oh, you get paid to do nothing and try all these products.' That's not what I do." We contend that such social devaluation rests on the presumed feminization of the influencer space, wherein the categories of fashion, beauty, and lifestyle tend to be populated by more "brand-friendly creators" than such genres as animals/pets, gaming, and health/fitness (Cunningham and Craig 2019, 106).

Despite the ambivalent understanding of influencers in the popular imagination, fashion/lifestyle/beauty influencers are rife on Instagram—a trend that challenges the presumed platform agnosticism of influencer culture (Lorenz 2019). This is in part an upshot of the platform's status as a site of aspirational imagery, with lifestyle ideals hitched to feminized consumer culture. On Instagram, writes Alice Marwick, "persona itself is aspirational, in that such a person has the audience, the looks, the money, the access to celebrity, or the cultural capital an interested audience member might want" (2015, 157). Owing to the wider social media ideal of personal branding, Instagram influencers are paragons of self-promotion who pursue success in the currency of likes, clicks, follows, and other digital proxies for "reputation" (Gandini 2016; Hearn 2010). It is against this backdrop that some of the early prognostications of Instagram's so-called "like ban" focused on the potential impact on the influencer community (for example, Graham 2019). A common way that influencers earn income is through sponsorships or so-called partnerships, whereby they receive financial remuneration to integrate a brand's product, service, or message into their arsenal of social media content (see also Duffy 2017; Cunningham and Craig 2019; Stoldt et al. 2019). More often, though, professional influencers' income streams are cobbled together from product recommendations, affiliate marketing, and the provision of educational/training content—including podcasts, webinars, and online tutorials—all of which they target to influencer hopefuls.

From Labor to Service

Other popular formulations of Instagram influencers valorize their independent careers, casting social media content creation as a field that supplies creative autonomy, a flexible schedule, and perhaps even the glittering promises of fame and fortune. Yet the reality of this professional sector is much less auspicious, and recent academic writings have challenged these upbeat framings with attention to the labor-intensive processes of production and promotion (for example, Abidin 2016; Duffy 2017; Rocamora 2018). We contend, moreover, that social media content creation is tantamount to a traditional creative career—one that demands significant investments of time, energy, and capital while offering a system of rewards that is profoundly uneven (Duffy 2017).

The people we interviewed discussed the exhausting nature of professional Instagramming. Comparing an influencer career to a so-called normal job, Nora explained, "It's hard work. We're putting [in] more hours, doing more things by ourselves than people at a normal company." While Nora reflected on the individualized nature of the profession, Lana was surprised at the amount of behind-the-scenes labor required: "[It's been] definitely a lot harder than I thought it would be when I first started doing it. It just turned out to be more work. I guess on the outside it just kind of seems like throwing a picture up on Instagram and walking away. But there was so much more behind the scenes that I had no idea. . . . It seems so easy [to] do it, and it's not. *You're not famous overnight*" (emphasis added).

At the same time that Lana's comment dispels the well-worn myth of overnight success, it raises the question of labor *for whom*. In other words, what value are influencers supplying as part of a vast, largely feminized service economy? And who benefits? By shifting our focus from the labor provided by influencers to their provision of services for other social actors, we can challenge the singular flow of influence and instead highlight the coconstructed meaning and valuations of Instagram's creator community. In what follows, we explore the services that Instagram influencers provide for or exchange with three distinctive groups, including the "three masters" of audiences, fellow creators, and advertisers.

Servicing Audiences: Advice, Aspiration, and Community

The services that influencers provide to audiences include the supply of information, entertainment, inspiration, and social connectivity—although these are inextricably interwoven. However, their most explicit function is the provision of product advice and recommendations amid a sprawling digital advertising economy. It is in this capacity that digitally networked "influencing" offers continuity with earlier forms of mediated communication, most especially the nineteenth- and twentieth-century "service magazines" that circulated to an almost exclusively female audience. Similar to the advice and recommendations furnished by these print-bound texts, today's influencer content is unequivocally in the "service of consumerism" (McCracken 1993).

That Instagram's user base skews female (Perrin and Anderson 2019) helps reproduce the (problematic) conflation of femininity with consumerism. Moreover, marketing surveys report that women who use social media to engage with the brands themselves or with influencer content are more likely to purchase products than they might otherwise be (*Retail Touch Points* 2016).

Some of our interviewees were quite candid about their roles as socially networked cultural intermediaries in the consumer domain (see also Arriagada and Ibáñez 2020). As the lifestyle influencer Renee explained, "I feel like people are really utilizing me as a tool to know what's new and what are good ideas." Olivia acknowledged, "People come to me because they see what I do, how I'm living, and that's exactly what they want to do or be able to do." Eva, meanwhile, emphasized the importance of "giv[ing] what your audience wants" by "listening to them." Such quotes indicate that content creators often have an "imagined audience" in mind while creating content (Litt and Hargittai 2016), and thus they seek to anticipate the impact—and influence—of such content on their followers.

To this end, a number of our interviewees explained how their understandings of audiences—including information about them gleaned from analytics—steered the direction of the creative process. Lana, for instance, started her Instagram account to share ideas and images about the book-production process; however, her social media audience exhibited greater interest in her style-related content. She recalled, "I was posting pictures of books I was reading and notebooks that I was writing in and stuff, and those photos weren't getting as much traction as when I posted my outfit. . . . The pictures where I had more outfit focus, even if there was a book in it, just did better." As a result, she explained, "I just started posting more style-based photos." Shanna, similarly, told us that her desire to produce a consistent "theme" was guided by audience feedback. "Once I started posting more about fashion," she told us, "I got way more likes and way more people following me for sure." In both cases, the content creators felt compelled to respond to the perceived interests and expectations of the audiences—regardless of whether this dovetailed with their own creative impulses.

At the same time, interviewees eschewed images that were deemed overtly commercial or unabashedly self-promotional, as they believed such content held the potential to alienate audiences. Tiffany, for instance, expressed concern that idealized imagery could make audiences feel bad about themselves. She shared, "I try to be as lighthearted and as fun as I can when I'm projecting that image on my social media, because . . . I don't want to be depressing. . . . I know a lot of people wish they could live a different life than they have." Renee, meanwhile, shared,

> I've gone back and forth between using [Instagram] to promote my blog and then promoting—I don't want to call it promoting my life—but also putting my life out there. Because I like to keep it as genuine as possible. . . . I have caught myself a couple times putting stuff out there that makes it look like I have a perfect life. So it has been a little bit of a reality check for me, in a sense, because I'm just . . . It's constantly that battle between, "Okay, is this what's really happening, or is this what I want people to think is what's happening?"

Renee's exposition is quite telling of the way content creators sought to respond to the social media ideal of authenticity (see, for example, Marwick 2015; Cunningham and Craig 2017; Duffy 2017) without disrupting Instagram's ethos of aspirationalism.

Not only did Instagram influencers rely on audience feedback to help determine the content they shared on social media, but they also underscored the value of the sharing process. For Olivia, responding to audience feedback was an expression of respect: "If someone wants to take the time to reach out to me, especially a lot of people ask me questions, I think the least I can do is respond. Like some people message me asking whatever it is, nutrition or training, and I reply, and they're like, 'Oh, I didn't think you'd reply.'"

Other interviewees, meanwhile, cast such engagement as "part of the job"—or what Nancy Baym has described as "relational labor." Compared to emotional labor, Baym notes, relational labor is "much more about the performance and creation of feeling" (2018, 19–20). Lana, accordingly, felt pressure to engage in relationship-building activities "all the time." She explained,

> Engaging is one of the most important, if not the most important, thing. Like when people are saying, "Oh, I'm really stuck [growing my audience], what should I do?" And it's just engaging, so I'll sit down and put on a movie or a TV show, and I'll just engage for two or three hours a day just commenting on the blogger friends that I've made, other bloggers, bloggers who are smaller, bloggers who are larger, people who follow those bloggers, random people on the explore page. So I just kind of sit there and just go through and like and comment for two hours.

Eva's description of engagement was similarly strategic: "All [the] people that comment on my photos, I respond to. I respond to every comment. At least if it's within the first two days. . . . [And] whenever I have the time, I will go a step further and visit that person's profile and like some of their photos as well to keep that engagement going."

The labor-intensive function helps to explain why some content creators seemed frustrated with the service demands of audiences (Baym 2018). As Shanna admitted, "When I come home from work, I'll be on Instagram for like an hour after, which kind of sucks because sometimes I don't want to be doing it. But at the same time, like, I wanna grow as a blogger, so you have to do these things."

Servicing the Creator Community: Knowledge, Collaboration, and Presumed Reciprocity

Content creators on Instagram are, at once, individual and communal, with influencers often cast as members of *community*. Their connections to one another differ from traditional coworker configurations in that influencers—with the exception of those signed to influencer marketing agencies or other intermediaries (Stoldt et al. 2019)—work independently but remain joined together by the commonality of their content goals. Moreover, while "content creation" covers a vast swath of consumer categories, the influencer role is broadened by its knowledge requirements, including the affordances of the platforms on which influencers work. For instance, platforms' incessant efforts to "tweak" their algorithmic systems mean that content creators must engage in constant upkeep to ensure that their content remains visible (Bishop 2018; Klawitter and Hargittai 2018; Cotter 2018; Cunningham and Craig 2019; Petre, Duffy, and Hund 2019).

Reflecting on the necessity of continuous algorithmic learning, Lana offered, "It's way harder to grow [because] the algorithm is always changing. So people are always trying to find ways . . . [to] get more followers and get noticed more and beat this algorithm that nobody really knows." Lana then pointed to the conjectures that seem to circulate among the Instagram creator community: "I don't think anybody really knows for sure, and so the groups that I'm in with other bloggers, it's just kind of like, 'Hey, I've noticed this' and 'Hey, I've noticed that' and 'If you do this, Instagram will punish you' and 'If you do that, Instagram will reward you.' So it's kind of just word of mouth, and nothing's really confirmed or denied."

Lana's account reveals that much of the learning that comes with being an influencer does not follow a platform manual or how-to guide. Instead, the people pursuing this type of career are left to rely on their own educational resources, which often amount to "folk theories" about the inner workings of algorithmic systems (DeVito, Gergle, and Birnholtz 2017). Because of their reliance on these folk theories, influencers service—and derive service from—the wider creator community.

Zoe's exposition of the role of Instagram's algorithm in the business accounts feature shows the assumptions that guide these folk theories:[3]

Instagram has completely changed its algorithm. . . . Everything is about paying for ads or paying for growth or paying for engagement. Like, you promote yourself on there, and that's what they're trying to do. If you have a business account, which I do because it's required . . . to be involved with a lot of these platforms or partner with a lot of the brands. . . . And having a business account completely really stops the amount. It puts a ceiling on the amount of engagement that you can get without promoting or without doing, like, organic engagement that you can get.

Zoe's perception—and one that seemed to circulate among many of our participants—is that Instagram is more interested in profiting from influencers' efforts than in facilitating them. As Nora summarized, "I think it's hard because Instagram is such a difficult platform, the algorithm itself."

As our participants observed, the strategy structuring the platform's feed feature—from reverse chronological to algorithmic—is frustratingly puzzling. Once a straightforward sequence of posts organized according to the times at which they were uploaded, the feed now follows a proprietary sorting method. Allegedly, the algorithm organizes posts according to one's past reactions to profiles (Murray 2017). Such algorithmic precarity—with posts pinballing between recency and relevance—along with the premium the site places on visibility (through, for instance, its prime real estate "discover" page), makes the Instagram algorithm especially enigmatic.

In an effort to circumvent or "game" Instagram's incessantly changing algorithm (Gillespie 2016; Petre, Duffy, and Hund 2019), influencers increasingly partake in strategic collaborative practices. As Grace stated, collaborations materialize "because it's really hard to kind of build yourself up on Instagram as it is, especially alone. And it's kind of become to the point where it's essential now to kind of make relationships with other people on Instagram and support each other to get to where you want to be." Accordingly, some influencers organize themselves into what our interviewees described as engagement "pods," or coordinated groupings of influencers who agree to interact with one another's posts—all in the hope of boosting their content to the top of their followers' feeds. These groups organize via Facebook page, Instagram direct message, and other social media features (see also Cotter 2018). After Olyssea noted her participation in one of these so-called engagement pods, she described the group's composition and guidelines:

So, actually, we have a group message. Like, there are people who are creatives or people who do music and want to run their views up. . . . Right when we make a new post, we go and comment in there that we made a new post so everybody goes and comments on it, right? So that way you've got like twelve comments all from people you know on there, right? And if you reply back to every single one of them, well now you've got twenty-four comments. So you just doubled your comments just by replying back to people. So now you're moving up on the timeline.

Olyssea's comment underscores the value of reciprocity, noting that her pod's success relies on its members' commitment to exchanging comments.

Renee, meanwhile, reflected on the slippage between individual and collective promotion that sustains these reciprocal Instagram relationships—many of which involve relative strangers: "We also are really supportive of one another, where if I have a new blog post, I can throw it up there, and people will comment on it, or they'll pin it or retweet it, or something like that. So it's a matter of just, pretty much, I don't want to call it, like, self-promoting because we're promoting each others, but we're self-promoting because it's all in the same content area. We're all lifestyle bloggers or all beauty bloggers or that type of thing."

Giveaways constitute another type of mutual collaboration that is powered by mutually beneficial outcomes. Several informants touched on this dynamic, indicating that influencers combine efforts in order to expand their audiences and engagement rates. Tiffany shared her understanding of this activity: "You can do stuff like giveaways to draw in more followers. So there's a lot of different ways that you can grow, not just your account base, like, your followers, but also your engagement." Tiffany's comments reiterate the importance of engagement and capture the joint benefits that giveaways may facilitate. Regarding the nature of these giveaways, Lana offered an example:

A lot of times there will be . . . there'll just be one random person, just anybody who will start an Instagram account, and then they'll reach out to people, like, your direct messages or through email, and say "I'm having this giveaway. Do you want to join?" Then you just buy into it. I still get those messages that are just like, "We're giving away a Gucci bag. It's

$50 for a spot." So a lot of times when you do the giveaways, you don't necessarily know the people in person, or they're not people that you connected with; they're just kind of people who also want to do a giveaway.

Like pods, Instagram giveaways operate according to myriad degrees of social distance—suggesting that personal relationships are not a prerequisite for collaboration. Furthermore, Lana's example contends that influencers' wider networks and financial resources play key roles in their access to giveaways and ability to participate. As Lana clarified, though, some giveaways are more productive than others. She observed that influencers "are a lot more focused and careful about who they choose to associate with" than in the past, because "you want to share an audience with people who have similar audiences and not just gain random followers." As we discuss more in the following section, this push for audience quality and consistency over purely quantified follower counts remains fraught.

Engagement groups, giveaways, and other collaborations demand a consistent dedication to involvement. As such, an influencer's participation can feel labor-intensive. Several of our informants described the work involved in maintaining their commitments to pod members while balancing the demands of their personal lives. While discussing the laboring function of influence on Instagram, Shanna recounted her experiences as a content creator, pod member, and full-time worker:

> At first, like, I thought it [engagement groups] was a good idea, but now I feel like it's just, like, a lot of work for me, because I work. And I feel like a lot of bloggers—well, at least the ones I'm friends with—I don't know if it's their job or if they just have, like, work part-time, but it seems like they have a lot of free time, so they're always on their phone. But I work until 6:30, so I only have like half an hour lunch too, so I don't comment on anyone's stuff until late that night.

Renee described a similar situation, noting the difficulties of this proverbial balancing act: "I honestly think it's me, because recently I have been really busy with work. My other job has been popping up a lot more, so I've been off Instagram. I've been putting stuff up there, but I haven't been commenting back or engaging back or liking back, that type of thing. Because Instagram is a very engagement type of platform, where if you're not talking to people, people aren't going to talk to you. It's kind of how the app reads it."

As Shanna's and Renee's reflections suggests, influencers may conceive of their engagement contributions in relation to those of their friends and/or fellow influencers. Given the argument that making sense of algorithmic culture is its own workload (Cunningham and Craig 2019; Petre, Duffy, and Hund 2019), influencers' asymmetrical personal schedules—with some working fewer hours outside the platform while others, like Shanna, navigate major time constraints—fracture the uniformity of an "ideal" collaborative group structure. As a result, service among influencers is issued, received, and experienced unevenly.

Servicing Brand-Clients: Knowing—and Selling—the Audience

It is perhaps axiomatic to describe the service that influencers supply to consumer brands: they hype the latter's goods or services, assuring networked audiences that such brand advocacy is sincere and authentic—in other words, that it is *a product they would own or use even without financial compensation*. And, so, much like the role of traditional media companies in the production of the "audience commodity" (Smythe 1977, 4–5), it is imperative for current and aspiring influencers to "know their audience" in order to profit from them (Ang 1991; see also Turow 1997). Against this backdrop, most of our interviewees offered up distinctive categorical segments in describing their Instagram "followers." Grace, for instance, explained her desire to provide advice on "travel and lifestyle for the young professional millennial woman." Recalling the process of learning about this imagined consumer segment, she added, "I started to really research it more and study more and try new things and really curate the content I posted on there to present this image that I wanted the people I was trying to target to see." Grace's uncritical use of marketing lexicon like "target" as well as marketing segmentation (that is, "young professional millennial women") highlights how imaginations of the audience shape not only industrial routines (Turow 1997) but also the work of *individual* content creators.

Other interviewees described their calculated efforts to learn about audiences as "research." Olivia's so-called research involved learning when her audience "is mostly online, when they are most responsive, [and] what hashtags work the best for what days." Similarly, Nora described the process of content creator skills acquisition as "all research": "Hours, upon hours, upon hours of research. Also, doing studies on my own account. Running two posts at the same time. Replying to all of my comments first, versus replying to them the next day."

In other instances, content creators relied on audience analytics furnished by Instagram to better understand *who* was engaging with their online content. Tiffany described the insights page: "You can actually look how your followers, if it's going up, if its going down, where people are from, your different demographics." Olyssea, who professed to "love" monitoring her platform analytics, explained, "[My Instagram audience] is 59 percent female, 41 percent male. . . . Forty-eight percent of that audience [is] people twenty-five to thirty-four. That's basically my target for my clients." She concluded, "I ultimately want to promote to women around my age."

Olivia similarly praised the ability to have access to audience analytics: "[to] know when people on my Instagram are on my account, what times are most popular for people to be checking, or like how many people click on the link in my bio. It'll tell me all of that." As Olivia's comment makes clear, content creators felt compelled to learn not only *who* the audience was but—perhaps more crucially—how many people composed it. And, accordingly, they offered up metric benchmarks of success with remarkable regularity: Arielle's goal was to hit "a thousand likes for every photo," while Nora used numeric shorthand to describe the success of a friend who was "getting like three thousand likes on her photos" with a "pretty good" engagement rate. For Instagrammers vying for marketing "partnerships"—the industry euphemism for income-generating ad sponsorships—both quantifiable links and more qualified indexes of "engagement" are prerequisites. As Nora reasoned, "If you can get a 50 percent engagement rate but have three thousand followers, that's probably so much better to a brand. Because (a) you're cheaper, and (b) your engagement is better than people that have like 40K." In a similar vein, Isabella shared her understanding that "brands won't work with you if you're just with five hundred followers. . . . Maybe you have amazing content, but unfortunately the point of the brands working with you [is] so that they can market their products and not to advance ideas." Moreover, she explained, numbers could occlude the more meaningful experiences of content creation: "When [metrics do start to] bother me, I'm like 'don't.'" She added, "I didn't join this because I wanted to get a thousand likes on a photo. I joined it because I love colors, I love creating, and that's why I'm in it. So that's what I try to, like, where I try to stay focused."

Despite creators' ambivalent experiences with metrics, most recognized that these were a prerequisite for securing brand partnerships with clients. Yet, crucially, many of these so-called partnerships paid in the always-deferred promise of "exposure" (Duffy 2017). Noting the number of brands trying to harness the unpaid labor of social media content producers, Lila explained, "They're not paying. . . . I know so many people, especially in this field. And it really upset me because these people want to make a point to change fashion, they're supporting fair trade, animal rights, or sustainability, yet they are not getting paid." Others, meanwhile, suggested how demoralizing it can be when influencers with similar content secure a lucrative brand sponsorship. Shanna confessed, "If a company reaches out to one or two of us, and then they don't reach out to the rest, people seem really sad about it or [wonder], 'Why did they reach out to you and not me?' type of thing. . . . I feel like it discourages people when companies pick some and not the others, and I honestly, like, I don't know like how companies pick specific people versus others."

Nora expressed a belief that the unevenness of the influencer economy was predicated on the emergence of influencer talent agencies, which function as intermediaries. She shared, "The influencer agencies are making bank because they're like, 'Oh, well, I'll sort through all of [the aspiring influencers] for you. We'll find you influencers so you don't even have to deal with them.' They're making so much money off it. Then brands, they're not growing, and they're not making any money because everybody wants everything for free."

Conclusion: Servicing the Grand Master in an Era of Platform Precarity

Much like the cultural gatekeepers of the art world who struggle to manage the competing demands of the "three masters" of artist, audience, and investors (De Roeper 2008), current and aspiring social media influencers are compelled to simultaneously serve a trio of audiences, community members, and brand clients. The services they produce for these three social actors vary extensively—from advice and connectivity to reciprocal promotion to strategic brand communication—and thus the valuations of their labor are often displaced or diminished. Moreover, influencers' accountability to this trio of masters renders their cobbled-together careers even more tenuous. Among the sources of such precarity is the oversaturated market of influencer wannabes who, collectively, drive down the overall valuation of influencers. As Talia noted, "A good amount of people that you meet [today] are trying to be a blogger or an influencer or a YouTuber of some sort." Nora similarly explained, "Every person and their mom and their brother and their grandma and their aunt and their uncle, they're all trying to be Instagram influencers." Then, acknowledging the importance of other social actors in propelling the influencer system, she added, "I influence as a side job now, because there's no one left to influence."

An additional source of instability for content creators is, of course, the platform itself, and the aforementioned discussion of algorithm-related frustrations reveals how creators must constantly negotiate social networking sites' affordances. Such so-called platform precarity incites many content creators to produce content across a variety of channels and formats in order to mitigate the risk of platform dependence (Cunningham and Craig 2019, 94). Eva, for instance, noted how she shares more extensive videos of her travel adventures on YouTube "as opposed to just [her] Instagram." Nora was even more explicit about the value of sharing content across a multiplatform ecosystem: "Instagram is so oversaturated that people are going to different channels to consume the information. . . . [Maybe] they'd rather watch a YouTube video. Or they'd rather listen to a Podcast while they're running. So finding a way to re-purpose your content constantly is really, I think, a big key to Instagram and a key to influencing in general." Nora went on to prognosticate the uncertain future of Instagram, including its potential to "crash, big time." She explained, "I'm encouraging people that use Instagram as a blog to get [an actual] blog, . . . because when Instagram fails, . . . if you don't have a backup plan, you're done. You're gonna have to work at McDonald's, because [you don't have other] experience probably, and all you're gonna be able to say is, 'Oh, I had five hundred thousand followers.'"

Nora's comment points to a stark reality about the business of Instagram influencing: content creators do not own their content, and as such, they have little recourse when it comes to algorithmic tweaks and other so-called updates. In more extreme cases, Instagram engages in the demotion or concealment of a poster's content without their knowledge or consent (Myers West 2018; Petre, Duffy, and Hund 2019).

We conclude by drawing attention to Instagram content creators' service to a fourth social actor: the platform itself. In other words, influencers both serve and, in many ways, are beholden to the whims and vagaries of a billion-dollar Silicon Valley social network. Similar to Baym's reminder about who *really* profits from the music industry's uptake of social networking platforms—whereby "the money in social media flows between sites' owners, investors, and advertisers, not [cultural producers] and audiences" (2018, 158)—Instagram is the ultimate beneficiary of the circulation of influencer content. Therefore, critiques of influencer marketing—including White Banana's contention that it is not really *work*—ignore the fundamental interrelationships of value, labor, and service in the platform economy.

NOTES

1. Recruitment of participants took place on Instagram in 2018–2019. To solicit potential interviewees, we used various hashtags linked to influencers and then deployed a snowball sample to seek out additional participants. Interviews took place over Skype and/or the phone, and discussions were transcribed with the participants' permission. The topic of anonymity is especially fraught when doing research on a community that seeks visibility, and some of our informants saw our recruitment of them as a potential path to new followers and/or professional opportunities. However, we have opted to give all participants pseudonyms unless they expressly requested that we use their name in research output.

2. While we acknowledge the fraught nature of the terms, we use "content creator" and "influencer" interchangeably, given that there is little consensus among the communities we are studying.

3. Instagram business accounts afford users the ability to track their performance metrics and access their followers' demographics and usage patterns (Instagram Business Team 2017).

REFERENCES

Abidin, Crystal. 2016. "'Aren't These Just Young, Rich Women Doing Vain Things Online?': Influencer Selfies as Subversive Frivolity." *Society Media + Society* 2 (2): 1–17. doi:10.1177/2056305116641342.

———. 2018. *Internet Celebrity: Understanding Fame Online*. Bingley, UK: Emerald.

Ang, Ien. 1991. *Desperately Seeking the Audience*. New York: Routledge.

Arriagada, Arturo, and Francisco Ibáñez. 2020. "'You Need at Least One Picture Daily, If Not You're Dead': Content Creators and Platform Changes in the Social Media Economy." *Social Media + Society*. doi:10.1177/2056305120944624.

Baym, Nancy. 2018. *Playing to the Crowd: Musicians, Audiences, and the Intimate Work of Connection*. New York: NYU Press.

Bishop, Sophie. 2018. "Anxiety, Panic and Self-Optimization: Inequalities and the You-Tube Algorithm." *Convergence* 24 (1): 69–84. doi:10.1177/1354856517736978.

Cotter, Kelly. 2018. "Playing the Visibility Game: How Digital Influencers and Algorithms Negotiate Influence on Instagram." *New Media & Society* 21 (4): 895–913. doi:10.1177/1461444818815684.

Cunningham, Stuart, and David Craig. 2017. "Being 'Really Real' on YouTube: Authenticity, Community and Brand Culture in Social Media Entertainment." *Media International Australia* 164 (1): 71–81. doi:10.1177/1329878X17709098.

———. 2019. *Social Media Entertainment: The New Intersection of Hollywood and Silicon Valley*. New York: NYU Press.

De Roeper, Julia. 2008. "Serving Three Masters: The Cultural Gatekeeper's Dilemma." *Journal of Arts Management, Law, and Society* 38 (1): 51–70. doi:10.3200/JAML.38.1.51-70.

DeVito, Michael, Darren Gergle, and Jeremy Birnholtz. 2017. "Algorithms Ruin Everything: #RIPTwitter, Folk Theories, and Resistance to Algorithmic Change in Social Media." In *Proceedings of the 2017 CHI Conference on Human Factors in Computing Systems*, 3163–3174. ACM Digital Library.

Duffy, Brooke Erin. 2017. *(Not) Getting Paid to Do What You Love: Gender, Social Media, and Aspirational Work*. New Haven, CT: Yale University Press.

Duffy, Brooke Erin, and Emily Hund. 2019. "Gendered Visibility on Social Media: Navigating Instagram's Authenticity Bind." *International Journal of Communication* 13 (2019): 4983–5002.

Gandini, Alessandro. 2016. *The Reputation Economy: Understanding Knowledge Work in Digital Society*. London: Palgrave Macmillan.

Gillespie, Tarleton. 2016. "Algorithmically Recognizable: Santorum's Google Problem, and Google's Santorum Problem." *Information, Communication & Society* 20 (1): 63–80. doi:10.1080/1369118X.2016.1199721.

Graham, Megan. 2019. "As Instagram Tests Its 'Like' Ban, Influencers Will Have to Shift Tactics to Make Money." *CNBC*, July 21, 2019. www.cnbc.com.

Halpern, Megan, and Lee Humphreys. 2016. "iPhoneography as an Emergent Art World." *New Media & Society* 18 (1): 62–81. doi:10.1177/1461444814538632.

Hearn, Alison. 2010. "Structuring Feeling: Web 2.0, Online Ranking and Rating, and the Digital 'Reputation' Economy." *Ephemera* 10 (3–4): 421–438.

Instagram Business Team. 2017. "Celebrating a Community of 25 Million Businesses." Instagram Business, November 30, 2017. https://business.instagram.com.

Klawitter, Erin, and Eszter Hargittai. 2018. "'It's Like Learning a Whole Other Language': The Role of Algorithmic Skills in the Curation of Creative Goods." *International Journal of Communication* 12:3490–3510.

Litt, Eden, and Eszter Hargittai. 2016. "The Imagined Audience on Social Network Sites." *Social Media + Society* 2 (1). doi:10.1177/2056305116633482.

Locker, Melissa. 2019. "Don't Expect Free Stuff Just Because You Have 2,000 Instagram Followers." *Fast Company*, April 5, 2019. www.fastcompany.com.

Lorenz, Taylor. 2019. "The Real Difference between Creators and Influencers." *Atlantic*, May 31, 2019. www.theatlantic.com.

Marwick, Alice 2015. "Instafame: Luxury Selfies in the Attention Economy." *Public Culture* 27 (1(75)): 137–160. doi:10.1215/08992363-2798379.

McCracken, Ellen. 1993. *Decoding Women's Magazines: From "Mademoiselle" to "Ms."* New York: St. Martin's.

Murray, Daisy. 2017. "What Is an Instagram 'Pod,' and Do They Actually Help You Get More Likes and Followers?" *Elle*, May 16, 2017. www.elle.com.

Myers West, Sarah. 2018. "Censored, Suspended, Shadowbanned: User Interpretations of Content Moderation on Social Media Platforms." *New Media & Society* 20 (11): 4366–4383. doi:10.1177/1461444818773059.

Omnicore. 2019. "Instagram by the Numbers: Stats, Demographics & Fun Facts." July 18, 2019. www.omnicoreagency.com.

Perrin, Andrew, and Monica Anderson. 2019. "Share of U.S. Adults Using Social Media, Including Facebook, Is Mostly Unchanged since 2018." Pew Research Center, April 10, 2019. www.pewresearch.org.

Petre, Caitlin, Brooke Erin Duffy, and Emily Hund. 2019. "'Gaming the System': The Politics of Algorithmic Visibility in Digital Cultural Production." *Social Media & Society* 5 (4): 1–12. doi:10.1177/2056305119879995.

Retail Touch Points. 2016. "86% of Women More Likely to Make a First Purchase after Social Media Engagement." September 6, 2016. www.retailtouchpoints.com.

Rocamora, Agnès. 2018. "The Labour of Fashion Blogging." In *Fashioning Professionals: Identity and Representation at Work in the Creative Industries*, edited by Leah Armstrong and Felice McDowell, 65–81. London: Bloomsbury.

Smythe, Dallas W. 1977. "Communications: Blindspot of Western Marxism." *CTheory* 1 (3): 1–27.

Stoldt, Ryan, Mariah Wellman, Brian Ekdale, and Melissa Tully. 2019. "Professionalizing and Profiting: The Rise of Intermediaries in the Social Media Influencer Industry." *Social Media + Society* 5 (1): 1–11. doi:10.1177/2056305119832587.

Turow, Joseph. 1997. *Breaking Up America: Advertisers and the New Media World*. Chicago: University of Chicago Press.

White Banana Beach Club Siargao. 2019. "Good Day Everyone . . ." Facebook post, March 27, 2019. www.facebook.com/pg/whitebananabeach/posts/?ref=page_internal.

8

Toy Unboxing Creator Communities

JARROD WALCZER

Toy unboxing videos are a YouTube-native genre of internet content in which popular children's toys are unpacked and played with on camera, by children and their families. Some toy unboxing content creators have generated billions of video views and hundreds of millions of subscribers on YouTube. These video views have generated substantial profit and notoriety for some, notably seven-year-old Ryan of Ryan's World, who was YouTube's highest earner in 2019, at over $26 million for his 39 billion views and 25.1 million subscribers (Berg 2019). Many of these views are assumed to be coming from children and their families, given the substantial number of videos focused on the unpacking or unwrapping of toys, candy, surprise eggs, and other commercial products of interest to children, varying in price and cultural capital depending on individual channel practices (for more detail, see Walczer 2021).

Toy unboxing has undergone far more concentrated critique compared to other genres of social media entertainment. Both academic scholarship and popular press discourse on toy unboxing tend to be underpinned by a deficit model (that is, what are the ill effects that toy unboxing videos have on a child's well-being) informed by the psychology, medical, and media effects disciplines. Only to a much lesser extent do we encounter an agentic capabilities model (that is, what opportunities these videos present to people who make them and how people use them). Often kids' content on YouTube is considered as little more than program-length advertorials, or "highly personalised opinion-laden promotions of products and services that influencers personally experience and endorse for a fee" (Abidin 2015). Such exploitation of the child audience is deemed indefensible by critics of toy unboxing (for a review of popular media criticism, see Craig and Cunningham 2017). What is constructed as a commercializing limit case raises questions for academic critics regarding whether there is adequate disclosure of sponsored content and age-appropriate exposure (for example, Evans, Hoy, and Childers 2018). The majority of popular press coverage has focused on the top-performing toy unboxer in a given year (for example, DisneyToyCollectorBR, EvanTubeHD, and *Ryan's* World), who has either been a young child or a pseudonymous hand channel (the viewer only sees hands, not the person themselves)—leading to concerns about children's well-being as both creators and viewers (Abidin 2017).

However, this chapter takes a different, agentic capabilities, approach framed by the moral intelligence of twenty-four top-ranking toy unboxing content creators and their ideas about the necessity for governance in the face of algorithmic and platform-imposed precarity and concerns about commercializing childhood. This work does not set aside the concerns raised in other scholarly approaches but rather brings the creators (many of whom are parents themselves) into a discussion that is often occupied by experts to discuss how they handle concerns about kids' digital media on a daily basis through their creator families and organizations. The task is to understand the moral intelligence of YouTube's toy unboxing creator community and how it deals with both the production environment (typically the creators' homes) and the industry they are in. The concerns raised in the deficit model, as we will see, are very much factored in by the community.

This chapter draws from twenty-four long-form expert interviews with and observations of top toy unboxing and kids' content creators. The long interview method developed by Grant McCracken (1988) and followed for this research suggests that a researcher may need only to speak with eight creators for an hour each in length to reach statistical significance. However, many of the creators I interviewed for this research expressed interest in speaking for longer than an hour (averaging almost two hours) and invited me into their homes to do walkthroughs of their studios and various production processes on and off YouTube (using the method of Light, Burgess, and Duguay 2018). These creators (made up mostly of adult creators or parents of children who are child stars on YouTube) were self-selecting, critical of their own works and the genre writ large, driven to be prosocial through their content creation, and aware of the ethical challenges facing the genre. However, their insights also suggest that toy unboxing is far more than the first-glance nadir of consumer capitalism that it has been positioned as (see Hess 2017).

This chapter focuses on the community the creators and their parents construct among one another as well as with their viewers. Many of these creator-to-creator communities have emerged as gap-fillers and substitutes for the multichannel networks (MCNs), multiplatform networks (MPNs), and other intermediaries that many creators joined and, subsequently, left. Those creators who joined MCNs resoundingly cited them as being unresponsive or ineffective or as having failed to deliver on promises to provide brand deals and foster collaborations.

In the years that followed the MCN exodus (most notably from Maker Studios in the years that followed its being purchased by the Walt Disney Company in March 2014), some toy unboxing creator communities have reorganized and newly emerged. These creators have taken on the increasingly progressive mantle of providing quality YouTube-native content for kids after the ElsaGate scandal and KidPocalypse of 2017. During ElsaGate, the toy unboxing creator community found that its videos were being algorithmically recommended alongside videos in which characters from trusted children's brands were satirized and shown in violent and sexual acts that were entirely inappropriate for children. In an attempt to combat ElsaGate, protect the community of fellow creators, and ensure that the child audience was cared for, these creators formed online communities with one another to tackle these issues head-on. However, questions remain as to whether these creator-centric communities are just a second coming of multichannel networks bent on profitability and mass acquisition or whether they represent a new type of community management and creator governance formation that differentiates itself from excessive commercialization and questionable ethics in the post-ElsaGate era.

What Is an Online Community?

For the purposes of this chapter, I draw from the new media scholar Rosemary Avance's notion of community in a digital era, namely, as an assemblage of "disembodied souls unit[ing] in fellowship mediated by the digital" (2016, 68). Using Avance's groundwork, I see toy unboxing creator communities as groups of individuals, linked primarily through the mediation of YouTube, who despite lacking face-to-face communications initially, united as a consequence of networked relations to one another and YouTube's user-centered software architecture and who now share skills, trade, lifestyles, and ethical ties related to playing with toys (and, secondarily, unboxing them) on YouTube. These ties unite toy unboxing creators under a collective consciousness and moral code. This stems, in part, from these creators' need to join forces and defend the kids and family vertical and various kids' content genres against several factors.

First is the popular press discourse that frames the kids' content genre in a particularly unfavorable light, despite journalists often not speaking to creators directly or mischaracterizing what they say and do. Second are the changes to the YouTube algorithm that are unpredictable and frequent and result in volatility for creators' AdSense revenue and livelihoods. The third comes from lack of communications from YouTube itself to creators, with many creators arguing that they receive only scripted responses. Fourth is the threat of governmental regulation, complicated by lobby groups like the Campaign for Commercial-Free Childhood appealing to the Federal Trade Commission (FTC) and Federal Communications Commission (FCC) to regulate YouTube and YouTube Kids. However, even in the face of these various forces arrayed against my cohort of interviewees, they largely rally together and advance an ethical narrative around how and why they create their content that has rarely been heard before.

Neta Kligler-Vilenchik (2016, 108) has shown how civic engagement and political participation can emerge in response to the shared interest, practices, and relationships of fans (as seen with the Harry Potter Alliance). Many of the toy unboxing content creators I interviewed do the same with and for their creator community as well as for their community of viewers. This comes as a result of the flattened social hierarchy of YouTube's participatory culture and the assumption or knowledge that many of their viewers are children. Many of the toy unboxers in my cohort create content that fits their idea of "family-friendly" values on YouTube. They do this through shared genre conventions, production practices, and social interactions and frame their practice through metaphors drawn from their fannish loves of particular brand cultures (Banet-Weiser 2012), toys, and entertainment properties; through creating content *with* their children *for* other children; or through even a love of YouTube itself.

It should be noted that my cohort of creators is, to some extent, self-selecting and occupies a more prosocial moral universe than some of the more unscrupulous edges of the toy unboxing genre and kids and family vertical. The twenty-four creators and their (approximately) seventy channels reflect a cohort who are critical of their own works and are largely driven to be prosocial through their content creation. I sent out over three hundred requests to kids and family channels and acknowledge that some (though not all) creators who did not respond or who declined to be interviewed may have done so for fear of criticism or exposure during the long-form interview and observation method. My response rate is not surprising given the popular press discourse around the genre. What was surprising, and exciting, to me was the peer-to-peer sharing of information, the content and intellectual property collaborations, and other forms of informal and formal assistance that make up toy unboxing creator communities.

It is well known, of course, that tactical "co-opetition" is widespread in SME (for example, Postigo 2016; Cunningham and Craig 2019). But the stakes are raised inside a culture considered by critics to be the nadir of consumer hypercapitalism. It is here that these once-niche community members have worked to redistribute the power dynamics seen in the children's media industry in both tangible and intangible ways (for an analysis of this phenomenon, see Bryant 2007). I suggest that toy unboxing creators and their fannish offshoots of dominant brands in children's culture can be meaningfully separated from commodification determinism and are instead, first and foremost, "about *culture* as much as they are about economics"; "[they] are meant to invoke the experience associated with a company or product" and are "more than just the object itself," because "a brand is [a] perception—[a] series of images, themes, morals, values, feelings, and sense of authenticity conjured by the product itself" (Banet-Weiser 2012, 4, emphasis original).

Toy unboxing videos and their many permutations and iterations should be placed in the wider field of new internet genres. Toy unboxing videos can be considered a part of the broader unboxing genre, which comprises the unpacking of everything from consumer electronics with product reviews to beauty products in "haul" and "style" videos. They also are part of the wider spectrum of kid-centric content on YouTube ranging from viral nursery-rhyme videos like the Baby Shark song to more established educational children's media and entertainment properties like *Peppa Pig*. Toy unboxing creators have often attempted to straddle the conditions and expectations of this set of genres while using "filler" material (Abidin 2017, 4) such as confessions, reactions, family occasions, and developmental milestones to boost a given channel's algorithmic visibility and prominence in the audience attention economy. In this way, toy unboxing creators actively engage in what Nancy Baym calls "relational labor," which emphasizes the "effort that goes beyond managing others' feelings in a single encounter, as is usually the case in emotional labor, . . . to creating and maintaining ongoing conversations" (2015, 16). However, this type of relational labor is not just among content creators and their viewers but with the YouTube algorithm and their fellow creators as well. In order to solidify, maintain, and nurture these relationships, toy unboxing content creators must be enthusiastically authentic and actively engage in the practices of calibrated amateurism for their audience (Abidin 2017), algorithmic optimization, and courteous, if not collaborative, professionalism among their peers.

As Cunningham and Craig (2019) have established in defining social media entertainment, toy unboxing creators also need a certain amount of trust in or, at least, perceived interconnectedness (Abidin 2015) with each viewer to ensure a given video's or channel's success. It is my contention that such trust or perceived interconnectedness is often extended by toy unboxing creators to other creators as well as to the YouTube algorithm and any intermediaries joined by these creators through what Melissa Gregg (2011) calls a "presence bleed"—or the blurring of professional and personal boundaries as a result of working online. By forming a community of trust among one another, creators either form tighter social bonds with these actors or, at the very least, give the impression of more intimate understandings of the other. These interactions (be they commercial, interactive, reciprocal, or disclosive) help to bridge the algorithmic, networked, and personal distances and create resilience in the toy unboxing community. It should be noted that there are clear distinctions between preplatformized internet communities and those like toy unboxing content creators who work largely on and with YouTube. Influence is radically dispersed: no one creator, viewer, platform employee, or algorithm is fully capable of controlling any of the factors that make toy unboxing videos spreadable (Jenkins, Ford, and Green 2013), be it calibrated amateurism/authenticity (Abidin 2017), relational labor (Baym 2015), determination of fannish expertise (Hills 2015), or algorithmic visibility (Gillespie 2014).

Joining and Leaving Multichannel Networks

Multichannel networks (MCNs) have been described as a rapidly disappearing, merging, and changing "raft of firms [that] began to launch their own channels as well as sign creators to help them grow and monetize their own. YouTube also directly facilitated and subsidized many of these firms, seeing them as a way of managing the explosion of online 'partners'" (Cunningham and Craig 2019, 78). MCNs promised to link the often time- and resource-poor toy unboxers to new brand partnerships, collaborations with like-minded YouTubers, and other forms of audience development, while concurrently providing cutting-edge analytics and programmatics that are unavailable to the everyday "broadcast yourself" YouTuber.

It is unsurprising that the suburban families who make up the majority of the toy unboxing creator community would look to MCNs like Maker Studios (Brouwer 2014) for more rapid professionalization, given how many of them had little to no formal videography, media-production, or brand-management training (like those skills detailed by London 2007). Many of the creators interviewed for this research who joined MCNs reported joining to mitigate the general industry precarity facing online content creators. Joining an MCN meant paying substantial amounts of their YouTube AdSense revenue (between 15 and 30 percent) in exchange for branded and sponsored deals brokered by the MCNs. But many creators reported that such deals were largely not delivered. One creator explained that the MCN model provided a form of "YouTube insurance" for legal, especially copyright issues, flagged videos, or other algorithm issues that could prompt demonetized content but that all other forms of value return (specifically branded or sponsored partnerships and creator collaborations) were negligible at best.

In the early years of SME, this arrangement worked strongly in favor of the MCNs. Mathias Bärtl's overall characterization of the way video provision and consumption of YouTube have changed over the past decade shows the striking figure that the vast majority (on average 85 percent) of all video views go to 3 percent of channels (2018, 16). Aaron Smith, Skye Toor, and Patrick van Kessel's (2018) Pew Research Center data suggests that 10 percent of all YouTube views in 2016 came from kids' entertainment (in some cases representing more than half of a given country's entire view count), with more recent research suggesting that videos that feature young children get triple the views of videos that do not (van Kessel, Toor, and Smith 2019). However, as I now will outline, kid content creators making toy unboxing videos have had to take on the functions of intermediaries, which adds a further layer to the checkered story of multichannel networks (Cunningham and Craig 2019, 115–147).

Many of the creators I interviewed argued that the MCN agents or managers who *were* in contact with them largely failed to represent them—focusing only on the revenue figures being brought in rather than the ways that those revenues could be improved. Unlike Violaine Roussel's (2016) assessment of talent agents' deep valuation of working with creatives, many members of the toy unboxing creator community explained that the conditions of MCN agenting and management lacked the personal touches of a relationship—such as advocacy, balance, creativity, or nurturing. As the toy unboxing and kids' content market became saturated, so the unregulated nature of this world (Craig and Cunningham 2017) became even more unregulated over time (Rubin 2018). With many creators' MCN contracts ending in the months and weeks before the ElsaGate scandal broke in November 2017 (despite the content being flagged by the creators to YouTube for over two years), MCNs were either uninterested or ineffective in protecting creators' interests as they faced their greatest challenge. The ethical dangers that ElsaGate presented, paired with the breakdown of the multichannel system, led to a radical change in creator governance, with creators turning to one another rather than their former high-profile MCN partners.

Creator Community Management Post-ElsaGate and Pre-Regulation

In 2017, an article went viral detailing the "ElsaGate" scandal: videos of notable children's entertainment characters like Spiderman, Peppa Pig, and Elsa from Disney's *Frozen* were satirized, reedited, or otherwise mischaracterized through adult themes of sex and violence (for example, Spiderman impregnating Elsa or Peppa Pig drinking bleach) and were circulating on YouTube and YouTube Kids (Bridle 2017). This prompted a massive retraction of advertising support for YouTube, which substantially curbed creators' AdSense revenues—the "KidPocalypse" (echoing an earlier crisis, the so-called Adpocalypse; see chapter 14). In this case, there was additional difficulty for the toy unboxing creator community, whose largest issue up to this point, as we have seen, was the argument about the commercialization of childhood. The issue was that James Bridle wrote about the community's content in the same article as the ElsaGate content, thus tarring toy unboxing videos and the community of creators who make them with the same brush. This connection to more egregious content that they had no creative association with led to toy unboxing creators losing algorithmic visibility and advertising revenue and to their earning an even more negative reputation among children's media professionals and advocates.

After ElsaGate, broader questions about content moderation became a source of frustration for many content creators, with few understanding where they went wrong. Grievances over the YouTube and YouTube Kids algorithm had been aired by toy unboxing creators following their family-friendly content being algorithmically linked to ElsaGate content. For example, during this period, a toy unboxing video of a Peppa Pig doll would be frequently suggested alongside an ElsaGate video in which a poorly animated spoof of Peppa Pig could be seen swearing, drinking bleach, or cannibalizing her father. Despite not having any production linkages to these spoofs, toy unboxers would face scrutiny about their use of "Peppa Pig" as a branded keyword to signal their playing with a Peppa Pig toy (see Bridle 2017). With Bridle conflating the practices of the toy unboxing creators with those of ElsaGaters, questions were raised about whether YouTube-native creators have the right to use words relating to children's entertainment brands like Peppa in their video titles and metadata tags. Further questions were also raised about whether any YouTube-native content featuring trusted children's brands could constitute fair and transformative use (defined by Tushnet 2017, 88).

Here, too, many creators felt that the complicated appeal processes were either slow or noncommunicative and that the inability to interact with a YouTube employee or representative who had the power to change anything added to further frustrations. The critical technology and culture scholar Sarah Myers West explains that "content moderations systems [are designed to] remove content at massive levels of scale, but do not do much to educate users about where they went wrong," positing that many creators are left "feel[ing] confused, frustrated, and as though they are 'shouting into a void'" about why their content was flagged in the first place (2018, 4380). Among my interviewees, the frustrations and folk theories about platform moderation resulting from this lack of clarity led many to move beyond finger-pointing at their YouTube representatives and the YouTube algorithm. They felt that the YouTube platform they were deeply engaged in culturally, and dependent on, had left them without agency and that the MCN "insurance" they once had was either long canceled or ineffective.

Many top creators turned toward one another to try to salvage, and work to revitalize, the collective identity and moral position of the toy unboxing genre in a post-MCN era. The outcome has been two types of new creator "communities." Pocket.watch's strategy of offering four top kids' content creators an equity stake to join forces with former children's media and MCN executives shows how a creator-centric community can be formed within a pseudo-MCN structure. Family Video Network's strategy of being creator helmed and community governed offers a more horizontal approach than that of pocket.watch. These communities offer insight into the way future creators within the kids and family vertical might work to combat algorithmic precarity while also recalibrating the moral compass and collective identity in the vertical.

pocket.watch

In March 2017, pocket.watch launched as a "new studio creating global franchises from the YouTube stars and characters loved by Generation Alpha, . . . specializ[ing] in entertaining and inspiring kids and families through digital-first content and sparking their imaginations with life-styles products ranging from toys to toothbrushes" (pocket.watch, n.d.). The effort was led by the former Maker Studios chief audience officer Chris Williams, the former Nickelodeon president of film and television entertainment Albie Hecht, and the entertainment lawyer Jon Moonves (brother of the former CBS Corporation CEO Les Moonves). In searching for partners, Hecht explained, "We really want to embrace the people who have made it to the top of the YouTube ecosystem, and we are very excited about finding the cream of the crop in terms of creativity, branding, and audience influence," while simultaneously signaling to creators, "we don't want to build an MCN, but rather a group of real partners and collaborators, hence the equity piece" (Goldman Getzler 2017).

These entertainment executives approached numerous top toy unboxing channels throughout 2017 (some of whose creators were interviewed for this research and declined pocket.watch's offer) before signing their first partner, the HobbyKidsTV suite of channels, in later April 2017 (Goldman Getzler 2017). In September 2017, pocket.watch signed Ryan of the Ryan's World suite of channels, shortly after the channel topped the US-based view charts in August 2017. This investment paid off when Ryan eventually was named 2018's highest-paid YouTube star in the world, at a whopping US$22 million (Berg 2019). Rounding out 2017, pocket.watch signed the popular Minecraft player CaptainSparklez and the EvanTubeHD series of channels (Gutelle 2017). For a substantial portion of toy unboxing's history, Evan, and by association his sister, JillianTubeHD, was one of the most recognizable and commercially successful toy unboxers.

From 2017 to 2019, the former Maker Studios and Viacom executives ensured that their four partner families had a rather public and forward-facing presence both on YouTube and in the wider children's media industry. Drawing largely from Evan's prior popularity (2013–16) and Ryan's current popularity (2016 to present day), pocket.watch has been able to leverage its multichannel community into a sizeable hold of young people's viewing time and attention economy. It has branched out beyond YouTube with repackaged videos on Hulu and Amazon Prime; a tell-all book published by Simon and Schuster, titled *Watch This Book!*; a series of online video games; an animated series on Nickelodeon; a comedy sketch show with the former child star and *Saturday Night Live* comedian Kenan Thompson; and an exclusive toy and consumer product line debuting at the US retailer Walmart centering around Ryan's World. Ryan was slated into an original series on Nickelodeon, *Ryan's Mystery PlayDate*, which debuted in April 2019 and inspired other children's content creators on YouTube, like MarMar and the Onyx Family, to sign deals with pocket.watch. As pocket.watch signed a major motion-picture deal with Paramount Picture, teased in 2019 as *The Unboxing Movie*, some of the creators I interviewed have raised questions about the creator agency that pocket.watch affords and the values of the equity stakes it has been offered. Though the corporation is seemingly skyrocketing forward in terms of revenue as of 2020, several creators have wondered whether pocket.watch seeks to keep itself rooted in the more participatory and creator-centric models of YouTube or whether it simply seeks to take over Nickelodeon's existing programming block. Further, some creators wonder whether company decisions will be coming from the likes of Ryan and Evan (let alone the smaller creators) or whether these decisions will be negotiated largely from the top down. Questions arise over who might collaborate or compete with pocket.watch, as the current industry leader, or whether anyone will stand as an alternative to its efforts. Comparisons can be made by looking at another creator-centric multichannel community, the Family Video Network.

Family Video Network

Family Video Network (FVN) was founded by Melissa Hunter (the "Mommy" part of the Mommy and Gracie Show YouTube channel now known as Mommy's World) in November 2013 following concerns from creators and parents alike about complying with the Children's Online Privacy Protection Act (COPPA) and the FTC and FCC guidelines regarding kid-centric content on YouTube. Relying heavily on Hunter's position as a trusted creator and parent by fellow creators, parents, and YouTube corporate alike, the Family Video Network benefited early on from her expertise in leveraging the massive power of family video (FVN 2015) and turned to her in the crisis the followed kids and family content following the ElsaGate scandal in 2017 (FVN 2017). Her role as a vocal moral compass for the toy unboxing creator community on YouTube positioned Hunter as a veritable "fixer" in the post-ElsaGate era (regardless of whether the channels were part of the Family Video Network). In my interview with her, I learned that her willingness to provide this kind of guidance began far before ElsaGate in 2017 and was largely sought in the wake of the mass MCN exodus from 2014 onward.

These factors, in combination with the rebranding of the Mommy and Gracie Show channel to become the Mommy's World channel in 2018, have allowed the Family Video Network to take on a more targeted approach: "Family Video Network has created a family tree of channels that brands love and parents trust. We are a group of video creators who provide family-friendly video content that is loved by kids and parent alike. Our mission is to support our channels, help them grow, and connect brands with our network of content creators" (FVN, n.d.). This re-brand was run by Melissa Hunter as well as chief operating officer Ralph Vuono, creator of the Chase and Cole Adventures channel, both of whom express the importance of being creator-centric and creator-focused while at the same time being audience-focused and platform- and government-compliant. This ethics of care has seen the reformalization of Family Video Network's long-standing partnerships with channels like babyteeth4 and Toy Caboodle while also giving eight new strategic partners equity stakes in the company—most notably, Princess T of Princess ToysReview, the aunt of Ryan of Ryan's World—and subsequent opportunities for strategic partnerships with other established players in the kid space who are known for strong family values and "clean" content.

Some distinguishing characteristics of FVN governance are that all partners, current and incoming, sign an agreement to have their content vetted by an executive member at FVN to ensure COPPA and Article 17 compliance as well as to ensure that they are family-friendly. Family Video Network has taken on smaller, developing channels that were underprivileged by the YouTube algorithm and has embraced African American creators. The BeYou (Black Entertainment on YouTube) Network is made up of several successful African American family- and kid-centric creators and is headed by the creators of the Onyx Family channel (who also signed an animation deal with pocket.watch in 2019) and the Naiah and Elli Doll Show.

FVN's strategy acknowledges that the YouTube algorithm positions kids and family content made by African American creators differently than it does other, similar content. In conducting network and search-engine analyses, FVN identified that African American kids' content was often not featured as often as other popular children's brands on YouTube in generic searches but was served alongside other African American kids' content creators once a channel was specifically searched for by channel name. FVN hypothesized that African American kids' content creators occupied a separate section of the YouTube algorithm. As creator-centric communities try to reestablish the wider kids and family vertical away from the KidPocalypse, FVN presents the promise of creators standing up for their audience and those creators who want to make a difference but may be underserved by YouTube's algorithm.

Conclusion

pocket.watch's and Family Video Network's practices relating to community management offer two distinct modes of governance. David Hesmondhalgh and Leslie Meier (2015; see also Hesmondhalgh, Jones, and Rauh 2019) examine how the internet created new modes of autonomy and dependence for the music industry, and their analysis is relevant to considering pocket.watch's and Family Video Network's models. Both pocket.watch and FVN straddle a line between being "fairly well-established large independents . . . with close financing, distribution, and other connections to the majors" and "a world of amateur and precarious semi-professional[s]" (Hesmondhalgh and Meier 2015, 102), with one occupying a more corporate and the other a more independent ethos. It is too early in both companies' histories to compare the governance techniques of the former mainstream children's media and digital media executives at pocket.watch, who are used to more top-down management structures, to the more executive-cum-creator and peer-to-peer model of community governance at Family Video Network. However, it is noteworthy that these more creator-centric organizations both formed as a response to platform precarity, ethical challenges, and moral panics and may presage a new level of creator agency.

In both pocket.watch's and Family Video Network's cases, their creator-centricity has seen the development of internal content guidelines that are regularly reviewed and, purportedly, strictly adhered to so as to ensure quality thresholds. These guidelines build on existing You-

Tube policies and COPPA compliance in areas that are often overlooked or unknowable to an outsider looking in on kids' content. These creator communities are orders of magnitude smaller than the multichannel networks of old. This does not seem to have harmed pocket.watch's or FVN's bottom line. Despite the fact that their abilities to generate commercial interest are currently at very different stages, with differences in viewership, subscription base, and reach, the strategies under which these communities are governed, the intended goals for their content, and their fate over time deserve further exploration given the current precarity facing kids' content on YouTube after ElsaGate and KidPocalypse. Wrestling with the YouTube algorithm, YouTube Kids, government regulation, scrutiny from lobbyists, constant public criticism, and their own fears about aging out or burning out, these unboxing creators have deepened their ties to maintain an ethics of community, prosocial values, and commercial viability.

REFERENCES

Abidin, Crystal. 2015. "Communicative ♥ Intimacies: Influencers and Perceived Interconnectedness." *Ada: A Journal for Gender, New Media, & Technology* 8. https://adanewmedia.org.

———. 2017. "#familygoals: Family Influencers, Calibrated Amateurism, and Justifying Young Digital Labor." *Social Media + Society* 3 (2): 1–15. doi:10.1177/2056305117707191.

Avance, Rosemary. 2016. "Community." In *Digital Keywords*, edited by Benjamin Peters, 63–69. Princeton, NJ: Princeton University Press.

Banet-Weiser, Sarah. 2012. *Authentic™: The Politics of Ambivalence in a Brand Culture.* New York: NYU Press.

Bärtl, Mathias. 2018. "YouTube Channels, Uploads, and Views: A Statistical Analysis of the Past 10 Years." *Convergence* 24 (1): 16–32. doi:10.1177/1354856517736979.

Baym, Nancy. 2015. "Connect with Your Audience! The Relational Labor of Connection." *Communication Review* 18 (1): 14–22. doi:10.1080/10714421.2015.996401.

Berg, Madeline. 2019. "The Highest-Paid YouTube Stars of 2019: The Kids Are Killing It." *Forbes*, December 18, 2019. www.forbes.com.

Bridle, James. 2017. "Something Is Wrong on the Internet." *Medium*, November 6, 2017. https://medium.com.

Brouwer, Bree. 2014. "Maker Studios Adds Five Toy Channels with 300 Million Collective Monthly Views." *Tubefilter*, November 25, 2014. www.tubefilter.com.

Bryant, J. Alison. 2007. "Understanding the Children's Television Community from an Organizational Network Perspective." In *The Children's Television Community*, edited by J. Alison Bryant, 35–56. Mahwah, NJ: Lawrence Erlbaum.

Craig, David, and Stuart Cunningham. 2017. "Toy Unboxing: Living in a(n Un-regulated) Material World." *Media International Australia* 163 (1): 77–86. doi:10.1177/1329878X17693700.

Cunningham, Stuart, and David Craig. 2019. *Social Media Entertainment: The New Industry at the Intersection of Hollywood and Silicon Valley.* New York: NYU Press.

Evans, Nathaniel, Mariea Hoy, and Courtney Childers. 2018. "Parenting 'YouTube Natives': The Impact of Pre-Roll Advertising and Text Disclosures on Parental Responses to Sponsored Child Influencer Videos." *Journal of Advertising* 47 (1): 326–346. doi:10.1080/00913367.2018.1544952.

FVN (Family Video Network). 2015. "Leveraging the Massive Power of Family Video—StreamCon 2015 Presentation." YouTube video, November 4, 2015. www.youtube.com/watch?v=wDRWQbg56tg.

———. 2017. "YouTube Kids and Family Content Crisis." YouTube video, November 25, 2017. www.youtube.com/watch?v=SsSp-9eyRdo.

———. n.d. Home page. Accessed September 7, 2020. www.familyvideonetwork.com.

Gillespie, Tarleton. 2014. "The Relevance of Algorithms." In *Media Technologies*, edited by Tarleton Gillespie, Pablo Boczkowski, and Kirsten Foot, 167–193. Cambridge, MA: MIT Press.

Goldman Getzler, Wendy. 2017. "Moonves: pocket.watch Will Give Creators Equity Stake." *kidscreen*, April 26, 2017. http://kidscreen.com.

Gregg, Melissa. 2011. *Work's Intimacy.* Cambridge, UK: Polity.

Gutelle, S. 2017. "pocket.watch Adds EvanTubeHD, CaptainSparklez to Roster of Kid-Friendly Creators." *Tubefilter*, November 21, 2017. www.tubefilter.com.

Hesmondhalgh, David, Ellis Jones, and Andreas Rauh. 2019. "SoundCloud and BandCamp as Alternative Music Platforms" *Social Media + Society* 5 (4): doi:10.1177/2056305119883429.

Hesmondhalgh, David, and Leslie Meier. 2015. "Popular Music, Independence, and the Concept of the Alternative in Contemporary Capitalism." In *Media Independence: Working with Freedom or Working for Free?*, edited by James Bennett and Niki Strange, 94–116. New York: Routledge.

Hess, Amanda. 2017. "How Unboxing Videos Soothe Our Consumerist Brains." *New York Times*, August 29, 2017. www.nytimes.com.

Hills, Matt. 2015. "The Expertise of Digital Fandom as a 'Community of Practice': Exploring the Narrative Universe of Doctor Who." *Convergence* 21 (3): 360–374. doi:10.1177/1354856515579844.

Jenkins, Henry, Sam Ford, and Joshua Green. 2013. *Spreadable Media: Creating Value and Meaning in a Networked Culture.* New York: NYU Press.

Kligler-Vilenchik, Neta. 2016. "Decreasing World Suck: Harnessing Popular Culture for Fan Activism." In *By Any Media Necessary: The New Youth Activism*, edited by Henry Jenkins, Sangita Shreshthova, Liana Gamber-Thompson, Neta Kligler-Vilenchik, and Arely Zimmerman, 102–148. New York: NYU Press.

Light, Ben, Jean Burgess, and Stefanie Duguay. 2018. "The Walkthrough Method: An Approach to the Study of Apps." *New Media & Society* 20 (3): 881–900. doi:10.1177/1461444816675438.

London, Robby. 2007. "Producing Children's Television." In *The Children's Television Community*, edited by J. Alison Bryant, 77–94. Mahwah, NJ: Lawrence Erlbaum.

McCracken, Grant. 1988. *The Long Interview*. London: Sage.

Myers West, Sarah. 2018. "Censored, Suspended, Shadowbanned: User Interpretations of Content Moderation on Social Media Platforms." *New Media & Society* 20 (11): 4366–4383. doi:10.1177/1461444818773059.

pocket.watch. n.d. Home page. Accessed September 7, 2020. https://pocket.watch.

Postigo, Hector. 2016. "The Socio-Technical Architecture of Digital Labor: Converting Play into YouTube Money." *New Media & Society* 18 (2): 332–349. doi:10.1177/1461444814541527.

Roussel, Violaine. 2016. "Talent Agenting in the Age of Conglomerates." In *Precarious Creativity*, edited by Michael Curtin and Kevin Sanson, 74–87. Berkeley: University of California Press.

Rubin, Molly. 2018. "The World of Kids on YouTube Is Wild, Weird, and Almost Entirely Unregulated." *Quartz News*, December 21, 2018. https://qz.com.

Smith, Aaron, Skye Toor, and Patrick van Kessel. 2018. "Many Turn to YouTube for Children's Content, News, How-To Lessons." Pew Research Center, November 7, 2018. www.pewinternet.org.

Tushnet, Rebecca. 2017. "Copyright Law, Fan Practices, and the Rights of the Author." In *Fandom: Identities and Communities in a Media World*, 2nd ed., edited by Jonathan Gray, Cornel Sandvoss, and C. Lee Harrington, 77–90. New York: NYU Press.

van Kessel, Patrick, Skye Toor, and Aaron Smith. 2019. "A Week in the Life of Popular YouTube Channels." Pew Research Center, July 25, 2019. www.pewinternet.org.

Walczer, Jarrod. 2021. "Toy Unboxing in U.S. Children's Culture." In *Routledge Companion to Digital Media and Children*, edited by Lelia Green, Donnell Holloway, Kylie Stevenson, Tama Leaver, and Lessie Haddon, 562–571. New York: Routledge.

9

Beyond the Nation

Cultural Regions in South Asia's Online Video Communities

SANGEET KUMAR, SRIRAM MOHAN, AND ASWIN
PUNATHAMBEKAR

The global expansion of the internet through networked devices is enabling emerging cultures of production that are revealing new webs and patterns of cultural affinity based on language, culture, and region. Long-held notions of audience, consumer, producer, and culture shaped in largely predigital media ecologies are giving way to radically altered ways of thinking about those categories, acknowledging the distributed architecture of a medium in which culture is increasingly algorithmic and privatized (Striphas 2015). This chapter explores the consequences of this emerging digital mediascape within the South Asian region by focusing on particular practices of video production, consumption, and circulation on YouTube that leverage the affordances of new media to challenge normative ideas of nation while centralizing notions of culture and region.

We invoke the concept of affordances here to signal that media technologies allow for specific readings and uses (Hutchby 2001; Bucher and Helmond 2017) and that analyzing the ways in which YouTube enables the formation of regional patterns of circulation cannot elide the technological dimensions of the platform as well as the web of which it is a part. As with any other media technology, YouTubers too must leverage the potentialities and possibilities that the technology allows while also managing its "constraints on their possibilities for action" (Hutchby 2001, 30). YouTube's peer-to-peer architecture (benefiting from the web's design as a distributed network), its lack of restrictions on who can upload (and consume) content, its ability to circumvent basic attempts of state censorship (which no doubt sometimes succeed), its large reposi-

tory of cultural content ready to be reused, and its multimodal interface (despite the primacy of video on the platform) are some of the key
affordances around which "users' perceptions, attitudes, and expectations" (Nagy and Neff 2015, 5) get built in relation to the platform. Our
case studies show (in explicit and implicit ways) how new patterns of
cultural production and circulation emerge when these technological
features militate against established regulatory structures such as the
nation-state.

South Asia represents a distinct geographical and political space for
analyzing such emerging mediascapes, given that its historical ties based
on culture, language, and religion have continued to thrive despite postcolonial political fissures that have often seemed insurmountable. The
recent uptake of digital media in the region, not surprisingly, has further
helped circumvent some of those political divisions by allowing the expression of robust organic interlinkages that always existed beneath the
seemingly ossified political borders.

This chapter analyzes these emerging networks of culture that cut
across political boundaries and enable a new way of thinking about
South Asia on the peer video-sharing platform YouTube. These emerging networks reveal patterns of cultural exchange, such as between the
southern states of India and diasporic populations in the Gulf states
and Southeast Asia, between the northern parts of India and neighboring Pakistan, and between the Bengali-speaking regions in India and
neighboring Bangladesh, that are arguably denser than any of those regions of India have among themselves. The optic of linguistic and cultural "region" therefore emerges as a far more productive metaphor that
challenges notions of national identity and culture as the primary organizing category for cultural circulation. These networks have preexisted
YouTube no doubt, but their intensification in the digital era cannot be
divorced from the ways in which social media platforms provide new
avenues and channels to bypass state control and regulation.

By showing how historically rooted regional cultural dynamics find
expression through cultures of creation (Cunningham and Craig 2019)
on YouTube, we hope to deepen and extend analyses about the role of
platforms in solidifying and reinforcing dormant cultural linkages. In
the case of India and Pakistan, these linkages long predate the digital
moment, with crossover cultural texts such as Pakistani television shows

(Tyagi 2016), Hindi cinema, and music. Digital platforms have enabled an intensification of scale of those exchanges, led by amateur producers and consumers in a context marked by censorship and regulation of established industries and renowned artists. At the same time, in the case of the southern peninsular region of India, the platform enables the creation and circulation of texts that help project regional and linguistic identities that militate against hegemonic constructions of national texts and culture. In underscoring the limits of the nation as the organizing category of digital culture in South Asia, both these cases show us how the affordances of social media platforms change the relationship between audiences and texts, with enduring political consequences. These include the "abstract high-level" (Bucher and Helmond 2017, 245) affordances of YouTube, such as always-on connectivity, its networked architecture and large archive of culture, and the "concrete feature-oriented low-level" (Bucher and Helmond 2017, 245) affordances of downloading, sharing, and commenting on videos unrestricted by one's geolocation. The distributed architecture of the web that makes this global orientation possible also animates these videos with an intertextual reciprocity wherein their anticipation of user feedback and responses situates them far more directly within preexisting conversations about identity, politics, and power. Embedded within an interactive ecology that continues in user comments below the videos, in other videos responding to them, and in discussions and conversations on other platforms and media outlets, these texts instantiate how free-flowing cultural desire defies expected nation-centric patterns and is hence inherently subversive.

Platforms and Regions in Global Media History

With the second-largest number of internet users in the world and growing exponentially, thanks to the cheapest data prices in the world (McCarthy 2019), countries like India will surely feature prominently in the transformation of online entertainment cultures. Indeed, the meteoric growth of local-language internet users in India from 42 million in 2011 to 234 million by 2016 also signals the emergence of vernacular practices that challenge our Anglo-centric understandings of digital cultures (KPMG 2017). Marc Steinberg and Jinying Li's argument, that "digital platforms have given rise to a sense of media regionalism and a renewed regional media geography through both transnational and transmedial processes" (2017, 173), is an important reminder not to reinscribe the Anglophone North Atlantic region as the basis for universal claims about emergent screen cultures.

We build on this perspective here and highlight the spatial logics of platform localization to ensure that the study of digital media remains alive to regional histories and cultural dynamics that are, in turn, embedded in transnational exchanges (Tinic 2005; Venegas 2009). At a broader level, a critical-regional perspective also helps us respond to calls to attend to the implications of the digital world's no longer being a predominantly English-speaking technoscape. Gerard Goggin and Mark McLelland are right to argue that despite the global diffusion of the internet and digital platforms, we are yet to "systematically chart what is now most salient and significant about the Internet: its great cultural and linguistic variety" (2009, 5). In this regard, the "region," a scale and category of analysis that has been crucial for scholars who have tried to move past media and communication studies' methodological nationalism or what Ravi Vasudevan has called "territorial fatalism" (2010, 95), emerges as key to understanding the significance of language-based cultural regions as foundational for any digital platform's localization.

From the perspective of the media industries, regions are at times regarded as sites of cultural and political coherence but at other times as spaces that have to be actively policed and (geo)blocked (Lobato and Meese 2016; Elkins 2019). Studies of global media industries make it clear that any straightforward mapping of geographic territories onto media regions is a fraught endeavor. Early satellite television's ability to transgress and circumvent national regulatory controls and to create common markets had already begun to centralize the role of language and culture (as opposed to nation and geography) as the organizing criteria for thinking about media regions (Sinclair, Jacka, and Cunningham 1996). In the Indian context particularly, the region-language link does emerge as a powerful organizing principle, given that the purportedly "national" Hindi-English content producers have explicitly categorized the "South" not just as a market but as a distinctive cultural and political territory. Since this categorization has been held in place by film and television distribution practice for well over five decades, the digital moment only intensifies it further.

The reorganization of independent India's states and territories along linguistic lines in 1956 helped to produce within the country a set of "regions," which continue to guide media production and distribution practices to this day. This territorial imagination has also been contested from various diasporic sites for well over a century now. These diasporic Indian populations formed through indentured labor, trade, and economic migration in the colonial era (at sites such as East/South Africa, Latin America, and islands such as Mauritius and Fiji) and through India's emergence as a source of labor for the technology industry in the postcolonial era (primarily in the West) have ensured that the production and consumption of "Indian" culture has already been irreducible to the geographic and cultural region of India. Moreover, the forces of economic and cultural globalization that led to the emergence of numerous translocal television networks like Sun TV or the development of new and diffuse regional formations around Bhojpuri-language cinema (a language with origins in the Indian states of Uttar Pradesh and Bihar but today spoken by diasporic Indians as far apart as the Fiji Islands, the West Indies, and Mauritius, among other places) have also challenged this narrow mapping of region onto language and culture (A. Kumar 2013). As Kathryn Hardy points out, given that the "linguistic limits of Bhojpuri are always in question and the geographic limits of Bhojpuri have not been coterminous with any state," we cannot presume a neat mapping of language onto a geographic region (2015, 145).

Scholars have also pointed out that linguistic and cultural regions, far from being fixed and pregiven, have to be continually produced and performed. At one level, the understanding of language based cultural regions in the subcontinent is complicated by the postcolonial context, wherein language became a key vantage point, first for a struggle for the separate nation of Pakistan (Ayres 2009; Datla 2013) and then again for the carving out of Bangladesh to construct a national identity around language rather than religion. The legacy of partition divided linguistic communities (of Bengali, Urdu, and Punjabi speakers) across the nation-states of Bangladesh, Pakistan, and India, thus showing why language and region emerge as far more productive lenses through which to analyze online cultures of creation on digital platforms in South Asia today than the lens of nation. Just as in the case of linguistically shaped online communities in southern India, our focus on the transnational circulation of Hindi and Urdu texts on YouTube reveals subcultures of interaction and collaboration that frustrate hegemonic constructions of nation, identity, and belonging.

At another level, these dynamics also operate within the nation, as shown by Sumathi Ramaswamy's (1997) and Lisa Mitchell's (2009) charting of the way Tamil and Telugu identities and their regional moorings are stabilized through a history of emotional commitments to the language in question, made apparent through mass protests and even suicides. The creation of linguistically reorganized states in independent India must then be viewed as an accrual of these commitments over the nineteenth and twentieth centuries, with the South Indian states explicitly positioning themselves against the imposition of Hindi as a "national" language. These concerns are far from resolved and continue to play out on digital and social media platforms as well, with a variety of regional/nonnational formulations locked in material-discursive struggles against resurgent nationalism. It is not possible in the space of this chapter to detail the many inter- and intraregional struggles that define the history of language-based state formation in India and beyond, but it is worth considering contemporary cultural and political dynamics within a history that extends back, as Farina Mir (2010), Francesca Orsini (2013), and Christian Novetzke (2016) all argue, well into the fifteenth and sixteenth centuries.

Keeping this context in mind, we take our cue from film studies scholar Ratheesh Radhakrishnan, who has argued that "linguistically organized formations need to be deployed under erasure by students of contemporary culture" (2016, 702). As we contend with a rapidly evolving digital media landscape and, in particular, platform companies' claims about cultural resonance, Radhakrishnan's argument reminds us that media regions have to be continually imagined, produced, and maintained over time. In the following section, we outline the efforts undertaken by YouTube to manage these processes in South Asia.

YouTube in South Asia: Online Video Industries and the Nation-State

When YouTube India, the twentieth country-localized version of the online video platform, was launched in May 2008, press coverage of the announcement focused on institutional partnerships with top Bollywood content providers (Indiatimes News Network 2008). Google-owned YouTube ensured that it signaled its intentions clearly and lined up a series of partnerships including those with television news channels like NDTV, state institutions like the Ministry of Tourism and the Indian Institute of Technology, and sports content providers like Krish-Cricket. In bringing together a range of partners to provide content across specific genres, YouTube was once again mobilizing industry lore about Indian audiences' proclivities, that is, their preference for cricket and Bollywood and their investment in news and education. It has been clear that the emergent scene of online video production in India has a "codependent relationship with hegemonic cultural institutions by being both in competition with it but also gaining from the technical, cultural labor, as well its archive of readily available content to be used and reused" (S. Kumar 2016, 5609).

At the same time, even a cursory examination of archived copies of the YouTube India site a month after its launch reveals that there were efforts undertaken to surface content created by individuals (in the "Featured Videos" tab on the home page, for instance). Videos of fish at the Golden Temple in Amritsar were listed alongside those of Bengali graffiti, card tricks, and motorcycle stunts in Kerala (YouTube India 2008). As people began to take seriously YouTube's exhortations to "broadcast yourself," the notion of a YouTube star started becoming legible in the Indian context. Wilbur Sargunaraj, famous for his Tamil-accented English music videos on topics ranging from blogs to "love marriage," is often referred to as India's first YouTube star (Anwer 2010). Other notable examples of early success on YouTube India through music videos include the teen musician Shraddha Sharma, who went on to release albums with the Universal Music Group (Pahwa 2013), and the "karaoke master" Dr. K Choudhary (Hartmann 2013). Even as claims of YouTube India being "bigger than MTV India" were floated by the top brass at Google (Pahwa 2012), the online video platform was also building on the momentum around comedy, curating content from collectives like All India Bakchod (AIB) and The Viral Fever (TVF) alongside clips from films in various regional languages. By the time the national general election results were livestreamed on YouTube in May 2014 (yet another marker of its growing importance as a site for political speech and resistance), the platform could boast of significant depth with regard to content availability in genres ranging from cooking and makeup tutorials to gadget reviews and devotional music.

This depth, of course, was rendered possible by the broader move toward "platformization" (Plantin et al. 2018) of splintered infrastructures (of language, network connectivity, etc.) that YouTube exemplifies. While YouTube India introduced a Hindi interface about a year after its launch (J 2009), it took a few more years to broaden support for various Indic languages and expand the catalogue of content in regional languages apart from Hindi (Saxena 2012). But the biggest shift arguably was the introduction of the option to download videos for offline playback on Android phones in 2014, a feature that was initially introduced only in three markets (India, Indonesia, and Philippines) known for their mobile-phone-centric user base and unavailability of affordable high-quality data plans. These were also three nations with the slowest average internet connection speed in the Asia Pacific region (Bellman 2014). While Brian Larkin (2008) points to the way media infrastructures and networks of circulation in precisely these kinds of places can connect people into collectivities, YouTube's infrastructuring impulse appears to be driven by the need to recast people as users. This is evident in proclamations by senior YouTube employees that the "next billion users . . . are going to come from a market like India" (*Indian Television* 2015). This industry discourse about emerging markets is not off the mark, given that India is one of the biggest online video markets in the world, with YouTube viewership on mobile phones alone hitting 180 million in early 2017 (Menon 2017). As in other key territories around the world, YouTube India's growth as a dominant video platform has been shaped in important ways by multichannel networks (MCNs) that, in turn, have helped institutionalize creator culture(s) (Cunningham, Craig, and Silver 2016).

As distinct from India, the launch and uptake of YouTube in Pakistan has been enmeshed within contestations about statist notions of nation, religion, and culture (Arif 2014). From YouTube's entry as a global platform in 2006, censorship and outright ban in 2008 and 2012, the protracted civil society struggle, and finally, the official lifting of the ban after the launch of a local version in 2016 (Wilkes 2016), the platform's trajectory in Pakistan offers an instructive case in cultural conflicts arising during the localization of global platforms. Following the republication of caricatures of Prophet Muhammad and the reproduction of purportedly non-Islamic content on YouTube in 2008, the Pakistani state ordered local internet providers to block access to the platform, which created a configuration error that shut off the site to users *across the world* for a couple of hours (McCullagh 2008). YouTube's radically different trajectories in Pakistan and India, combined with its worldwide shutdown (caused by its ban in Pakistan), reiterate how a collection of regional internets come together to support the discursive and sociotechnical arrangement of the internet as a global network. Digital intermediaries like YouTube are increasingly central to scholarly efforts to read the "coming together" of such regional webs rather than the "taking apart" of a global monolithic network of networks. Such approaches to platforms are crucial to ensure that the study of digital media remains alive to regional characteristics and histories while being responsive to transnational exchanges and relays (Venegas 2009).

Further, thinking through the lens of platform localization nuances understandings of the enmeshing of curatorial and representational politics and its volatile and uncertain implications. For instance, the lack of a localized YouTube implementation (and, consequently, the lack of control experienced by the state in its efforts to monitor and moderate content) was repeatedly mobilized as the reason for the blanket ban on the platform in Pakistan from 2012 to 2016. In 2012, YouTube was banned in Pakistan after the site refused to take down the trailer of the film *Innocence of Muslims*, which was produced in the United States and provoked protests across the Muslim world (Rosenberg and Rahimi 2012). The tensions between the state's impulse to censor content that it deemed blasphemous and Pakistani civil society's opposition to such heavy-handed control of digital and news media then unfolded through persistent calls to reinstate platform access. Among many such protests, one that stands out is #KholoBC (*kholo* meaning "open" and *BC* being an acronym for an expletive), a transmedia campaign opposing state censorship and content regulation on the internet. Sparked by a "viral" rap song (Desmukh 2014) featuring the comedian Ali Gul Pir and the rapper Adil Omar, #KholoBC indexed a range of discontents about the limiting of the freedom of expression in Pakistan using religion and national security as smokescreens, culminating in a call to action specifically focused on removing the YouTube ban (Khatri, n.d.). #KholoBC found other expressions such as a video shot on the streets of Karachi featuring a person wearing a YouTube-branded cube walking the streets holding a sign reading, "hug me if you want me back." Men and women are shown approaching the friendly cube for hugs, as cries of "I love YouTube" and "God, please open YouTube" punctuate the soundtrack.

YouTube's different trajectories in the two national contexts of India and Pakistan nevertheless must not take away from its common role as a site for nonmainstream, subversive, and risky content that would not make it to the traditional media outlets. Moreover, its role in cultivating a culture of creation has enabled the blossoming of new genres, subgenres, and topics of content, thus creating conversations within and across traditional national boundaries. New genres such as rural cooking videos, spirituality, education/tutoring videos, trailer spoofs, and music and dance represent a small sample of a complex content ecosystem showcasing mutation, cross-fertilization, and regional/transnational patterns of cultural circulation. YouTube's radical promise, which posed a threat to the authority of sovereign states (for example, Pakistan), is also visible in its ability to foreground and intensify linguistic and cultural regions, as seen in the following section through the case studies of the South Indian peninsula and the Hindi- and Urdu-speaking northern region.

The Southern Peninsula of India as Practiced Place

In an interview rounding up developments on YouTube in India in 2017, Satya Raghavan, the company's head of entertainment for the country, revealed that Hindi, Tamil, Telugu, and English remained the top four languages for the platform (Mathur 2017). Less than a year later, he acknowledged a rise in demand for content in South Indian languages (like Tamil and Telugu), in another trade press article about the $700 million online video market in India (Singh 2018). Following David Hesmondhalgh (2012, 279), we consider such formulations of audience/user community discovery as an acknowledgment of the existence of a geocultural market, united by shared histories and cultural experiences and not by language. In the case of the South Indian states, this has often translated to the vision of a homogenized southern peninsula from the point of view of the postindependence Hindi film industry, dominated by Punjabi (North Indian) Khatri caste groups (Dwyer 2002). In the case of online video communities, the disruption of this homogenizing view has been enabled, in some instances, by a satirical embrace of this peninsular framework by creators from media capitals in the South Indian states.

On YouTube, a richly textured exemplar of the invocation of this regional solidarity is "South of India," the "viral" hit video produced by the Chennai-based theater company Stray Factory in association with an MCN called Culture Machine and uploaded onto a channel called Rascalas in November 2014. Set to the tune of Billy Joel's "We Didn't Start the Fire," "South of India" starts with the screen being split into a two-by-two grid and four actors in traditional attire occupying those spots, facing the audience. They then burst into song, listing the names of various states and union territories in the peninsula and briefly slipping into the four dominant South Indian languages before returning to register their plaints about the "Northies" in English. The peninsular mapping and its limits are echoed in the song's chorus ("We are South of India"), that South India is not a single state made up of *madrasi-s*; rather, they are all *padosi-s* ("neighbors" in Hindi). The rest of the song then proceeds with two verses highlighting widely regarded cultural, sociopolitical, and religious icons and places of note in each of the four large southern states, interspersed with the chorus, which catalogues both the legibility of the South Indian peninsula as a distinct entity and its role as a signifier of a more granular regional formation. As the performers mime their way through this survey of the South, their anger and frustration about being imagined as a monolith by Hindi-speaking northerners turns into pride and satisfaction at having set the record straight. The BBC's online magazine called the video "a musical guide to southern India" and declared it a "YouTube hit" (Brosnan 2014), with the song eventually clocking close to 2.6 million views on the online video platform and garnering press coverage in national and international news outlets.

Since the release of "South of India," the peninsular imagination has repeatedly been invoked by YouTube creators across India to varying degrees of success in terms of online circulation. For instance, even in 2019, upcoming South Indian creators like Nee Yaaruda Komali (Tamil) and Rey 420 (Telugu) posted comedy videos with titles like "*Hindi* v.

South India" and "North Indian vs South Indian." In addition, issues pertaining to language politics and rights of the South Indian states in a federal structure (for example, the imposition of Hindi-language teaching in schools nationwide through education policy changes) continue to be refracted through the peninsular frame, with YouTube channels like Temple Monkeys, Put Chutney, and Nakkalites all relying on shared experiences of alienation and negligence to spatialize their political satire.

As an early example of speaking back to this sense of othering, "South of India" represents what Michel de Certeau (1984) calls "spatial stories," where the text and its narrative enactments specify the practices organizing the peninsular space. Be it the song's reference to closing times of pubs in Bangalore or to watching cricket at the Chepauk stadium in Chennai, the peninsular space mobilized here, while distinctly middle class and largely urban, is actuated in the aggregation of places and the everyday practices associated with them. It is articulated as a set of possibilities, with the urban elements in question offered as examples of both specificity and simultaneity. For de Certeau, "space" does not possess the stability that "place" does. Instead, space, he argues, "occurs as the effect produced by the operations that orient it, situate it, temporalize it, and make it function in a polyvalent unity of conflictual programs or contractual proximities" (1984, 117). The narrators in "South of India" and the stories they tell, then, perform the labor of translating the peninsular space into a "practiced place," building off the territorializing impulse of the hegemonic Hindi-speaking North and establishing the itinerary charted *as* map. Central to these moves is the question of language, as the speech acts enabled by the narrators in service of region-making faithfully abide by the linguistic reorganization of states in postindependence India. In so doing, they encounter an essential contradiction; that is, the region-language mapping exceeds these territorial boundaries, as such mapping invariably has.

Humor and Prank Videos at the Junction of India-Pakistan

A different iteration of such regional dynamics, across historically arbitrary but increasingly vexed national borders, is visible in the case of India and Pakistan, where enduring undercurrents of cultural exchange that have withstood decades of political and military conflict find new resonance online. Following the division into two countries by a political boundary that sought to carve out a Muslim nation by separating it from a Hindu-majority India (in 1947), these ongoing cultural exchanges on digital platforms are both a testimony to the violence of political boundaries and a reminder of their limits in dividing intermixed communities into separate silos. The contentious political separation notwithstanding, the hybrid cultural terrain of the region bears witness to the millennia-old linkages in the region, whose common language and culture have ensured a rich cross-fertilization across genres, formats, and media. This is reflected in the strong footprint of Bollywood in Pakistan but equally in the large audiences that Pakistani television shows have historically attracted in India (Tyagi 2016). These institutional and formal cultural linkages between the two countries have frequently been disrupted by ongoing military skirmishes on the border and the geopolitical rivalry over the disputed region of Kashmir. These disruptions include decisions (by the Indian side) to ban Pakistani artists from working in Indian films and to stop the airing of Pakistani shows on Indian television (*India Today* 2016), as well as (by the Pakistani side) to bar Indian films and television shows from airing in Pakistani cinema halls and television networks. While these frequent disruptions have curtailed the formal flow of people and culture, they have also helped divert and rechannel the latent desire for cultural exchange into the less regulated online realm. While YouTube's growth in India can partly be explained by YouTube's emphasis on regional expansion (Mohan and Punathambekar 2019), its interrupted trajectory in Pakistan is a more complex journey of starts and stops leading to its gradual emergence as a site for "fragmented attachments, local desires and concerns, lazy provocation, and casual sociability" (Hashmi 2019, 254). Additionally, its rise as a site for more activist and politically subversive texts (Arif 2014) also ties into the contested relationship between the media and the state, resulting in frequent attempts to censor and mute the press (Hashmi 2012).

YouTube's distinct paths in the two countries notwithstanding, the platform today emerges as a common site for expressions of linguistic and cultural affinity between India and Pakistan, thanks in no small part to common transnational audiences for texts. At the juncture of India and Pakistan, emerging digital localities on YouTube cohere around exchange of texts across established genres such as humor, music, drama, and sports but also in subgenres such as prank videos. The emergence of the genre of humorous prank video in South Asia is in line with its global popularity among new audiences and creators; YouTube recently had to ban certain dangerous forms of it entirely from the platform (John 2019). While these videos represent the democratization of cultural production, their consumption and circulation patterns also show the ways in which cultural desires reflect a "search for cultural relevance or proximity" (Straubhaar 1991, 39) that is irreducible to assumed patterns of circulation either within nations or even from the dominant exporting West to the receiving East. We show this dynamic through a close analysis of the South Asian prank genre, whose viewership and interaction patterns reveal a symbiotic cultural imaginary in which the historical connections of language and culture trump differences such as nationality and religion.

Cultural texts produced in these genres reflect a constant awareness of the gaze of the other, a fact that is apparent in the cross-border references and traces within the text as well as the metatextual elements such as background music, appreciation fan videos, and reader comments. P 4 Pakao is a popular YouTube channel run by the Pakistani comedian Nadir Ali, who specializes in prank videos that create humorous real-life situations by confronting unsuspecting ordinary citizens going about their daily life. The videos re-create the globally popular prank genre in Pakistan; the humor arises from the candid responses of disbelief, shock, disgust, and other similar emotions from unsuspecting targets when confronted with a strange or out-of-the-ordinary situation. In Ali's videos, these scenarios include (among others) being asked to help Ali prepare for a boxing match on the street, aggressively asking people for the time and then challenging their response inside an elevator, providing on-the-job training to a barber cutting the hair of an unsuspecting customer, and posing as a television reporter and drawing passersby into intense debates on social and political issues.

Even though staged, created, and recorded on the streets of Pakistan, these videos have large audiences in India due to the similarities of language and social and cultural idioms and the common topics of interest in the two nations. Ali is quite aware of his transnational audience, and he intermixes his videos with constant references to India and particularly to Bollywood. One of his prank videos, for instance, features a burka-clad Ali repeatedly trying to catch a ride with motorcycle riders and capturing the riders' dazed responses as they try to fathom why a strange woman would try to ride along with them. As each such attempt is played out sequentially, an additional dash of humor is added through a famous Bollywood song ("Parde Mein Rahne Do" roughly translated as "let things remain behind the veil" and easily recognizable in the Hindi- and Urdu-speaking regions of the subcontinent) that is layered as the background music. In addition to the background music, Ali often jokingly refers to his victims as actors (Ajay Devgan, Anil Kapoor) and singers (Yo Yo Honey Singh) from Bollywood, pointing to their familiarity in Pakistan.

While most of Ali's videos have references to Indian culture, the discourse around P 4 Pakao's prank videos is another indication of the ways in which these texts represent instances of the way YouTube enables the expression of latent cultural desires that would otherwise find no outlet amid the reciprocal bans on cultural exchange arising from geopolitical conflicts in the region. The comment sections below the videos have a significant presence of Indian users, a sign as much of India's large digital population as it is of the popularity of these Pakistani comedy sketches in India. Comments by Indian viewers invariably make it a point to mention their nationality, thus calling attention to the paradox of Ali's large fan base in India, where he is unlikely to get a visa to perform under the present political situation. These attempts to let Ali know about his Indian fan base present a starkly contrarian discourse to the environment of distrust and fear created by political leaders and radical groups rehearsing routine threats at each other across the border. These attempts are further bolstered by video endorsements for Ali from Indian celebrities including Johnny Lever, Sanket Bhosale, and Sunil Pal.

Conclusion

Both the case studies analyzed in this chapter show the ways in which digital platforms such as YouTube intensify the contravention of assumed circuits of content circulation and reveal the limits of the nation as an analytic category for understanding patterns of cultural circulation and consumption. Our analyses of both the cultural exchanges within the Indian peninsular region and the interactions across India-Pakistan show that the interactive, immanent, always-on distributed architecture of the web, combined with the specific affordances of YouTube (described earlier), bolster the expressions of ground-up and organic cultural formations rather than being entirely shaped by top-down structures such as the nation-state. In this media ecology, the cultural analytic of the "region" emerges as a far more accurate descriptor of the ways digital media platforms are reshaping culture, bypassing the usual constraints of time and space. Our claim to rethink formations of creator culture beyond the nation is in line with the changing nature of sovereignty in the digital era (Kohl 2017). While this phenomenon has been analyzed in a varied range of areas such as commerce, law, security, and territoriality (among others), we reveal the workings of that process in the realm of online creator cultures.

By making linguistic and cultural regions the starting point (rather than an afterthought) for analyzing digital culture, our analysis is an invitation for more scholarship that seeks to retrace the linkages and communities that have remained suppressed amid the hegemonic primacy of the nation-state. The imposition of the modern nation-state in large parts of the world (often in relation to colonialism) disrupted existing community affiliations (Chatterjee 1993) by drawing a political boundary around and between organic and free-flowing cultural and linguistic communities. These affiliations have, however, remained latent and, as seen in both of our case studies, find renewed expression within emerging cultures of creation online.

REFERENCES

Anwer, Javed. 2010. "Meet India's First YouTube Star." *Times of India*, March 21, 2010. http://epaper.timesofindia.com.

Arif, Rauf. 2014. "Social Movements, YouTube and Political Activism in Authoritarian Countries: A Comparative Analysis of Political Change in Pakistan, Tunisia & Egypt." PhD diss., University of Iowa.

Ayres, Alyssa. 2009. *Speaking like a State: Language and Nationalism in Pakistan*. Cambridge: Cambridge University Press.

Bellman, Eric. 2014. "Chart: India's Internet Speed Is the Slowest in Asia." *Wall Street Journal*, June 30, 2014. https://blogs.wsj.com.

Brosnan, Greg. 2014. "A Musical Guide to Southern India Is a YouTube Hit." *BBC News*, November 8, 2014. www.bbc.com.

Bucher, Taina, and Anne Helmond. 2017. "The Affordances of Social Media Platforms." In *The Sage Handbook of Social Media*, edited by Jean Burgess, Alice Marwick, and Thomas Poell, 233–253. London: Sage.

Chatterjee, Partha. 1993. *The Nation and Its Fragments: Colonial and Postcolonial Histories*. Princeton, NJ: Princeton University Press.

Cunningham, Stuart, and David Craig. 2019. *Social Media Entertainment: The New Intersection of Hollywood and Silicon Valley*. New York: NYU Press.

Cunningham, Stuart, David Craig, and John Silver. 2016. "YouTube, Multichannel Networks and the Accelerated Evolution of the New Screen Ecology." *Convergence: The International Journal of Research into New Media Technologies* 22 (4): 376–391. doi:10.1177/1354856516641620.

Datla, Kavita. 2013. *The Language of Secular Islam: Urdu Nationalism and Colonial India*. Honolulu: University of Hawaii Press.

de Certeau, Michel. 1984. *The Practice of Everyday Life*. Translated by Steven Rendall. Berkeley: University of California Press.

Desmukh, Fahad. 2014. "Pakistani Artists Say Their Country's YouTube Ban Is about Politics, Not Religion." *Public Radio International*, February 28, 2014. www.pri.org.

Dwyer, Rachel. 2002. *Yash Chopra*. London: British Film Institute.

Elkins, Evan. 2019. *Locked Out: Regional Restrictions in Digital Entertainment Culture*. New York: NYU Press.

Goggin, Gerard, and Mark McLelland. 2009. "Internationalizing Internet Studies: Beyond Anglophone Paradigms." In *Internationalizing Media Studies*, edited by Daya Thussy, 3–17. New York: Taylor and Francis.

Hardy, Kathryn. 2015. "Constituting a Diffuse Region: Cartographies of Mass-Mediated Bhojpuri Belonging." *BioScope: South Asian Screen Studies* 6 (2): 145–164. doi:10.1177/0974927615600623.

Hartmann, Graham. 2013. "Old Doctor from India Performs Classics by Metallica, Guns N' Roses + AC/DC." *Loudwire*, February 7, 2013. http://loudwire.com.

Hashmi, Mobina. 2012. "At the Limits of Discourse: Political Talk in Drag on *Late Night Show with Begum Nawazish Ali*." *South Asian History and Culture* 3 (4): 511–531. doi: 10.1080/19472498.2012.720065.

———. 2019. "Private Publics: New Media and Performances of Pakistani Identity from Party Videos to Cable News." In *Global Digital Cultures: Perspectives from South Asia*, edited by Aswin Punathambekar and Sriram Mohan, 245–260. Ann Arbor: University of Michigan Press.

Hesmondhalgh, David. 2012. *The Cultural Industries*. London: Sage.

Hutchby, Ian. 2001. *Conversation and Technology: From the Telephone to the Internet*. Cambridge, UK: Polity.

Indian Television. 2015. "'The Next Billion YouTube Users Are Going to Come from India': Ajay Vidyasagar." December 4, 2015. www.indiantelevision.com.

Indiatimes News Network. 2008. "YouTube Launched in India." *Economic Times*, May 7, 2008. https://economictimes.indiatimes.com.

India Today. 2016. "Sad News! Zee to Ban All Pakistani Shows." September 25, 2016. www.indiatoday.in.

J, Preethi. 2009. "YouTube India Embraces Hindi; No Transliteration; Subtitles?" *MediaNama*, August 17, 2009. www.medianama.com.

John, Tara. 2019. "YouTube Bans Dangerous Pranks and Challenges." *CNN*, January 16, 2019. www.cnn.com.

Khatri, Sadia. n.d. "#KholoBC." *Pakistan For All.* Accessed July 13, 2019. http://pakistanforall.org.

Kohl, Uta, ed. 2017. *The Net and the Nation State: Multidisciplinary Perspectives on Internet Governance.* Cambridge: Cambridge University Press.

KPMG. 2017. "Indian Languages—Defining India's Internet." April 26, 2017. https://home.kpmg.com.

Kumar, Akshaya. 2013. "Provincialising Bollywood? Cultural Economy of North-Indian Small-Town Nostalgia in the Indian Multiplex." *South Asian Popular Culture* 11 (1): 61–74. doi:10.1080/14746689.2013.764642.

Kumar, Sangeet. 2016. "YouTube Nation: Precarity and Agency in India's Online Video Scene." *International Journal of Communication* 10 (18): 5608–5625.

Larkin, Brian. 2008. *Signal and Noise: Media, Infrastructure, and Urban Culture in Nigeria.* Durham, NC: Duke University Press.

Lobato, Ramon, and James Meese. 2016. *Geoblocking and Global Video Culture.* Amsterdam: Institute of Network Cultures.

Mathur, Nandita. 2017. "We Have a Content Ecosystem That Is Wide, Deep, Well Balanced: YouTube." *Mint*, December 11, 2017. www.livemint.com.

McCarthy, Niall. 2019. "The Cost of Mobile Internet around the World." *Forbes*, March 5, 2019. www.forbes.com.

McCullagh, Declan. 2008. "How Pakistan Knocked YouTube Offline (and How to Make Sure It Never Happens Again)." *CNET*, February 25, 2008. www.cnet.com.

Menon, Bindu. 2017. "YouTube Mobile Viewership Hits 180M in India." *Hindu BusinessLine*, March 23, 2017. www.thehindubusinessline.com.

Mir, Farina. 2010. *The Social Space of Language: Vernacular Culture in British Colonial Punjab.* Berkeley: University of California Press.

Mitchell, Lisa. 2009. *Language, Emotion, and Politics in South India: The Making of a Mother Tongue.* Bloomington: Indiana University Press.

Mohan, Sriram, and Aswin Punathambekar. 2019. "Localizing YouTube: Language, Cultural Regions, and Digital Platforms." *International Journal of Cultural Studies* 22 (3): 317–333. doi:10.1177/1367877918794681.

Nagy, Peter, and Gina Neff. 2015. "Imagined Affordance: Reconstructing a Keyword for Communication Theory." Social *Media + Society* 1 (2): 1–9. doi:10.1177/2056305115603385.

Novetzke, Christian. 2016. *The Quotidian Revolution: Vernacularization, Religion, and the Premodern Public Sphere in India.* New York: Columbia University Press.

Orsini, Francesca. 2013. *The History of the Book in South Asia*. London: Routledge.

Pahwa, Nikhil. 2012. "YouTube India Is Bigger than MTV India in Revenues—Rajan Anandan." *MediaNama*, January 18, 2012. www.medianama.com.

———. 2013. "YouTube Star Shraddha Sharma Signs Album Deal with Universal; YouTube Deal with Culture Machine." *MediaNama*, November 28, 2013. www.medianama.com.

Plantin, Jean-Christophe, Carl Lagoze, Paul Edwards, and Christian Sandvig. 2018. "Infrastructure Studies Meet Platform Studies in the Age of Google and Facebook." *New Media & Society* 20 (1): 293–310. doi:10.1177/1461444816661553.

Radhakrishnan, Ratheesh. 2016. "The 'Worlds' of the Region." *Positions: Asia Critique* 24 (3): 693–719.

Ramaswamy, Sumathi. 1997. *Passions of the Tongue: Language Devotion in Tamil India, 1891–1970*. Berkeley: University of California Press.

Rosenberg, Matthew, and Sangar Rahimi. 2012. "Protests over Contentious Film Spread to Afghanistan." *New York Times*, September 17, 2012. www.nytimes.com.

Saxena, Anupam. 2012. "YouTube Adds Support for More Indic Languages." *MediaNama*, February 27, 2012. www.medianama.com.

Sinclair, John, Elizabeth Jacka, and Stuart Cunningham. 1996. "New Patterns in Global Television." In *Media Studies: A Reader*, edited by Paul Marris, Sue Thornham and Caroline Bassett, 170–190. New York: NYU Press.

Singh, Manish. 2018. "Netflix and Amazon Are Struggling to Win over the World's Second-Largest Internet Market." *CNBC*, July 5, 2018. www.cnbc.com.

Steinberg, Marc, and Jinying Li. 2017. "Introduction: Regional Platforms." *Asiascape: Digital Asia* 4 (3): 173–183. doi:10.1163/22142312–12340076.

Straubhaar, Joseph. 1991. "Beyond Media Imperialism: Assymetrical [*sic*] Interdependence and Cultural Proximity." *Critical Studies in Mass Communication* 8 (1): 39–59. doi:10.1080/15295039109366779.

Striphas, Ted. 2015. "Algorithmic Culture." *European Journal of Cultural Studies* 18 (4–5): 395–412. doi:10.1177/1367549415577392.

Tinic, Serra. 2005. *On Location: Canada's Television Industry in a Global Market*. Toronto: University of Toronto Press.

Tyagi, Amit. 2016. "10 Landmark Pakistani Shows That Were Hugely Popular in India." *India Today*, October 5, 2016. www.indiatoday.in.

Vasudevan, Ravi. 2010. "Geographies of the Cinematic Public: Notes on Regional, National and Global Histories of Indian Cinema." *Journal of the Moving Image* 9:94–116.

Venegas, Cristina. 2009. "Thinking Regionally: Singular in Diversity and Diverse in Unity." In *Media Industries: History, Theory, and Method*, edited by Jennifer Holt and Alisa Perren, 120–131. Malden, MA: Wiley.

Wilkes, Tommy. 2016. "Google Builds Local Version of YouTube Just for Pakistan to Circumvent 3-Year Ban." *VentureBeat*, January 18, 2016. https://venturebeat.com.

YouTube India. 2008. Home page. Wayback Machine. June 10, 2008. https://web.archive.org.

10

Creativity and Dissent in Arab Creator Culture

MOHAMED EL MARZOUKI

Over the past decade, the role of information and communication technologies in societies of the Middle East and North Africa (MENA) has been studied in close connection to Arab Spring uprisings. Today, there is a growing multidisciplinary body of research that examines the role of digital media technologies in popular protest, dissent, and social movements (Honwana 2013; Douai and Moussa 2016; Tufekci 2017; Zayani 2018). Much of this work highlights the significance of digital media platforms in furnishing online spaces for contentious politics, online protest, and the expression of dissent (Zayani 2015). The affordances of digital media platforms in this literature are celebrated for facilitating participation in public life through creative and politically inflected forms of creator content (cf. Kraidy 2016). In a region where cultural production has largely been dominated by state institutions in the era of national and satellite broadcasting, digital media platforms were taken up by early adopters in the aftermath of Arab Spring protests to build spaces for producing and circulating alternatives to the staged, professionally executed content of state media. While state-controlled television, radio, and print media were marshaled by postcolonial states across the Arab world to achieve political integration and to build homogeneous national identities, the arrival of digital media technologies ushered in a new era of creative expression. The emerging creative media practices and the amateur cultural forms they spawn are gradually and steadily coalescing into a semiprofessional field of creative cultural production and consumption driven by young creators and their fans across the MENA region.

The aim of this chapter is to introduce an emerging field of creative cultural production that makes use of participatory media practices to build repositories of user-generated content on platforms like YouTube,

Facebook, Instagram, Twitter, and Snapchat. In the MENA region, such content consists mainly of videos and photos, covering a wide spectrum of entertainment genres including comedy sketches, fashion and makeup tutorials, cuisine and cooking guides, travel vlogs, gaming, and DIY video. Almost a decade after the first Arab Spring mass protests, the "users" who create, curate, and circulate social media entertainment content are gradually maturing into semiprofessional media entrepreneurs, often referred to as social media influencers (SMI), YouTubers, vloggers, or creators. To describe the emerging field of cultural production fueled by this new generation of professionalizing amateur creators, Stuart Cunningham and David Craig use the phrase "social media entertainment" (SME), in contrast to "Hollywood-like content" produced and distributed by online streaming services like Amazon Video, Hulu, and Netflix (2019, 12–13). Building on their definition, this chapter uses the phrase *creator culture* to refer to the myriad content forms, media practices, and digital spaces that constitute the field of social media entertainment.

In mapping this field of creator culture in the MENA region, I draw on fieldwork and in-depth interviews I have conducted in Morocco between 2016 and 2018 with more than twenty prominent social media creators whose work is increasingly circulated across different social media platforms (primarily YouTube, Facebook, and Instagram). The creators I interviewed produce a variety of content genres, including music remix and parody, political satire and comedy, animated cartoons, makeup and lifestyle, information communication technology (ICT) hacks and DIYs, and popular science, among others. The fieldwork informing this chapter includes visits to production studios, live performances, cafés, and homes where creators worked, socialized, and lived in nine Moroccan cities. In addition to these interviews, this chapter is informed by published interviews and my immersion and analysis of the media texts that my respondents create. Using methods of critical media industry studies (Havens, Lotz, and Tinic 2009), the chapter presents two case studies that investigate the meanings and contradictions shaping the ideological struggles and entrepreneurial aspirations of social media creators in the MENA region.

The significance of the emerging field of digital creator culture in the Arab world is twofold. First, from a media industry perspective, youth creator culture is changing the media landscape in the region. The popularity of creator culture among young users and early adopters of social media is challenging established national television and pan-Arab satellite broadcasters. Creator culture is increasingly localized and speaks to the everyday lives, aspirations, and frustrations of youth in the region compared to national television and satellite programming, which are dominated by state-aligned productions and dubbed foreign content, respectively. Second, from a social-change perspective, the significance of digital creator culture lies in its potential to challenge existing social and political hierarchies and to provide a space for expressing and rehearsing new identities. The political import of these emerging spaces of youth-driven cultural production lies in setting forth an incremental process of change centered on new-identity formation.

In order to trace the development of digital creator culture in the Arab world, I first outline the social, political, and technological developments that furnished the conditions of possibility for the rise of youth digital media culture across the region. I discuss the deteriorating socioeconomic conditions of youth in light of decades of political authoritarianism and state monopolies in media and cultural institutions. Second, I present a case study of #ZeroGrissage, an online protest campaign led by digital content creators. This section examines the political role of creator culture as a space for rehearsing new practices and expressions of youth citizenship. The third section discusses the Arab multichannel network Kharabeesh as an example of the entrepreneurial form that creator culture in the MENA region is evolving into. The last section of the chapter summarizes some of the counterdiscursive tropes and meanings of youth digital culture, based on my fieldwork and media analysis of creator content. I conclude with a discussion of how creator content is differentiated by gender and political ideology and is fraught with contradictions.

Origins of an Arab Creator Culture

What is the larger backdrop for the emergence of a networked space of creative media production and consumption in North Africa and the Middle East? Of the 380 million people who live in the Middle East and North Africa (excluding Iran and Turkey), over 30 percent are between the ages of fifteen and twenty-nine years, amounting to 100 million people, while the population between the ages of fifteen and twenty-four is estimated at 74 million (Kronfol 2011). By these estimates, youth in Arab societies is often the fastest growing segment of society, making the MENA region one of the most youthful regions in the world, with a local median age of twenty-two years, compared to twenty-nine years globally (YouthPolicy.org, n.d.). According to World Bank data, the youth bulge that characterizes the region will not change anytime soon, as the youth population is expected to surge by 10 million between 2015 and 2030. This rapidly growing youth population across countries in the MENA region, however, faces serious challenges and frustrations with regard to access to quality education, health care, employment, and political participation. Illiteracy rates in the region are among the highest in world, reaching more than 30 percent among youth (fifteen to twenty-four years old) in countries like Morocco, Egypt, and Yemen and being more rampant among women and youth in rural areas (Magin 2010). Some of the highest rates of unemployment are also found in the Arab world. Unemployment rates dip to 6.3 percent in UAE, for example, and rise to 38.9 percent and more than 40 percent among youth in Egypt. Among youth, frustration with education and employment is deepened by inadequate health provisions and lack of access to health-care facilities. Much like illiteracy rates, lack of access to health care is especially rampant among women, people with disability, and rural dwellers.

Politically, despite Arab Spring protests, young people still face limited access to decision-making processes. Combined with feelings of resentment against dysfunctional social services and institutions, lack of access to political decision-making and frustration with political corruption and authoritarianism fuel expressions and practices of what Mohamed Zayani calls a "networked politics of contention" (2015, 8) that are key to understanding processes of social and political change in the region. In response to the destabilizing potential of these spaces, state backlash against insurgent online activity has ranged from violent repression (for example, in Egypt and Syria) to the enforcement of more insidious measures like online surveillance and youth-targeted conscription programs.

The preceding sociodemographic and politico-economic context coincides with the expansive adoption and proliferation of information and communication technologies among youth in the region. The Middle East and North Africa counts some 280 million internet users, for whom Facebook is the most popular social media platform, with 200 million subscribers (Internet World Stats n.d.). The majority of users in the region are generally youthful, with 64 percent of social media users being under thirty years of age (Salem 2017). The young demographic makeup of the region, combined with increased access to social media platforms as facilitated by the proliferation of smartphones and wireless mobile infrastructure, is driving a cultural trend of localization. A recent survey of twenty-two Arab states reports that for the first time Arabic has become the language of the majority of social media activities in the region, as North African counties have witnessed the strongest growth in Arabic-language use on social media since 2015 (Salem 2017). The appetite for local content drives the rise of Arabic digital content on the web and, in turn, fuels a youth-driven phenomenon of avid short-video consumption and creation. By some estimates, the MENA region uploads two hours of video to YouTube every minute, while in certain countries like Saudi Arabia, users clock up to ninety million views per day (Arab Media Outlook 2018).

With smartphone penetration rates reaching near-saturation levels in the Arab Gulf countries and maintaining a steady increase across the region, photo-sharing and video-sharing platforms are emerging as hubs for creating and sharing entertainment content. A 2017 social media entertainment survey of six Arab countries reports that while 59 percent of Arab internet users maintain an account on YouTube, eight in ten subscribers use the platform to find and share entertainment content (Dennis, Martin, and Wood 2017). A hub for online video creation and consumption, YouTube is in competition with Instagram and Snapchat, two important players in the circulation of social media entertainment in the region. In 2015, Arab social media users spent on average more than one hour per day watching online video, while youth (fifteen to twenty-four years old) spent two hours a day between online videos and social network. In line with these trends, industry reports identify the MENA region as one of the biggest consumers of online video worldwide, with Saudi Arabia being YouTube's largest market in per capita video consumption (Arab Media Outlook 2018).

In fact, high numbers are not unique to Saudi Arabia but are indicative of a broader trend of a booming digital creator culture across the Middle East and North Africa. The soaring popularity of Google's video-streaming giant in the region prompted it to introduce a series of investment initiatives and development programs for its prominent content creators, including technical training and logistical support. In 2012, YouTube launched the Middle East and North Africa's first You-Tube Space in Dubai. YouTube Spaces are a global initiative aimed at building a number of production-studio facilities in select global metropolises and are made available to prominent YouTube creators. In Dubai, the creative production studio offers YouTube creators access to soundstages, special production programs and sets, and advanced education and training opportunities. While access to production facilities and equipment is limited to creators with at least ten thousand subscribers, the studio offers a number of workshops, production classes, and community events that are open to all creators and tailored to specific content categories.

The politically volatile context surrounding the Arab Spring led to a broad expansion in freedom of expression and the proliferation of computing and mobile technologies, and rising internet penetration rates resulted in a deluge of artistic and cultural production. It is important to note that such youth-driven creator culture is emerging against the backdrop of a traditional media landscape that is heavily intertwined with the interests of politically corrupt elites and/or authoritarian state regimes. Traditional national media across much of the Arab world have for decades adopted varying degrees of authoritarian development media models guided by the old politics of educating the gullible masses, modeling "good" citizenship, and favoring consensus over debate in nation building (see, for example, Abu-Lughod 2005). For post–Arab Spring youth, online creator culture is experienced as an alternative to (and a relief from) a traditional media programming that is heavily packaged in statist hegemonic discourses that do not reflect the artistic and sociopolitical aspiration of younger generations. To this extent, Arab youth-driven digital culture is both a space of alternative artistic and cultural expression and a site of power struggle increasingly marked by public contention and contestation of traditional social norms and political orthodoxies. The next section presents the case of an online protest campaign to illustrate Arab creator culture's potential for mobilizing fans and creators in contestation of official state discourse and policies.

#ZeroGrissage: Insurgent Creativity

With the consumption of three billion plastic bags a year, the North African country of Morocco is said to be the second-largest consumer of plastic bags in the world after the United States, with an average annual consumption of nine hundred bags per capita (Alami 2016). After years of failed attempts to curtail the informal production and distribution of plastic bags, in July 2016 Morocco put into effect a controversial law that bans the production, import, sale, and distribution of plastic bags across the country. The ban was part of a concerted campaign involving a coalition of semiofficial environmental associations, government ministries, and a swath of professional communication and media strategists. For a month, state-controlled mass-communication channels, from television, radio, billboards, and newspapers to Friday mosque sermons, all hailed the ban as an important initiative and promised the availability of biodegradable alternatives. The nation's political ether was filled with a euphoric sense of commitment to protecting the environment as all chanted, "Zero Mika," indicating the campaign's aim to bring the proliferation of plastic bags (*mika*) to zero percent. With propaganda-style television and radio advertisements, expert testimonies on broadcast news segments, and professionally designed billboard posters, #ZeroMika bombarded the public with anti-plastic-bag messages.

Yet despite the state's efforts to garner support from the public for this ostensibly unifying, noble cause, the campaign failed miserably. A strong sense of distrust and resistance permeated the citizenry, raising questions as to why the government should choose to address the minor issue of plastic bags while there are much weightier and more urgent problems engulfing the country: youth unemployment, a dysfunctional educational system, a failing health-care system, rampant crime, endemic political corruption, high levels of illiteracy, and crumbling roads and infrastructure. The air of distrust and resistance to the #ZeroMika campaign was especially felt in public disengagement with the message of the campaign on social media. Followers of the campaign's Facebook page, for example, did not exceed 900 users; a meager 108 viewers subscribed to the campaign's YouTube channel; the #ZeroMika Twitter hashtag was dominated by sarcastic and satirical tweets that criticized and poked fun at the campaign; and the campaign's official website attracted no more than 30,000 unique visitors at its peak.

Yet, contrary to the lack of positive engagement with the campaign's social media messages, the launch of #ZeroMika triggered an online countercampaign that satirized the government's call to ban plastic bags and mobilized social media users behind an alternative cause: #ZeroGrissage. The unplanned, informal countercampaign espoused the eradication of violent street mugging (*grissage*, from French *aggression*) and drew so much support from social media users and activists that it became an expressive social movement in its own right. *Grissage*, or mugging, is a phenomenon that plagues almost all Moroccan cities, and while it has origins in youth unemployment and the failing national education system (among other causes), *grissage* is an experience that almost all Moroccans can relate to regardless of their gender, age, profession, class, or race. In fact, the countercampaign #ZeroGrissage capitalized on this common everyday experience and harnessed the communicative affordances of social media to unleash a spontaneous digital movement that undermined the state-sponsored campaign aimed at enforcing a ban against plastic bags.

It is important to note that the digital counterpublic behind #ZeroGrissage was not necessarily against a green public policy per se but was rather opposed to the political hypocrisy of the state regime. The extent of such hypocrisy soon became evident through press reports and social media posts about the context surrounding the introduction of the ban on plastic bags. Building on international sustainability measures that place Morocco in a position of leadership in the green policy arena in the developing world, the country undertook a global public relations campaign to brand itself as a green and eco-friendly tourist attraction and investment hub. The ban against plastic bags was read against the background of state aspirations and in light of the fact that the city of Marrakesh was due to host a global climate-change conference in November 2016—COP22, the twenty-second conference of the parties to the United Nations Framework Convention on Climate Change (UNFCCC).

Raising more suspicion about the already-thin grounds supporting the ban, social media activists revealed that July 1, the day when Morocco chose to put the ban into effect, was the same day that France, the host of COP21 and Morocco's former colonizer, imposed its ban on plastic bags. It became clear that the regime's rush to ban plastic bags was further clouded by its ambition to brand itself as an environmentally conscious state and by the fact that it was hosting a global conference on climate change a few months after the ban went into effect.

However, no sooner had #ZeroGrissage picked up momentum than the government offered the already distrusting social web a priceless gift. Leaked government documents revealed that in the middle of tooting its own horn of green public policy and environmentally responsible governance, the government was scheduled to receive twenty-five hundred tons of plastic and rubber waste from Italy. This was part of a three-year deal in which Morocco would import five million tons of refuse from the waste-crisis-stricken region of Campania, Italy (*EuroNews* 2016). The first shipment of the arguably toxic waste was scheduled to arrive in Morocco one month after the ban on plastic bags went into effect, but news of the impending arrival of this cargo became available less than a week after the ban on plastic bags went into effect. News of the government's signed deal to import Italian waste broke in the midst of state media efforts to peddle propaganda-style advertisements about the need for a public commitment to a clean and nontoxic environment as part of the #ZeroMika campaign.

In every sense of the word, this was a farce. And a farce was all that a skeptical digital public needed to fuel its countercampaign, #ZeroGrissage, for humor is a valuable tool to achieve online virality for what otherwise may be seen as dull and boring political news. #ZeroGrissage quickly became an expressive digital movement focused on two fronts: one that ridicules and protests the duplicity characterizing official discourse and public policy and a second that advocates the clampdown on street mugging as a desired alternative course of action. On the first front, YouTube political satirists, vodcasters, bloggers, activist Facebook pages, and social media influencers all joined in jamming the web with posts that ridiculed the state. Delegate Minister of the Environment Hakima el-Haiti came under stinging criticism and ridicule. In a news conference, the minister attempted to defend her decision and contextualize the latest importation of Italian waste by acknowledging that Morocco indeed receives 450,000 tons of foreign waste annually. Initially, the government insisted on justifying the importation of waste by citing its use as refuse-derived fuel

(RDF) in industrial ovens for drying concrete, but under growing public pressure, the government rescinded the deal; and consequently, the burning of the 2,500 tons of Italian waste in Moroccan cement factories was suspended, along with all importation of foreign waste.

On the second front, young social media actors urged the state, addressing their messages and petitions to King Mohamed VI and the Directorate of National Security, to end physical assaults in Moroccan cities following the killing of a teenage boy in the northern city of Ksar Lkbir. The Facebook page of the campaign offered a space where citizens posted pictures, videos, and short anecdotes about their experiences with armed physical assault. Within days of the launch of the Facebook page of #ZeroGrissage, it reached 120,000 followers, and the page's wall was awash with harrowing stories and graphically shocking images and videos of violent knife attacks and bleeding victims of *grissage*. In response to wide popular engagement with #ZeroGrissage, the national security service made numerous arrests and took to social media to report on the intensity of its antiassault arrest campaign. Through local citizen journalism websites, the national security service reported daily arrest figures from different cities and gave instructions to officers to use live ammunition against armed and threatening *grissage* suspects; in the month following the launch of the social media campaign, security services reported arrests of more than 40,000 suspects, according to a local news report.

Although the policing of a crisis like *grissage* does not necessarily address the deep socioeconomic problems that spawn street violence and crime, the effectiveness of a social media protest to generate a quick response from the most entrenched of state apparatuses, the security service and the Ministry of Interior, was until recently almost impossible in authoritarian Arab regimes. Philip Howard (2010) describes the range of online media practices and oppositional cultural forms that disrupt the official rhetoric of authoritarianism as the harbingers of an emerging political culture, born out of the marriage between ICTs and the local dynamics of democratization in the Arab, Muslim world. Political culture, in this sense, comes to include "not just the most obvious political content, news and information, but more broadly the range of social activities that take on political importance in societies where ruling elites work hard to manage cultural interactions" (Howard 2010, 18). Online cultural practices in authoritarian and transitioning states are politically inflected, in that they involve negotiations of gender norms, questioning of authority, and critiques of marginality, poverty, and corruption. Yet, while they are political in nature, their counterhegemonic undertones happen to be expressed in cultural forms and practices that are gradually evolving into a new creative media industry that caters to a growing youth appetite for daring, nonconformist entertainment content and banks on its commitment to youth representation to build fan loyalty, a capital that is the bedrock of digital monetization. The Arab multichannel network Kharabeesh is a case in point.

Kharabeesh, Entrepreneurial Creativity

In Arabic, the noun *kharabeesh* means "scribbles." Kharabeesh is also the name of a YouTube multichannel network (MCN) that produces politically inflected, Arabic-language animated cartoons, comedy sketches, music videos, and talk shows in the Arab world. The network specializes in youth-oriented online media content designed to critique and satirize social, political, and religious issues across the Arab world. With offices in Tunisia, Egypt, United Arab Emirates, and Jordan, Kharabeesh is a network of about one hundred YouTube channels counting more than fifty-five entertainment shows in five major content streams: Toons (adult animation), Dawsha, (music production), Tahsheesh (comedy), Kharabeesh Street (talk shows and vlogs), and Rusoom (comedy and caricature). Founded in 2008 by Wael Attili and four other young Jordanian men, Kharabeesh benefited from a growing internet penetration rate in the region, especially in Saudi Arabia and Egypt, and from the Arab Spring political climate that allowed youth wider margins of political and cultural expression. In a statement on the network's official website, Kharabeesh prides itself on its commitment to "create artistic videos with high sense of humor, . . . dedicated to gauge the pulse of the people of the Arab World, to express their despairs, frustrations, aspirations and hopes" (Kharabeesh 2015). With Arabic being one of the fastest growing languages on the web, Kharabeesh has become one of the most popular YouTube creative networks in the region, with the Jeddah Comedy Club channel being the top-viewed YouTube channel across the region in 2019.

According to Wael Attili, the Palestinian founder of Kharabeesh and a longtime activist and blogger, the network operates on a unique business model that creates high-quality content with low-cost production and zero-cost publishing. In return, the content that Kharabeesh creates has a bigger profit margin and is monetized in three ways. First, through investing in quality content, the network attracts more viewers and thus sells more product-placement spots to high-profile companies in the region, like Samsung, Pepsi, and Axiom Telecom. Second, as a YouTube partner company, the network receives 45–55 percent of advertising revenue shares from Google up to a cost-per-mille (CPM) threshold of $18 to $24, after which all advertising revenues go to the content creator (Spangler 2013). While other video-on-demand (VOD) platforms like Apple traditionally gave 70 percent of advertising revenues to content creators, YouTube argues that the majority of its user-generated content does not have advertising and, thus, that the video-sharing powerhouse has to recuperate the millions of dollars it spends on storage, bandwidth, and localization infrastructure through retaining 45 percent of advertising revenue. Third, in addition to selling product-placement spots and Google ad-share revenue, Kharabeesh also monetizes its content through reselling its shows to other platforms such as television and mobile.

Kharabeesh in hailed in the region as an entrepreneurial success story, and its founding members tour regional economic capitals, giving inspirational speeches and sharing their stories of innovation with start-ups and young media creators. In a media interview, Kharabeesh CEO Mohamed Asfour attributes the success of the network to its perseverance in finding new creative talents and nurturing them (Kataya 2015), while Attili explained the popularity of Kharabeesh in terms of the originality of its script writing (TEDx Talks 2011), which draws on the everyday experiences of Arab youth to inspire its sketches and cartoons. The success of Kharabeesh, he adds, benefited from the confrontational and daring originality of the ideas and messages that motivate its content. The taboo political, social, and religious issues that Kharabeesh critiques and satirizes in its online video content were absent on traditional media content, given that most broadcasting television and radio programming across the Arab world has long been subject to the close scrutiny of state censorship. The online platform allowed Kharabeesh a margin of freedom of expression unknown on regime-controlled broadcast media and accessibility to transnational young Arab audiences at zero cost.

Kharabeesh capitalized on the immaterial spatiality of social media platforms to produce content that speaks to the aspirations and frustrations of youth across the region. While its video content is highly entertaining, its political undertones contest authoritarian politics in its social, cultural, and religious dogmas and reflect Arab youth's aspirations for meaningful political and social change. In a TED talk in Ramallah, Attili spoke of Arab youth's resentment against the forces of political and social stagnation that overdetermine the lives of youth in the MENA. While the Arab Spring protests were driven by a refusal to live in dictated "templates," the content of Kharabeesh, he explained, succeeded because it broke many rules and templates that impinged on the lives of young people for decades (TEDx Talks 2011). Such breakthroughs find expression in the proliferation of edgier online entertainment content across such genres as cartoon animations, miniseries, short film, comedy sketches, stand-up monologues, and music videos. As the hallmark of a post–Arab Spring creator culture, this budding semiprofessional entertainment industry highlights and caters to the changing tastes, politics, and aspirations of youth in the region.

Indeed, the role of oppositional online media content in nurturing contentious politics and setting the tone of citizen-state relationships in the Arab world is key to understanding the entanglement of information and communication technologies with the cultural, social, and political lives of youth in Arab creator culture. As Attili concluded his TED talk, he urged his largely young audience, "If you want glory and greatness, reject other people's templates, make your own, and redefine yourself" (TEDx Talks 2011). Just as the Arab Spring could be understood as the uprisings of "affective publics" (Papacharissi 2015)—newly expressed political subjectivities, identities, and structures of feeling—so those suppressed energies are now being called on to be articulated through social media entertainment creator culture. Creator culture in the MENA region at its current juncture is both a space for exercising renewed modes of citizenship and discursive struggles and an entrepreneurial creative project, experimenting with new monetization models and facilitating global-local flows of culture and technology.

The political undertones of creator culture are intertwined with entrepreneurial commitments to a burgeoning creative industry that banks on "authentic" representations to strengthen its commercial viability. The ostensibly contradictory logics of public-spirited activism and entrepreneurial commercialism seem to complement each other in this regard. Creator culture's commitment to express and represent the "real" lives, aspirations, grievances, and tastes of Arab youth brands digital creators as authentic, pure, and committed to public causes (Banet-Weiser 2012, 12–14). Through representations of and participation in collective expressions of resistance, like #ZeroGrissage, digital creators cultivate an air of authenticity that accumulates into an immaterial capital (or social relations) of credibility and trust that binds them with their networked fan communities. As those social relations of trust enhance the online popularity and visibility of "authentic" creators, they become the basis for attracting lucrative collaboration deals with advertising and marketing companies, organizing tours and live performances, and appearing on traditional media outlets. The commercial aspirations of digital creators, however, have to always be balanced with a genuine commitment to local micropolitics of representation. For instance, Kharabeesh's parodies, shows, cartoons, vlogs, and music are politically inflected, in that they involve negotiations of gender roles, questioning of authority, and critiques of marginality, poverty, and corruption that a political economy analysis of the macroeconomic structures and business model of the internet cannot begin to unravel.

Conclusion: Complexities of Creator Culture

The salient tropes and meanings of youth-produced social media entertainment in the MENA region are saturated with adversarial rhetoric and expressed through diverse cultural forms and practices. From political satire shows, animated sitcoms (El Marzouki 2015, 2016), rap music (Moreno Almeida 2017; Ben Moussa 2019), and mashup videos to beauty and fashion channels, youth creator culture is defined by articulations of counterpublicity and counterpower. On the one hand, the textual import of these cultural forms contests the social, political, and cultural domains of state power, especially as they relate to hegemonic constructions of the nation and institutional practices that produce marginality and social inequality. On the other hand, the performative aspect of producing and circulating these participatory media texts are productive of oppositional identities and networked communities (Mohamed, Douai, and Iskandar 2019). The emergence of these communities of amateur digital production and consumption is indicative of a changing political culture among youth. Increasingly, youths' experience of and contribution to national politics are mediated by their participation in the production and circulation of a vernacular, creative form of public culture. In short, the tropes and meanings that define creator culture in the MENA region center around microexpressions of resistance, social critique, and counterpublicity shrouded in ridicule, humor, and carnivalesque performances of everyday life.

The counterdiscursive meanings of creator-culture texts are articulated along vectors of class, ideology, and gender. Looking through the twin prisms of social class and ideology, the counterpublicity of young digital media practices emerges from the value/belief systems of a conservative popular class *and* a progressive, liberal middle class. In North Africa, the ideological underpinning of content produced by youth from poor working classes—the so-called *classes populaires*—is often populist nationalism referencing Islamic conservatism and patriarchy. YouTubers from popular classes, defining themselves against the "inauthentic" tastes and styles of French-educated middle-class creators, present themselves as the true sons and daughters of the soil and the nation (*wlad sha'ab*). Building on these claims, digital media practices of populist and conservative sentiments harness the symbolic resources of the abject, nitty-gritty everyday life and channel their rhetorical power to produce carnivalesque performances of marginality and poverty. While the rhetorical and aesthetic styles of populist digital media practices are reminiscent of the vulgar and crude styles of the unrefined gullible masses in scholarly critiques of popular culture in the West, the way they manifest themselves in North African creator culture combines registers of religion, social class, patriarchy, language, and cultural taste.

Competing with populist conservatism as an ideological reference point is a liberal cosmopolitan belief system. Middle-class creators tend to have a higher educational level and to reside in major metropolitan cities, often in affluent neighborhoods. Their education, multilingual skills, and cosmopolitan cultural capital allow them to consume global media, arts, philosophy, literature, and theater. As brokers of a cosmopolitan aesthetic and a progressive outlook in politics, digital media creators from affluent backgrounds espouse liberal attitudes in their digital practices. Although their claim to the nation is no less than that of their conservative populist counterparts, progressive creators do not have strong affinities for religion, tradition, and local *sha'bi* culture. Unlike the rustic *'aroubi* styles of populist digital media discourses, cosmopolitan aesthetics and styles tend to deploy refined language and emphasize scientific rationalism, and their content generally has higher production values. The topics most broached in cosmopolitan digital media practices include science, feminism, national development, literacy, democracy and rights, and technology.

It is important to note, however, that the populist and cosmopolitan ideological anchor points are not mutually exclusive, as the two often bleed into each other. This tendency is also reflected in offline coalition politics, as was the case with Arab Spring protests, which unified Islamists, Marxist and socialist factions, feminists, workers, ethnic activists, and independents in protest against corruption and inequality.

Looking through the prism of gender, the digital media spaces spawned by the production and circulation of creator culture contain segregated modes of participation. Overall, access to social media remains male dominated in the MENA region; only one-third of Facebook users, for example, are female, and penetration rates among Arab female users have consistently remained lower than the global average (Salem 2017). Female creators are especially discouraged from discussing and critiquing issues of public policy and national politics because they attract trolling and cyberbullying to a harrowingly greater extent.

Because female creators' participation in and contribution to national political debates is seen as incongruent with traditional offline gender norms, the social web seems to have devised creative instruments for enforcing social norms in online space. To evade male trolling and cyberbullying, young female creators use content specialization as a strategy to insulate themselves in gender-segregated online spaces. The majority of prominent female creators on YouTube in Morocco produce content related to feminine cosmetic consumption, lifestyle, health, and fashion. Not only do these strategies drive away male users and spare female creators trolling and hate comments, but they also lead to gender-segregated YouTube channels. Yet gender-segregated online spaces not only are enforced from outside but, in some instances, are sought and preferred by female creators themselves to create female-inclusive spaces—to evade male trolling and cyberbullying. Yet, despite the ostensibly disempowering nature of female-gendered spaces, they have their own politics: the politics of building knowledge repositories to enable female participation in offline public space. Such gendered cultural practices carry potential for women's agency and empowerment and extend beyond North Africa and the Middle East to other postcolonial contexts. Sangeet Kumar (2016) identifies similar patterns in studying YouTube creators in India. He argues that such emerging digital media practices are indicative of the rise of an entrepreneurial logic of "agentic subjectivity" that enables young female creators to secure extra income to support independent lifestyles in cosmopolitan centers.

The ideologically bifurcated, gendered, and classed character of creator media practices reflects the adversarial social processes that are at the heart of social and political change in the region. The economy of information exchange that sustains creative youth media production and circulation spawns social relations and communities of trust. As sites that generate opportunities for the exercise of social counter-power at the margin of society, these networked counterpublics have a significant political import. They seek to undermine state legitimacy by circulating counterhegemonic texts and competing with state figures and institutions for social capital, loyalty, and trust. On the one hand, the signs, texts, practices, relations, and subjectivities that overflow in these networked communities of trust act as vectors of resistance and incremental social change. On the other hand, an examination of the monetization models and processes that sustain creator culture reveals a more nuanced reality.

Youth creative media practices on YouTube and other platforms are rooted in complex and unequal economic processes. In producing free video content, young male and female creators also produce themselves as social media celebrities and social influencers. Creators' presumed ability to influence the attitudes, opinions, and styles of their followers consolidate into an immaterial form of capital that creators exploit in pursuit of collaborations and partnerships with local media and advertising industries. This economic model has recently been identified in similar studies of social media production as "hope labor" (Kuehn and Corrigan 2013) or "aspirational labor" (Duffy 2015). But while macro-level political economy analysis of creative digital media practices emphasizes the exploitative, coercive, and alienating aspect of "digital labor," investigating the personal experiences, meanings, and identities involved in practices of cultural production at the granular, ethnographic level yields a more empowering account. Digital practices of producing and circulating social media entertainment content are important sites of ideological and power contestation. Yet the oppositional identities, texts, and practices that populate these online sites tend to reproduce asymmetrical economic relations at the macro-level. These equally valid observations capture some of the contradictions that define creative digital media practices of producing and circulating creator culture in the MENA region.

REFERENCES

Abu-Lughod, Lila. 2005. *Dramas of Nationhood: The Politics of Television in Egypt.* Chicago: University of Chicago Press.

Alami, Aida. 2016. "Going Green: Morocco Bans Use of Plastic Bags." *Aljazeera*, July 2, 2016. www.aljazeera.com.

Arab Media Outlook. 2018. *Youth, Content, Digital Media.* 5th ed. Dubai, UAE: Dubai Press Club and Dubai Media City.

Banet-Weiser, Sarah. 2012. *Authentic™: The Politics and Ambivalence in a Brand Culture.* New York: NYU Press.

Ben Moussa, Mohamed. 2019. "Rap It Up, Share It Up: Identity Politics of Youth 'Social' Movement in Moroccan Online Rap Music." *New Media & Society* 21 (5): 1043–1064. doi:10.1177/1461444818821356.

Cunningham, Stuart, and David Craig. 2019. *Social Media Entertainment: The New Intersection of Hollywood and Silicon Valley.* New York: NYU Press

Dennis, Everette, Justin Martin, and Robb Wood. 2017. *Media Use in the Middle East, 2017: A Six-Nation Survey.* Education City: Northwestern University in Qatar. www.mideastmedia.org.

Douai, Aziz, and Mohamed Ben Moussa, eds. 2016. *Mediated Identities and New Journalism in the Arab World: Mapping the "Arab Spring."* London: Palgrave Macmillan.

Duffy, Brooke Erin. 2015. "Amateur, Autonomous, Collaborative: Myths of Aspiring Female Cultural Producers in Web 2.0." *Critical Studies in Media Communication* 32 (1): 48–64. doi:10.1080/15295036.2014.997832.

El Marzouki, Mohamed. 2015. "Satire as Counter-discourse: Dissent, Cultural Citizenship and Youth Culture in Morocco." *International Communication Gazette* 77 (3): 282–296. doi:10.1177/1748048514568762.

———. 2016. "Citizens of the Margin: Citizenship and Youth Participation on the Moroccan Social Web." *Information, Communication and Society* 21 (1): 147–161. doi:10.1080/1369118X.2016.1266373.

EuroNews. 2016. "Moroccans in Uproar over Imported Italian Waste." July 12, 2016. www.euronews.com.

Havens, Timothy, Amanda Lotz, and Serra Tinic. 2009. "Critical Media Industry Studies: A Research Approach." *Communication, Culture & Critique* 2 (2): 234–253. doi:10.1111/j.1753-9137.2009.01037.x.

Honwana, Alcinda. 2013. *Youth and Revolution in Tunisia*. London: Zed Books.

Howard, Philip. 2010. *The Digital Origins of Dictatorship and Democracy: Information Technology and Political Islam*. Oxford: Oxford University Press.

Internet World Stats. n.d. "Internet Usage in the Middle East." Accessed September 11, 2020. www.internetworldstats.com.

Kataya, Abdulghani. 2015. "How Animation Studio Kharabeesh Drew Its Own Success." Wamda, April 29, 2015. www.wamda.com.

Kharabeesh. 2015. "We Create Outstanding, Funny, Edgy and Innovative Video Shows." May 1, 2015. http://kharabeesh.com.

Kraidy, Marwan. 2016. *The Naked Blogger of Cairo: Creative Insurgency in the Arab World*. Cambridge, MA: Harvard University Press.

Kronfol, Nabil. 2011. "The Youth Bulge and the Changing Demographics in the MENA Region: Challenges and Opportunities?" DWA-HSG Discussion Paper Series on Demographic Issues No. 2011/8. www.wdaforum.org.

Kuehn, Kathleen, and Thomas Corrigan. 2013. "Hope Labor: The Role of Employment Prospects in Online Social Production." *Political Economy of Communication* 1 (1): 9–25.

Kumar, Sangeet. 2016. "YouTube Nation: Precarity and Agency in India's Online Video Scene." *International Journal of Communication* 10 (18): 5608–5625.

Magin, Shawn. 2010. "Illiteracy in the Arab Region: A Meta Study." *GIALens* 4 (2): 1–18.

Mohamed, Eid, Aziz Douai, and Adel Iskandar. 2019. "Media, Identity, and Online Communities in a Changing Arab World." *New Media & Society* 21 (5): 1035–1042. doi:10.1177/1461444818821360.

Moreno Almeida, Cristina, ed. 2017. *Rap beyond Resistance: Staging Power in Contemporary Morocco*. London: Palgrave.

Papacharissi, Zizi. 2015. *Affective Publics: Sentiment, Technology, and Politics*. New York: Oxford University Press.

Salem, Fadi. 2017. "Social Media and the Internet of Things towards Data-Driven Policymaking in the Arab World: Potential, Limits and Concerns." The Arab Social Media Report, Dubai: MBR School of Government, February 6, 2017. https://papers.ssrn.com.

Spangler, Todd. 2013. "YouTube Standardizes Ad-Revenue Split for All Partners, but Offers Upside Potential." *Variety*, November 1, 2013. http://variety.com.

TEDx Talks. 2011. "TEDxRamallah—Wael Attili—Rejecting Templates." YouTube video, July 6, 2011. www.youtube.com/watch?v=BNwXFVF_Al4.

Tufekci, Zeynep. 2017. *Twitter and Tear Gas: The Power and Fragility of Networked Protest*. New Haven, CT: Yale University Press.

YouthPolicy.org. n.d. "Middle East and North Africa: Youth Facts." Accessed August 13, 2017. www.youthpolicy.org.

Zayani, Mohamed. 2015. *Networked Publics and Digital Contention: The Politics of Everyday Life in Tunisia*. Oxford: Oxford University Press.

———, ed. 2018. *Digital Middle East: State and Society in the Information Age*. Oxford: Oxford University Press.

PART III

Industries and Governance

11

Wanghong

Liminal Chinese Creative Labor

ELAINE JING ZHAO

The evolution of social media platforms in China has witnessed the blossoming of vernacular creativity online. From bulletin boards and blogging to microblogging and online video platforms, social media entertainment has become a mainstay of the cultural repertoire and propelled a diverse range of online creators to heightened visibility. Many have gone from obscurity to fame—or notoriety. Some are transient; others are more enduring. *Wanghong*, literally "internet famous," has featured prominently in both media and industry discourses in recent years. The term made the top-ten buzzwords list in China in 2015 in the linguistics periodical *Yaowen Jiaozi*.

Wanghong is a polysemic term not only because it embodies a diverse range of individuals who attain fame native to the internet with various possibilities for commercialization and different levels of sustainability but also because it is celebrated and stigmatized at once. The economic potential of the *wanghong* economy has attracted growing attention. Advertising and virtual gifts have become the main revenue sources for *wanghong*. The technology company Alibaba used the phrase "*wanghong* economy" for the first time in 2015 to highlight the economic potential of *wanghong* in converting internet traffic into revenue through e-commerce integration. According to CBNData (2016), a commercial data company affiliated with Alibaba, the *wanghong* economy was worth RMB 58 billion in 2016, exceeding China's movie box-office revenue in 2015. Top-tier *wanghong* have reportedly outperformed showbiz A-listers in China (Tsoi 2016). Meanwhile, negative connotations of *wanghong* abound in journalistic and regulatory discourse, dismissing them as frivolous, silly, bizarre, vulgar, morally questionable, or socially menacing.

Generations of *wanghong* have come under the spotlight with the evolution of internet infrastructure and affordances. The history of *wanghong* can be traced back to the late 1990s, following China's connection to the internet in 1994. With little professional training and financial ambition, literary enthusiasts found a path to fame on internet forums, which offered an alternative space beyond the state-controlled publishing system for amateurs to express their creativity and address popular taste (Hockx 2015). The space became more formalized in the early 2000s, with the freemium business model, micropayment system, and tiered contracting mechanism (Zhao 2011). Since then, a growing number of more entrepreneurially minded writers started to produce genre fictions online in the hope of reaping financial gains from the fan economy. Many writers are, however, caught in "ambivalent identities between writers and writing hands, between professionals and amateurs, between glamorous creative class and low-level labourers as promises of democratization and empowerment of creativity are adulterated by precarious conditions" (Zhao 2017, 1249).

As the internet became more visual, photo sharing has offered an avenue to quick digital fame. *Wanghong* started to tap into the opportunities in lookism (Berry 2007) and gender performativity (Butler 1988) to attract large followings. Shi Hengxia (widely known as Sister Furong), for example, became widely known in 2004 for her photos, which showed her awkward attempts to appeal to the male ideal of female beauty (Roberts 2010). Zhang Zetian (popularly known as Sister Milk Tea), in contrast, became an overnight sensation in 2009 for her innocent and sweet looks in an online photo of her holding a cup of milk tea. Oftentimes such instant and seemingly accidental fame is facilitated by much less visible agents designing and executing social media promotion.

With the availability of faster broadband and the increasing adoption of smartphones, video sharing has become a prominent space where creators rise to fame. While earlier generations of creators distributed content mainly on various internet forums, digital platforms have become a prominent site of content distribution and monetization. From spoof and parody videos that are connected to China's *shanzhai* culture (often associated with copycat production, creative remix, grassroots entrepreneurialism, and antiestablishment ethos) to the recent reincarnation of user-generated content in livestreaming and short videos, a growing number of professionalizing amateurs have seen their creative energies find purchase among their fan base and advertisers (Craig, Cai, and Lv 2016; Zhao 2016).

While coevolving with internet infrastructure and affordances, *wanghong* operate in the broader context of China's approach to digital creative economy. The state's will to develop the internet as a new engine of economic growth is evident from its elevating the role of the ICT industry as a pillar of the Chinese economy in the early 2000s to the "Internet Plus" blueprint unveiled in 2015. This interest parallels the state's cultural logic of tight regulation over the internet. Meanwhile, the state has started to promote the development of creative industries since the turn of the century, with the hope of accelerating economic growth and innovation (Cunningham 2009; Keane 2013). In this context, celebratory discourses about creative labor abound. Meanwhile, in 2015, the state released a strategy to stimulate "mass entrepreneurship and innovation" in the hope of revitalizing the economy. This strategy further promotes an entrepreneurial ethos as a desirable quality, adding to the romanticized image of creative labor, often featuring freedom, flexibility, autonomy, self-actualization, and economic prosperity. Such celebratory discourse manifests a strong influence of proponents such as Richard Florida (2003) and John Howkins (2001) in the Western context. Literature on creative labor has, however, seen growing critique regarding precarity in creative labor under neoliberalism (Gill and Pratt 2008; Ross 2009; de Peuter 2011; Hesmondhalgh and Baker 2011). Importantly, China's adoption of the creative industries discourse does not come without a cautionary aspect. In other words, creativity has its boundaries under the state's gaze.

This chapter focuses on online video production as a part of the broader *wanghong* phenomenon, not only for its scale in China's social media entertainment but also for the insights it affords into various aspects of creative labor experiences, where multiple platforms, modalities, and business models coexist in the broader context of the state agenda of developing and disciplining the internet and the creative economy. In the following section, I provide a brief history of China's online video space and the fluctuating place of amateur creativity in it. Then I draw on the concept of liminality (V. Turner 1967) to analyze creator experiences. Specifically, I discuss how creators occupy a liminal space in several aspects: (1) between the professional and amateur, (2) between authenticity and performance, (3) between public and private, and (4) between being harnessed and being disciplined. The discussion reveals the diversity and contestation in the process of navigating these ambiguous borders, involving both agency and precarity. In doing so, I aim in this chapter to address a gap in the emerging scholarship on internet-famous creators in cultural production, where studies in Anglophone contexts dominate the discussions (Marwick 2013, 2015; Abidin 2015; Duffy 2017; Burgess and Green 2018; Cunningham and Craig 2019), and to enhance understanding of the way aspiring creators experience multiple layers of liminality as internet fame is gained, lost, or transformed in China.

Locating Amateur Creativity in Video-Sharing Platforms in China

While an important distinction exists between the two approaches in the new screen ecology outside China—namely, the Hollywood-like intellectual-property-centric approach and the platform strategy connecting content creators with advertisers and other intermediaries, or "SoCal" versus "NoCal" culture (Cunningham and Craig 2017, 2019)—the picture in China is different. With a few exceptions, platforms in China initially showed initial enthusiasm toward user-generated content, which was quickly dampened, leading to a more suspicious view, before a revisionist approach emerged (Zhao 2016). More recently, vernacular creativity has not only returned to the strategic map of online streaming sites but also witnessed a new generation of platform players.

When video-sharing sites such as Tudou, Youku, 56, and ku6 emerged between 2005 and 2006, they championed the vision of facilitating and profiting from a thriving community of amateur creators. Google's acquisition of YouTube in 2006 further boosted the industry's confidence in user-generated content. Platforms were quick to discover and recruit creators, who became well known for their works circulating in the online forums and on file-sharing sites. Among this generation of *wanghong* are Backdorm Boys, known for their lip-synching performances; Hu Ge, known for his spoof videos mocking official and elite culture; and Jiaoshou, known for his satire and self-mockery. Initial fame launched Backdorm Boys into the music industry, with a five-year contract from China's top label, Taihe Rye Music, although they struggled later. Monetization became possible for Hu Ge with a turn to custom-made advertising. Jiaoshou became a cofounder of a start-up dedicated to online video production, UniMedia (Wanhe Tinyi).

Despite these high-profile examples, the uneven quality of user-generated content and the potential risk of copyright infringement made advertisers wary. In the meantime, increasing traffic incurred high costs in bandwidth for video-sharing platforms. This scenario led Tudou's founder, Wang Wei, to refer to user-generated content as "industrial waste water" in 2008, indicating its disappointing capacity to generate revenue while exacerbating cost pressure (Zhao 2016, 5447). Meanwhile, the state's licensing regulations and the crackdown on copyright infringement led video-sharing platforms to become more like portals, investing in licensed professional productions (Zhao and Keane 2013). The competition for content resulted in soaring licensing costs and a significant industry shakeout.

In this context, exclusive rights to popular content became more prohibitive in terms of cost, resulting in a limited catalogue of content for any one platform. For surviving platforms, this raised yet another challenge: enhancing viewers' loyalty. Therefore, the professionalization and commercialization of user-generated content became a strategic move to elevate the originality of content at relatively lower costs. Aspiring creators experimented with different genres, such as sketch comedies and made-for-web series. For some, digital platforms became a springboard to the incumbent media industry. Subsequent years have seen further attempts among platforms to launch advertising revenue-sharing plans and to promote an entrepreneurial ethos to attract aspiring creators (Zhao 2016).

In contrast to platform portals, which approach amateur creativity with fluctuating attitudes, livestreaming and short-video platforms are more determined to professionalize and commercialize amateur productions. Prominent players in livestreaming have emerged in various verticals, such as showrooms (for example, 9158 and YY), gaming (for example, Douyu and Huya), and e-commerce (for example, Taobao Live); performers or creators receive a share of the revenue from virtual gifts, advertising, or sales. Moreover, amateur creativity, and its professionalization, has gained further momentum with the emergence of smartphone apps such as Miaopai (embedded in the 4.0 version of Sina Weibo as a result of its acquisition in 2013); Kuaishou (known as Kwai internationally), launched in 2012 and now backed by Tencent; and Douyin (known as TikTok internationally), launched by ByteDance in 2016. Video lengths are usually from around ten seconds to under a minute. Creators can easily use filters, special effects, and editing tools to create and share videos online. These creative tools, together with fun challenges that the platforms present to users, lower the barrier to entry for content creation and facilitate a sense of community among users. The mediating role of platforms lies not only in creating challenges for users to respond to but also in algorithm-driven content distribution. This is a crucial difference from previous generations of video-sharing platforms. Apart from platform players, incubators and training camps have mushroomed, hoping to taking a slice of the *wanghong* economy. These intermediaries add complexity to creators' experiences.

Liminal Creative Labor

In order to analyze aspiring creators' experiences in China's online video space, I draw on the concept of liminality. Initially introduced in anthropology by Arnold van Gennep (1909) in his classic analysis of the middle stage in ritual passages in traditional societies, the notion of liminality has opened up new lines of inquiries in various fields through the writings of Victor Turner (1967). According to Turner's interpretation, liminality refers to any "betwixt and between" state or experience, where individuals "are neither one thing nor another; or may be both; or neither here nor there; or may even be nowhere" (1967, 97). Media scholars have found liminality a useful concept to analyze the consumption of media messages, the production of media events, and the role of media in historical transition (Dayan and Katz 1992; Couldry 2003; Coman 2008; Moore 2009).

In critical accounts of contemporary creative labor, researchers have drawn inspiration from the concept of liminality to illuminate the ambiguous space and experiences in creative industries (Borg and Söderlund 2014; O'Brien 2018). By bringing the concept to the emerging line of inquiry into internet-famous creators, the following section focuses on *wanghong* in China's online video space and analyzes how they experience several aspects of liminality as they seek fame and fortune on social media.

Between the Professional and the Amateur

As entrepreneurial creators cultivate their own brands, many are strategically crafting and enacting their personae. This often involves navigating the ambivalent line between the professional and the amateur. While user-generated content is usually associated with the ordinary, as Patricia Lange (2008) reminds us, it is lazy to assume that people who post videos on YouTube were, are, and always will be "ordinary" with regard to professional training, aspirations, and reputation. Similarly, Ramon Lobato, Julian Thomas, and Dan Hunter (2011) point out that user-generated content moves between the formal and informal over time.

Amateurism can serve the purpose of building an approachable persona, which helps build and monetize a personal brand. More importantly, easy-to-emulate performance, often associated with amateurism, helps drives participatory culture in the context of algorithm-driven distribution. Consider Daikula K, a university student from northeastern China who became famous on Douyin and accumulated over ten million fans within a month. Best known for her dancing, she has received no professional training in dancing. Yet the video featuring her signature performance received over one hundred million views, over ten million likes, over two million forwards, and two hundred thousand comments by October. Her girl-next-door image, with a sweet smile, is perceived by her incubator company as crucial to her rise of fame. As Nie from that company, Onion, said, "There are so many professional dancers on Douyin, but Daiguka K is different. For viewers, she is like their friend. There's not that much of a distance between her and the viewers" (personal communication, 2018). More importantly, the easy-to-emulate dance moves in the amateurish performance have led to mimetic production on Douyin, which in turn boosts their popularity in the context of algorithmic distribution.

Other creators harbor more aspirations to be recognized for professional expertise. Feng Ya'na(n), known online as Feng Timo, was one of the most popular performers on the livestreaming platform Douyu. Her cover of pop songs and adorable looks won her over sixteen million subscribers on Douyu, over twenty-two million on Douyin, and nearly nine and a half million on Weibo. Her internet fame further opened doors for her to China's leading entertainment shows, including *Happy Camp* and *Day Day Up*, both produced by Hunan TV. The attempt to extend her fame beyond the internet is evident. Feng is a signed performer at Douyu, and her reach out to incumbent media is part of the platform's initiative to promote contracted *wanghong* across multiple media and to elevate their visibility. This in turn enhances the perceived capacity of the platform to nurture talent, which helps maintain and attract more creators. In this sense, the move toward the incumbent media is both an individual aspiration and a platform strategy.

Feng's negotiation with her *wanghong* status in relation to the professional-amateur axis is particularly evident in a singing game show broadcast by Jiangsu Satellite TV, *The Masked Singer* (*Mengmian changjiang caicaicai*). The show followed the format of a South Korean show, where celebrities perform songs while wearing masks on stage. Feng referred to the mask as a protector for her. As she said onstage, "Since I wear the mask, the audience forms their opinion of my performance by listening to me instead of judging me based on who I am." She alluded to the fact that some audiences did not think highly of her because she is only a *wanghong* instead of a professional singer. While *wanghong* like her can monetize their content, some audiences still draw a clear line between *wanghong* and professional performers. Thus, for her, the mask offered an opportunity to prove her singing skills and untag herself as *wanghong*, a notion carrying perceived inferiority. The aspiration to achieve perceived professional status, however, does not mean distancing herself from online platforms. In fact, despite her expanding career boundaries, Feng did not reduce the frequency of her performance online.

For other creators, liminality between amateurism and professionalism can be artfully mobilized in self-branding. Jiang Yilei, better known as Papi Jiang, serves as a good example. Papi Jiang started posting original short videos online in September 2015, when she was still a graduate student at China's Central Academy of Drama. She quickly rose to fame owing to her satirical style, with brutal honesty and deep cultural resonance, as well as her low-maintenance image in 2016. She is known for her tagline, "I am Papi Jiang, a woman who has both brains and beauty." In her videos, she comments on everyday social and cultural issues, sometimes playing a variety of characters in a single video. She wears minimal makeup, and the videos are usually shot in her home with little regard to its messiness. Such gestures of amateurism, however, are only part of the picture. Her professional training in directing underpins her work in script writing, performance, and postproduction, all done by herself. The amateurish setting and the everyday look are strategically combined with professional skills, attracting a large following.

Between Authenticity and Performance

The ideal of authenticity is pervasive in contemporary brand cultures (Banet-Weiser 2012). For influencers or microcelebrities on social media, authenticity allows them to cultivate a sense of intimacy, accessibility, and relatability, which is fundamental to establishing affective relationships with followers (Marwick 2013, 2015; Abidin 2015; Cunningham and Craig 2017; Duffy 2017). The use of authenticity as a strategic advantage distinguishes these creators sharply from the branding logic of traditional media and celebrities.

Authenticity is a highly nuanced concept. In China, while using filters to beautify *wanghong* faces or livestreaming from studios turned into home-like rooms is not unusual, performed authenticity is a strong currency in the market. It carries significant weight in many ways, and creators constantly negotiate the boundaries with their followers in content production and commercialization.

For internet-famous creators, maintaining authenticity means being consistent with their image before the fame. Take Jiaoshou, for example, who has turned himself into an entrepreneur and cofounded UniMedia. His rise to fame has coevolved with the need for online video platforms to professionalize and capitalize on amateur production in the emerging field. The journey saw Jiaoshou producing made-for-web series and movies, earning himself a name in the incumbent media industry. It remains crucial for him to maintain an unpretentious image and maintain connectedness with audiences. When the story of UniMedia was written into a book, Jiaoshou's only request was not to turn him into a pretentious figure (Zhang 2014).

Despite the conscious effort to maintain consistency in the staged persona, the creator's aspiration to venture beyond the comfort zone can trigger the paradox of authenticity. Jiaoshou was known for spoofing, and his attempt to go beyond his well-known style encountered push-back from audiences. While hesitating at first, Jiaoshou decided to compromise and sharpen his signature style of spoofing and self-mocking. Thus, although the entrepreneurially minded creator may hope to experiment with content creation and brand extension, the risk lies in the perceived inauthenticity as a result of inconsistency. In other words, the effort of seeking a possible future self as a creator is discouraged. This paradoxically challenges the notion of being authentic, as many selves are yet to be found.

As a diverse range of revenue including advertising deals becomes possible, persona-brand alignment is crucial for creators to maintain authenticity. Papi Jiang's popularity and commercial prospects, for example, do not come without backlashes. Notably, her partnership with the luxury brand Jaeger-LeCoultre was perceived as a misalignment between the brand and her persona. Her professional image and tone in the advertising does not align with her persona, which is known for humorous and sharp online rants. Moreover, the brand was perceived by many people as reserved for "real" celebrities and stars. Here, *wanghong* are caught in the hierarchy of fame.

Further, when the staged persona is overly or carelessly edited, authenticity becomes questionable. As the *wanghong* economy becomes a burgeoning phenomenon, agencies and incubators play an important role in producing *wanghong* in China. This often involves persona design, which guides creators' performance. For aspiring creators contracted with agencies, their looks, personality, talent, and life experience allow incubators to establish their online persona. This possibility, however, does not often turn out to be a carefully considered approach in reality. Oftentimes it involves only simplified tags such as "innocent and cute," "cool," or "comedic." These tags work with the playbooks, which inform how creators should enact the persona from content production to viewer engagement. Moreover, persona design provides guidelines about whom the creator should network with in the creator community. Such instrumental sociality with both viewers and other creators serves the purpose of maintaining the persona. As one creator previously working with an agency revealed anonymously, "Being a *wanghong* means being ready to mingle with other creators who you don't like or not even know well. The agency may even assign a best friend or a boyfriend to a creator, and we need to interact frequently with these people and perform intimacy to attract traffic" (personal communication, 2018). For creators, this is a part of their job that they have to live with. When incubators are too much in the way, some creators have demonstrated their agency out of the concern over loss of autonomy. For example, @Anna_ZhuXuan, a creator previously contracted with PapiTube, quit the incubator within a year. As she explained on her social media (WeChat) account on August 22, 2018, "Now I am on my own again, mainly for more freedom, more control over what I want to do, and over content creation."

Misalignment with the designed persona in online performance can lead the creator into the danger zone of inauthenticity. A Yi, a livestreamer specializing in playing *League of Legends* (*LOL*), is a telling example. Working on the video-game livestreaming platform Douyu, she is branded as a sophisticated female gameplayer, which provides a niche positioning and helps her to stand out from the crowd. The persona draws attention, as it refutes the common perception that female players are weak in the male-dominated space. However, the persona collapsed when she was found to be cheating by using a shadow player in 2016. Initially she responded with an adamant denial, only to see mounting evidence published online by internet users. The evidence resulted from a "human-flesh search engine," where internet users devoted significant amounts of time and labor in extensive online and offline collaborations to piece information together and verify findings. The evidence included various inconsistencies between A Yi's posture and her gaming performance, identification of the gaming account, and her unbelievably quick rise to the high rank. This eventually led A Yi to livestream, with the camera capturing her operation on a keyboard to prove her gaming skills, on May 30, 2016, only to face five consecutive failures with obvious mistakes. Facing live comments from users who felt disappointed and betrayed, A Yi said, "I know what I should do, but I have no option." Before she ended the livestreaming session, A Yi left a quick remark: "I cannot fake it anymore."

A Yi confessed on Sina Weibo on June 9, 2016, that she had purchased the account from a sophisticated player for use in livestreaming and had been using a shadow player. Two hours after her confession, the statement from *LOL* regarding the investigation appeared on its official website and Sina Weibo account, announcing the decision to freeze involved accounts for ten years, stop the collaboration with A Yi, and prohibit her from entering any official *LOL* competition.

As well as viewers, many livestreamers also expressed their indignation. It was the dishonesty, and more importantly the inequality, that irritated many gameplayers. In the broader context of social inequality in China (Sun and Guo 2013), such indignation is augmented. While many players face only a slight chance of winning contracts from digital platforms despite their hard work, a performer earned huge amounts of money from fans by working with a shadow player. As one viewer said in a comment, "We all work hard to improve our skills and rank, but we lose to a cheater. This is so disappointing!" Another rightfully questioned, "If it were not for her public persona of a sophisticated female player, can she attract so many fans? Can her Taobao store deliver the revenue?"

The penalty enforced on A Yi by *LOL* was perceived as weak by many internet users. What was surprising to some viewers was that A Yi restarted her livestreaming at Douyu. The performance continued to lure audience, be they adamant supporters or indignant detractors. Evidently, the economic logic of the platform in the context of an attention economy was a strong motivator to tolerate creators' misbehavior. This was, however, short-sighted. As many users published negative comments on the app store, the rating of the app significantly dropped. Transgressions on the part of creators not only tarnish their fame but also hurt the reputation of hosting platforms when such transgressions are tolerated.

Creators can, however, be resilient, hoping to relocate their fame by reconfiguring their persona and reconstructing authenticity. After A Yi finished her contract with Douyu, she left for another platform, Quanmin TV. As she revealed in a post on Sina Weibo, she wanted to start a new journey and "just be an entertainment show host." Evidently, this was an attempt to reconfigure her persona by moving on from the image of a sophisticated gameplayer. Whether such attempts to relocate or transform fame will work is, however, uncertain.

Between Public Personae and Private Selves

As social media collapse contexts (Marwick and boyd 2010), *wanghong* operate in a liminal space where the line between public personae and private selves is blurred. "Celebritisation of the ordinary" (G. Turner 2013) in China means that *wanghong* are subject to scrutinization in the context of the Chinese public's preoccupation with the moral virtue of prominent individuals (Jeffreys and Edwards 2010). The human-flesh search engine in China is a relentless force in collapsing the boundaries between public personae and private selves.

Powered by collaborative internet users, the human-flesh search engine can target individuals ranging from officials to celebrities. Oftentimes, suspected immorality and injustice trigger the crowd-powered engine into operation, as private information is hunted down and disclosed online. Through this form of cyber vigilantism, internet users often seek to enforce social norms and moral values (Ong 2012; Gao and Stanyer 2014). DIY justice is, however, only part of the story. The dark side of the human-flesh search engine is manifest in privacy infringement and cyberbullying (Cheung 2009).

Wanghong are easily targeted in the human-flesh search engine, subject to public shaming, humiliation, and harassment. One comment from a creator who had quit the business is revealing: "It's no easy job. To be a *wanghong*, you need to bear the risks of being targeted in the human-flesh search engine" (personal communication, 2018). A Yi's case, as discussed previously, is also a telling example. In this context, some creators/performers have resorted to hiding their faces in videos to maintain anonymity.

For livestreamers, the challenges double, as they have to muster the courage to carry on while facing attacks or harassment by viewers through live comments. As one livestreamer mentioned, "When negative comments flash right in front of me across the screen as I am livestreaming, I have to stay calm and appear unaffected. I find it the hardest part of being a live streamer" (personal communication, 2018). Another echoed, "Live comments can be unfriendly attacks. Some are more vehement than others, but I have to move on" (personal communication, 2018).

Some creators hope to maintain the right to privacy in order to circumvent the challenge in relation to authenticity. Feng Timo, one of the most popular performers on Douyu, experienced a difficult situation when her marital status stirred up a storm. She was accused of keeping her marriage a secret while cashing in on a public persona of a cute, innocent, single girl with singing talent. When hinting at her single status, she often emphasized the importance of fans in her livestreaming: "I haven't met someone I can be in a long-term relationship with, but I have my friends and fans. I'll accompany you for as long as I can." When the details of her identification, her marriage, and her divorce were disclosed as a result of the human-flesh search engine, Feng was put under great pressure. She stayed offline for almost a month before resuming her livestreaming and coming up with a response: "This is my privacy, and it's none of your business."

Clearly, Feng hoped to draw a clear line between her private self and her public persona. However, the revenue model of showroom livestreaming added complexity to the risk arising from the liminal space between the public and the private in this case. Given that livestreaming has earned the nickname of "the industry of virtual girlfriends" (Aynne Kokas, quoted in Kaiman and Meyers 2017), which relies on virtual gifts for revenue, hiding one's marital status while profiting from fans' contributions is perceived as morally questionable. In Feng's case, she reportedly pulled in RMB 30 million from her fans in 2017 (*Sina* 2018). When her carefully crafted public persona was found to be misleading, her followers started to question her inauthenticity and morality. Thus, creators' experience in the liminal space between the public persona and the private self is entangled with platform affordances, business models, and community culture.

Disciplined and Harnessed at Once

Wanghong are situated in a liminal space as they are both disciplined and harnessed by the state as well as by corporate platforms. Apart from digital platforms, incubators, and creators themselves, the state is a force that cannot be neglected in producing *wanghong*. This dynamic mirrors China's broader celebrity culture, which is marked by the influence of the party-state (Jeffreys and Edwards 2010). Moreover, the state's approach to *wanghong* governance mirrors its broader approach to internet governance in China, in which economic, political, and cultural logics are all at work (Zhao 2019).

On the one hand, multiple government agencies have started to regulate the market by targeting transgressing creators. A warning sign in this previously loosely regulated space emerged when the state targeted Papi Jiang. Soon after Papi Jiang rose to fame and attracted venture-capital funding of RMB 12 million (around US$1.84 million) and sold a spot in her video ads for RMB 22 million (around US$3.4 million) at an auction, she was singled out by the national regulator. In April 2016, China's media watchdog, the State Administration of Press, Publication, Radio, Film, and Television (SAPPRFT) (2013–2018), ordered some videos of Papi Jiang containing "foul language and vulgar content" offline and demanded that the content be deleted before the videos could be put back online.

Clearly, with fame comes money and influence but also increasing scrutiny from the state. An editorial published by *Global Times* argues that Papi Jiang's elevated status in the *wanghong* economy has turned her into a role model and that she has to take some "social responsibilities" (Yu 2016). In response to the state's rectification requirement, Papi Jiang quickly published a statement on her Weibo account, stating that she would make amendments to her videos accordingly, pay more attention to her use of language, and convey *zhengnengliang* (positive energy) in the future.

The regulation has since become systemic. The Ministry of Culture (MoC), for example, released "Measures for the Administration of Online Performance Operating Activities" in December 2016 to regulate showroom livestreaming activities (*Xinhua News* 2016). The measures require that all online live-performance operators apply for a permit from the relevant provincial cultural affairs authority, with performers to register their real names. Both Cyber Administration of China and MoC have stressed the regulatory responsibility of platforms (*China Daily* 2016; *Xinhua News* 2016). The growing scrutinization by the state has prompted more intense industry self-regulation. China Netcasting Services Association, the national-level industry association in the streaming sector, published "Management Regulations for Online Short Video Platforms" and "Detailed Standards for Content Review of Online Short Video" in January 2019 (*People's Daily* 2019).

Apart from disciplining creators' performance and content, the state is promoting and harnessing the influence of *wanghong*. Instead of blatant propaganda, *wanghong* on corporate social media platforms are being mobilized by the state to wield their influence among youth in everyday entertainment. The fact that Papi Jiang's videos are not completely censored or removed altogether is testament to this intention of the state. A more telling example is Feng Timo. As well as the expansion of her career boundaries in the entertainment industry, her influence among Chinese youth has led Chongqing Municipal Committee of the Chinese Communist Youth League (CCYL) to appoint her as its ambassador. This is one of many initiatives by CCYL to command the online space to enhance its influence among youth. In an interview with *Chongqing Daily*, Feng Timo pledged to unconditionally advocate for Chongqing Municipal Committee of CCYL, to transmit positive energy to youth, and to inspire young people with her own stories. Since then, Feng has started to repost or comment on content published by CCYL as well as the state media *People's Daily* to spread positive energy on social media. Politics thus becomes increasingly infused into everyday social media entertainment.

As the state adopts this two-pronged approach to *wanghong* governance, platforms implement the state logic and launch self-regulatory initiatives. In the context of the intense debate on how platforms should be governed, platforms often adopt self-regulation to preempt state regulation or stronger approaches (Zhao 2019). Governance by platforms ranges from guidelines to terms of use to much less transparent algorithms (Gillespie 2018). All these mechanisms influence content visibility and potential monetization for creators. Douyu, for example, has released very detailed guidelines regarding livestreamers' dress code, with corresponding penalties in case of violations. Many of these guidelines are designed to discipline female streamers. Such guidelines paradoxically entrench the already stigmatized image of female creators. This is a major reason why some female *wanghong* do not like to be addressed as such, as female *wanghong* are often crudely equated with showroom performers, whose productions are reduced to appealing to male viewers and chauvinist aesthetics. In fact, some female creators manifest agency in challenging conventional tropes (Zhang and Hjorth 2017). Moreover, algorithmic distribution pushes aspiring creators to adopt an aspirational mind-set in the hope of placing themselves in a good position in the hierarchy of visibility—another challenge for creators.

Conclusion

As social media become a breeding ground for internet celebrities, *wanghong* as both a cultural and economic phenomenon flourishes in China's own social media ecology. As a prominent part of this broader phenomenon, video sharing is a space where multiple platforms, modalities, and business models coexist in the broader context of the state agenda of developing and disciplining the internet and the creative economy. This chapter has discussed the liminal experiences of creators on video-sharing platforms in China as a case of the broader *wanghong* phenomenon in the country.

By bringing the concept of liminality (V. Turner 1967) into dialogue with critical creative labor studies, I have discussed how *wanghong* and *wanghong* aspirants experience the liminal space in several ways— between the professional and the amateur, between authenticity and performance, between public and private—as they are being harnessed and disciplined at the same time. While approached separately in the analysis, these four layers of liminality can become infused with each other, influencing creators' experience. Together, they constitute an explanatory framework to achieve a more textured understanding of creators' experiences as they negotiate individual aspirations with platform affordances and constraints, sociocultural resonance, and governance approaches by both the state and platforms. The ambiguous borders carry both opportunities and challenges for creators. The process of navigating the liminal space is a process in which creators mobilize agency and experience precarity as fame is gained, lost, relocated, or transformed in the process.

Given the broader ecology of the *wanghong* economy, the four layers of liminality can be used as an explanatory framework to investigate creators' experiences in different sectors of social media, where technoeconomic and cultural characteristics may engender differentiated experiences. This may add complexity to the existing research that addresses the intersecting space of creative labor and internet fame.

REFERENCES

Abidin, Crystal. 2015. "Communicative ♥ Intimacies: Influencers and Perceived Interconnectedness." *Ada: A Journal for Gender, New Media, & Technology* 8. https://adanewmedia.org.

Banet-Weiser, Sarah. 2012. *Authentic™: The Politics of Ambivalence in a Brand Culture.* New York: NYU Press.

Berry, Bonnie. 2007. *Beauty Bias: Discrimination and Social Power.* Westport, CT: Praeger.

Borg, Elisabeth, and Jonas Söderlund. 2014. "Moving In, Moving On: Liminality Practices in Project-Based Work." *Employee Relations* 36 (2): 182–197. doi:10.1108/ER-11-2012-0081.

Burgess, Jean, and Joshua Green. 2018. *YouTube: Online Video and Participatory Culture.* 2nd ed. Cambridge, UK: Polity.

Butler, Judith. 1988. "Performative Acts and Gender Constitution: An Essay in Phenomenology and Feminist Theory." *Theatre Journal* 40 (4): 519–531. doi:10.2307/3207893.

CBNData. 2016. "2016 Zhongguo dianshang hongren dashuju baogao" [2016 Report on *Wanghong* in China's E-commerce Market]. May 23, 2016. https://cbndata.com.

Cheung, Anne. 2009. "China Internet Going Wild: Cyber-Hunting versus Privacy Protection." *Computer Law and Security Review* 25 (3): 275–279. doi:10.1016/j.clsr.2009.03.007.

China Daily. 2016. "China to Regulate Online Streaming Services." November 4, 2016. www.chinadaily.com.cn.

Coman, Mihai. 2008. "Liminality in Media Studies: From Everyday Life to Media Events." In *Victor Turner and Contemporary Cultural Performance*, edited by Graham St. John, 94–108. New York: Berghahn Books.

Couldry, Nick. 2003. *Media Rituals: A Critical Approach.* London: Routledge.

Craig, David, Heng Cai, and Junyi Lv. 2016. "Mapping and Managing Chinese Social Media Entertainment: A Conversation with Heng Cai, Chinese Media Entrepreneur." *International Journal of Communication* 10 (2016): 5463–5472.

Cunningham, Stuart. 2009. "Trojan Horse or Rorschach Blot? Creative Industries Discourse around the World." *International Journal of Cultural Policy* 15 (4): 375–386. doi:10.1080/10286630902977501.

Cunningham, Stuart, and David Craig. 2017. "Being 'Really Real' on YouTube: Authenticity, Community and Brand Culture in Social Media Entertainment." *Media International Australia* 164 (1): 71–81. doi:10.1177/1329878X17709098.

———. 2019. *Social Media Entertainment: The New Industry at the Intersection of Hollywood and Silicon Valley.* New York: NYU Press.

Dayan, Daniel, and Elihu Katz. 1992. *Media Events: The Live Broadcasting of History.* Cambridge, MA: Harvard University Press.

de Peuter, Greig. 2011. "Creative Economy and Labor Precarity: A Contested Convergence." *Journal of Communication Inquiry* 35:417–425. doi:10.1177/0196859911416362.

Duffy Brooke Erin. 2017. *(Not) Getting Paid to Do What You Love.* New Haven, CT: Yale University Press.

Florida, Richard. 2003. *The Rise of the Creative Class.* New York: Basic Books.

Gao, Li, and James Stanyer. 2014. "Hunting Corrupt Officials Online: The Human Flesh Search Engine and the Search for Justice in China.: *Information, Communication & Society* 17 (7): 814–829. doi:10.1080/1369118X.2013.836553.

Gill, Rosalind, and Andy Pratt. 2008. "In the Social Factory? Immaterial Labor, Precariousness and Cultural Work." *Theory, Culture and Society* 25 (7–8): 1–30. doi:10.1177/0263276408097794.

Gillespie, Tarleton. 2018. *Custodians of the Internet: Platforms, Content Moderation, and the Hidden Decisions that Shape Social Media.* New Haven, CT: Yale University Press.

Hesmondhalgh, David, and Sarah Baker. 2011. *Creative Labor: Media Work in Three Cultural Industries.* London: Routledge.

Hockx, Michel. 2015. *Internet Literature in China.* New York: Columbia University Press.

Howkins, John. 2001. *The Creative Economy: How People Make Money from Ideas.* London: Penguin.

Jeffreys, Elaine, and Louise Edwards. 2010. "Celebrity/China." In *Celebrity in China,* edited by Louise Edwards and Elaine Jeffreys, 1–20. Hong Kong: Hong Kong University Press.

Kaiman, Jonathan, and Jessica Meyers. 2017. "Chinese Authorities Put the Brakes on a Surge in Live Streaming." *Los Angeles Times,* June 24, 2017. www.latimes.com.

Keane, Michael. 2013. *Creative Industries in China: Art, Design and Media.* Cambridge, UK: Polity.

Lange, Patricia. 2008. "(Mis)Conceptions about YouTube." In *Video Vortex Reader: Responses to Youtube,* edited by Geert Lovink and Sabine Niederer, 87–100. Amsterdam: Institute of Network Cultures.

Lobato, Ramon, Julian Thomas, and Dan Hunter. 2011. "Histories of User-Generated Content: Between Formal and Informal Media Economies." *International Journal of Communication* 5 (2011): 899–914.

Marwick, Alice. 2013. *Status Update.* New Haven, CT: Yale University Press.

———. 2015. "Instafame: Luxury Selfies in the Attention Economy." *Public Culture* 27 (75): 137–160. doi:10.1215/08992363-2798379.

Marwick, Alice, and danah boyd. 2010. "I Tweet Honestly, I Tweet Passionately: Twitter Users, Context Collapse, and the Imagined Audience." *New Media & Society* 13 (1): 114–133. doi:10.1177/1461444810365313.

Moore, Candace. 2009 "Liminal Places and Spaces: Public/Private Considerations." In *Production Studies: Cultural Studies of Media Industries,* edited by Vicki Mayer, Miranda Banks and John Caldwell, 125–139. New York: Routledge.

O'Brien, Anne. 2018. "(Not) Getting the Credit: Women, Liminal Subjectivity and Resisting Neoliberalism in Documentary Production." *Media, Culture & Society* 40 (5): 673–688. doi:10.1177/0163443717734405.

Ong, Rebecca. 2012. "Online Vigilante Justice Chinese Style and Privacy in China." *Information & Communications Technology Law* 21 (2): 127–145. doi:10.1080/136008 34.2012.678653.

People's Daily. 2019. "Management Regulations for Online Short Video Platforms and Detailed Standards for Content Review of Online Short Video." October 1, 2019. http://politics.people.com.cn.

Roberts, I. D. 2010. "China's Internet Celebrity: Furong Jiejie." In *Celebrity in China*, edited by Louise Edwards and Elaine Jeffreys, 217–236. Hong Kong: Hong Kong University Press.

Ross, Andrew. 2009. *Nice Work If You Can Get It: Life and Labor in Precarious Times.* New York: NYU Press.

Sina. 2018. "Feng Timo Responds to in Relation to Her Marital Status." May 29, 2018. http://ent.sina.com.cn.

Sun, Wanning, and Yingjie Guo. 2013. Introduction to *Unequal China: The Political Economy and Cultural Politics of Inequality*, edited by Wanning Sun and Yingjie Guo, 1–11. London: Routledge.

Tsoi, Grace. 2016. "Wang Hong: China's Online Stars Making Real Cash." *BBC News*, August 1, 2016. www.bbc.com.

Turner, Graeme. 2013. *Understanding Celebrity.* Thousand Oaks, CA: Sage.

Turner, Victor. 1967. *The Forest of Symbols: Aspects of Ndembu Ritual.* Ithaca, NY: Cornell University Press.

van Gennep, Arnold. (1909) 1960. *The Rites of Passage.* Chicago: University of Chicago Press.

Xinhua News. 2016. "'Measures for the Administration of Online Performance Operating Activities' Released to Move the Industry towards Healthier Development." December 13, 2016. www.xinhuanet.com.

Yu, Jincui. 2016. "Pai Jiang Is Smart Enough to Work Clean." *Global Times*, April 23, 2016. www.globaltimes.cn.

Zhang, Ge, and Larissa Hjorth. 2017. "Livestreaming, Games and Politics of Gender Performance: The Case of Nüzhubo in China." *Convergence: The International Journal of Research into New Media Technologies*, December 8, 2017. doi:10.1177/1354856517738160.

Zhang, Yingqi. 2014. "The Anxiety of Our Times behind the Popular Series." *Sina*, December 3, 2014. http://news.sina.com.cn.

Zhao, Elaine. 2011. "Social Network Market: Storytelling on a Web 2.0 Original Literature Site." *Convergence: The International Journal of Research into New Media Technologies* 17 (1): 85–99. doi:10.1177/1354856510383364.

———. 2016. "Professionalization of Amateur Production in Online Screen Entertainment in China: Hopes, Frustrations and Uncertainties." *International Journal of Communication* 10 (2016): 5444–5462.

———. 2017. "Writing on the Assembly Line: Informal Labour in the Formalised Online Literature Market in China." *New Media & Society* 19 (8): 1236–1252. doi:10.1177/1461444816634675.

———. 2019. *Digital China's Informal Circuits: Platforms, Labour and Governance.* London: Routledge.

Zhao, Elaine, and Michael Keane. 2013. "Between Formal and Informal: The Shake-out in China's Online Video Industry." *Media, Culture & Society* 35 (6): 724–741. doi:10.1177/0163443713491301.

12

Content Creators and the Field of Advertising

ARTURO ARRIAGADA

Carlos is a thirty-four-year-old university lecturer based in Santiago, Chile. He started creating content online—specifically on a blog—to share his interest in fashion, commenting on garments and trends. During that time, he built an audience online that followed his content, providing comments and sometimes sharing on social media. One day, he received an email from an advertising agency inviting him to promote a brand of men's clothing. The requirement consisted of sharing a press release on his blog about the brand's new collection and taking pictures modeling different clothes. The agency's idea was to give Carlos an opportunity to share his experience with the clothes by writing a review on his blog and social media. In compensation, he received a set of pants, shirts, and socks as a gift. Carlos was happy about this proposal, because it was an opportunity to convert his hobby into a more professional activity, receiving products for free. He knows that he will not receive payment for this activity now, but it works as a point of entrance for future deals. During our conversation, he still was surprised about that email: "Why me?" he constantly asks. Then that surprise evolved into confidence, having a clear idea about the reason why brands are interested in people like him: "As content creators, we are offering a real experience with products. I have talked personally with advertising agencies. . . . Brands hire agencies, and then agencies contact us to promote those brands. Even though agencies can hire 'celebrities' that give more visibility to brands, they also are looking for YouTubers, bloggers, and Instagrammers because we have *a real and honest perspective* to promote brands and products."

This chapter explores how creators and advertising agencies work together as dual markets within the industry of advertising. These markets can be approached as a field where different actors compete to legitimize their forms of knowledge, expertise, and taste classifications for the promotion of brands and products. The notion of a field—borrowed from the French sociologist Pierre Bourdieu (1993a)—refers to bounded spaces of action and interaction. In this chapter, we will consider advertising and content creation as cultural and economic activities that increasingly interact with each other in a bounded space—the field of advertising—operating according to rules, strategies, players, and capitals.

Carlos's story reveals a process through which creators look to claim a position of authority within the field of advertisement, challenging the identities and values of advertising agencies in trying to legitimize *their* forms of knowledge around the communication of brands. In competing with advertisers to distinguish a set of values within the field, creators feel compelled to diminish information asymmetries between brands and consumers (Arriagada and Ibáñez 2019) and feel more in touch with consumers because of their familiarity with consumer interests and their content-creation abilities, which help them to legitimize their knowledge around communicating brands. Creators do this by defining themselves as experts in authenticity (showing who you are) and affect (creating a sense of intimate and close communication with audiences; Abidin 2016; Duffy 2017). In contrast, advertisers claim authority in the form of cultural capital—the ability to create consumer needs for audiences—such as secondary data (for example, surveys, focus group, and other research techniques) and "intuition" to connect consumers' interests with brand values (Ariztía 2015). Advertisers are dealing with an overall industry undergoing transformation and affected by declining revenues, where money is moving from traditional TV, radio, or newspapers to social media, blogs, and websites. In the latter market, the work of content creators is increasingly valuable for advertising agencies. For instance, 80 percent of advertising agencies consider creators—for example, influencers—effective in marketing terms (Mediakix 2018).

While the advertising industry is embracing creators as part of this new media ecology, the embrace is not without tensions. With the spread of social media, communicating brands increasingly incorporate "amateur experts" (Baym and Burnett 2009), consumers who are actively engaged in promoting brands and products on blogs, social media, and online forums. Some authors describe this process as blurring the lines between production and consumption (Bruns 2009), where a "reputation" industry emerges online (Hearn 2010). However, these studies frequently ignore the way the practices and knowledge of content creators like bloggers or influencers are becoming part of consolidated industries like advertising. In analyzing how the roles of traditional intermediaries are challenged within the contemporary advertising industry, this chapter contributes to an understanding of the evolution and mutual constitution of content creator and advertiser activities.

This chapter draws on participant observation at an advertising agency that hires creators, as well as thirty-five semistructured interviews with Chilean content creators in the field of fashion and lifestyle. I discuss how advertising agencies and content creators appear to have a mutually constitutive influence on each other in a rapidly evolving set of economic and cultural relations, while generating dynamic shifts in industrial power asymmetry. On the one hand, creators challenge the power of advertisers by configuring their knowledge-based labor to validate the online content-creation economy. On the other, advertisers work to accommodate creator authenticity—the basis for extracting value from their relationship with their fan communities—even as they continue to exert power over creators through low payment schedules and through controlling commercial relations with clients.

Advertising as a Field of Cultural Production

Following Bourdieu, we may theorize advertising and the practices of advertising executives as part of a field of cultural production. Fields are "bounded spaces of action and interaction" (Bourdieu 1990, 72) where the social world is conceived as a "game." In this game, fields operate according to forces, rules, players, different types of capital (economic, symbolic, cultural), and strategies. In this sense, as Bourdieu proposes, "in order for a field to function, there have to be people prepared to play the game, endowed with a *habitus* that implies knowledge and recognition of the imminent laws of the field, the stakes, and so on" (1990, 72).

When actors enter fields, they are establishing power relations in order to accumulate different types of capital (economic, symbolic, cultural, and social), which will enable them to achieve a position in the field. Fields and various types of capital are the result of individuals' practices; they are not conceived as preexisting categories. Practices are bodily performances that are based not on rational calculation but on a practical and embodied rationality (Bourdieu 1990).

Bourdieu (1993a, 1993b) identified different fields of cultural production, for instance, the fields of art, education, or "high fashion," where actors compete to accumulate and exert power. For instance, the latter field is structured by the unequal distribution of what Agnès Rocamora calls "fashion capital," which "consists essentially of familiarity with a certain milieu and of the quality conferred by the simple fact of belonging to it" (2002, 351). In the case of my work in this chapter, advertising agencies compete for and accumulate cultural and economic capital through their ability to be involved in social, cultural, and economic mediations and their ability to connect brands' values and product qualities with consumers' demands (Kelly 2014). In my framework, the field of advertising is one of large-scale production (Bourdieu 1993b), oriented to commercial success and for the masses. For instance, in creating ads, advertisers consume, mediate, and incorporate, for example, the social world—trends, forms of consumption, and lifestyles; cultural forms, like movies and art; and economic relations with clients—to accumulate economic capital.

In fields, where actors compete to achieve positions of distinction and to accumulate different forms of capital, challengers define new values that allow them to legitimate a new specific capital, "for the exclusive power to constitute and impose the symbols of legitimate distinction on the subject" (Bourdieu, quoted in Rocamora 2002, 237). For instance, in the field of high fashion, new actors that enter the field (for example, new designers) challenge the rules established by consolidated designers (or *couturiers*) (Bourdieu 1993a). From the perspective of advertising agencies they rely on "creativity" as a form of cultural capital to exert power in the field of advertising, based on their ability to connect brands' values with consumers' demands (Kelly 2014). Creators are challengers in the field of advertising in their claim to better, more pertinent cultural capital, being more in touch with consumers via their ability to create attractive content for their audiences, and their claim to more digital savoir faire than advertising agencies, striving to become the authentic and affective "face" for brands and products (Abidin 2016; Hearn and Schoenho 2016).

Creators are a challenge to advertising executives in their role as what Bourdieu calls "cultural intermediaries" (1984, 359), or "occupations involving presentation and representation, . . . providing symbolic goods and services . . . in the context of a new economy . . . whose functioning depends as much on the production of needs and consumers as on the production of goods" (1984, 310). Cultural intermediaries have a significant role in the reproduction of consumer economies, between the production and consumption of goods, as "shapers of taste and the inculcators of new consumerist dispositions" (Nixon and Du Gay 2002, 497). In this sense, Bourdieu's conceptualization highlights the social positions of cultural production professionals in endowing symbolic meaning to goods.

Advertising agencies have, traditionally, converted cultural capital into economic capital by possessing the means of production, and today they hold positions of power in the field, determining what brands or products are good or should be consumed. Advertisers deploy their ability and knowledge to connect brands' values with potential consumer demands—a powerful cultural capital that distinguishes advertising executives' social position within the field of advertising. Today, however, as we will see, this position is challenged by creators, by the new media ecology that values creativity and authenticity (Duffy 2018), and by the new forms of communicating brands' values and qualities (Arriagada and Concha 2019). In this context, advertising agencies try to adapt to this new environment by incorporating the activities of creators as part of their business in order to create value for brands and for themselves as experts in connecting consumers' demands and brands.

Content Creators and the Field of Advertising

The activities of content creators are without doubt immersed in discourses about the potential role of digital technologies in changing power relations. Traditional media (for example, television, newspapers, and radio) are adapting to technological transformations around the production and circulation of content that empower consumers (Jenkins 2006). Content creators facilitate this move toward a "participatory culture," which gives a voice to underrepresented groups or demands (Duffy 2018) and challenges traditional leadership from advertising executives. The emergence of creators happens in a context of transformation for media and advertising industries—with regard to audience attention, content consumption patterns, and revenues (Cunningham and Craig 2019).

The activities of content creators have caught the eye of the advertising industry, which seeks to commodify them to represent brands and their value chains (for an analysis of the political economy of influence, see chapter 13 in this volume). According to recent data, the global influencer industry—constituted by creators who integrate "advertorials" into their social media content (Abidin 2016)—was worth $6.5 billion in 2019 and will be worth $10 billion in 2020 (Mediakix 2018). Instagram, the leading influencer platform, was worth $1.07 billion in 2017 and will reach $2.38 billion by 2020 (Statista 2019).

Content creators compete with advertisers through two imperatives that work as strategic advantages for their commercial activities: authenticity and entrepreneurial spirit (Marwick 2013; Abidin 2016). Being authentic also works for creators as a form of distinction from media celebrities (Duffy 2017), changing radically what agencies look for as the "face" of brands. The entrepreneurial ideal, which contributes to such authenticity, is based on creators constantly working to promote themselves, to succeed, and to be profitable (Banet-Weiser 2012; Duffy 2017). Their entrepreneurial spirit is a form of self-promotion of a productive and exciting future (Neff 2015). In the same vein, the entrepreneurial spirit of creators involves building their identity around work (Gill 2010; Duffy 2017).

Advertisers cannot emulate content creators, who construct an audience by presenting themselves as authentic and affective consumers (Marwick 2013; Duffy 2017). A qualified reputation for authentic lifestyles or acts of consumption can indeed be measured through a set of metrics (for example, likes, shares, and reproductions), which are in fact subject to valuation by advertising agencies or other commercial entities (Carah 2014; Gandini 2016; Hearn and Schoenho 2016). Social media platforms like Instagram, YouTube, or Facebook thereby become "attention economies," in which attention is an "intrinsically scarce resource," and in this vein, "money flows to attention" (Goldhaber 2006). Those who can levy their self-presentations to sustain audience attention accumulate cultural capital and compete as intermediaries. It is this context that has changed the advertising industry. Brands' advertising budgets are moving from traditional forms of media (TV, radio, magazines, and newspapers) toward digital media (social media, websites, and blogs) (Barthel 2019), and so advertising agencies work to get audiences' attention with less cultural capital in the new digital ecology. The technical infrastructure of new media further challenges the traditional power of advertising agencies. Today, advertisers are evaluated by clients according to new metrics—for example, online audience engagement—in addition to TV ratings or newspaper readership. Clients with more information may thus constantly evaluate advertising agencies and the impact of commercial messages, and so social media is transforming the commercial relation between clients and advertising agencies. In short, agencies are competing in a new social media scenario of empowered clients and audience attention.

Playing the Promotional Game: An Analysis of Content Creators in the Field of Advertising

How are the practices of advertising agencies challenged by content creators in the field of advertising? How do advertisers incorporate creators' practices? How are creators struggling compared to other forms of creative and digital labor, particularly against advertisers? This chapter answers these questions through an analysis of the "rules of the game" around online content creation and the promotion of brands in the social media age. I delve into the case of advertising executives who hire creators for the promotion of brands and products and the experiences of a group of thirty-five content creators—mostly fashion and beauty bloggers—based in Santiago, Chile (for more detail, see Arriagada and Ibáñez 2019). Most creators are professionals with university degrees in communication, marketing, or advertising and in some cases with stable jobs in digital-marketing agencies, newspapers, or fashion agencies. Only a small group of participants work as content creators full-time.

A New Actor in the Field of Advertising: When Advertising Agencies "Have" to Work with Creators

There are two primary ways in which creators and agencies relate to each other to promote brands. When creators are interested in contacting agencies, they send their "media kit"—a portfolio with text and images that describe creators' work—with information about their target audience, the type of content they create (videos, social media posts, Instagram stories, and so forth), and their topics of interest. The second form is when agencies contact creators after following their work online for a period and they consider creators' content and self-brand can fit with their clients. This is a trial-and-error process, in which advertising executives rely on their own instinct and on creators' public metrics (for example, number of followers, content comments, and audience engagement). In some cases, clients give agencies a list of creators they "hear" or "feel" fit with their brands. This can present a conflict for advertising agencies: even if they consider a suggestion detrimental to their clients, they may not always want to contradict them. Similarly, clients may ask for a specific type of content. For instance, according to an advertising executive, "Clients love pictures of influencers or bloggers in front of the [brand] store, but that kind of content doesn't work for audiences; it's not authentic." This dynamic reflects a change with regard to the relation between a client and an agency: clients may demand including the work of creators as part of a campaign, imposing on advertising agencies. As such, agencies feel pressured to include creators in their proposal to clients—directly diminishing their own role in their creative and commercial services to promote brands online.

It is in the best interest of agencies, then, to try to limit creators' establishing direct relationships with brands. When agencies are interested in the work of creators—or indeed feel obligated from clients' demands—they contact creators to collaborate with the brand. When creators are not on the radar of advertising agencies, they are treated as "amateurs" in promoting brands and products. Advertisers here exert power over creators by controlling the conditions of commercial deals. For instance, during the participant observation at an agency for this study, the word "collaboration" was commonly used to describe the relation between the agency and a group of creators. That word denies the existence of a commercial relation, replacing an "equally beneficial partnership" with the "opportunity," given by the agency, to a group of creators to become part of the field of advertising. At the same time, creators see "collaboration" as reflecting the entrepreneurial spirit of doing "what they love" while gaining agencies' confidence, working for free, or receiving invitations to marketing events or a stock of products as an exchange for that collaboration. Advertisers set trial periods and suggest they may later pay for creators' content, thus maximizing their position in the field. They charge clients for hiring creators, paying little or nothing to the latter or giving them gifts, products, or discount coupons. Agencies may also invite creators to marketing events to promote products in front of creators, influencers, and potential consumers. They ask creators to promote the product on social media and provide them with a press release of the qualities of the product and its story. Again, advertising executives structure their relationship with content creators as a collaboration, an opportunity for the creators to have "new content" for their audience. Such gatekeeping activities reflect the tension that advertising agencies have in relation to the work of creators—they feel that their creative activities around commercial communication are threatened by these new actors who have knowledge of the new media ecology and online audience behavior, which is valuable for clients.

And so, as advertisers are aware of their position in the field of advertising—following Bourdieu's terminology—they start playing the game. And vice versa. Indeed, at this stage, creators follow the (as yet hidden) rule in the field by constantly building relations with (and, at times, being submissive to) advertising executives in their role of promoting brands and products. As a fashion blogger describes, building relations with advertising executives means "building a network of potential collaborators," something that includes being constantly involved in self-promotion, at events and at meetings, sending their media kits to executives, and creating content related to those exchanges. As Rosalind Gill (2010) suggests, life is a constant "pitch" where everything is work and a potential working relation. Creators cannot be seen as conflictive or as challenging the reputation of advertising executives as experts in the communication of brands. However, they are aware that these relations are not always honest. As a blogger describes, "It can feel fake sometimes—you have to understand that you are useful for them [agencies]. . . . But there is a lot of hypocrisy. People from agencies flatter you and then talk shit behind your back." And so, at least at this stage, creators defer to traditional cultural capital, presenting themselves to agencies as proactive workers, although they may not feel totally comfortable with their relegated positions.

"Fighting" over the Control of Commercial Messages: The Competition between Creators and Agencies

After enough "collaboration," creators start to negotiate with advertising executives about how a brand can be promoted, especially in relation to the type of content and the messages agencies and creators consider useful for brand promotion. For instance, Danielle is a lifestyle blogger and has paid and nonpaid collaborations with advertising agencies (and brands). For her, agencies are looking for creators who are capable to publish "authentic" and "real" opinions about products, so they can build credibility around their content. However, according to her, advertising agencies are "lovely" before working together, empowering creators as "experts" communicating their own content. Then, when they have the creator's attention, they try to control how branded content is communicated. For instance, agencies send products and a press release they want creators to publish on blogs or Instagram accounts; however, creators, who have begun to understand their position as cultural intermediaries, challenge this rule by proposing different forms of promoting brands. They start "fighting" over the control of the commercial messages they will communicate; or, as Bourdieu (1993a) describes, they are actors competing to accumulate and exert power.

Here, the changes in the media landscape, in agencies' relevance to consumers, redefine agencies' business models, the role their cultural capital plays in the form of creativity—indeed, borrowing Bourdieu's term, their "weapons" (1993a)—in competing to connect brands with consumers. Agencies strive to control the communication and content that a creator may circulate about a brand through a press release, especially with creators whose audience may not fit with what agencies consider "the brand's consumer target." Creators see this practice as a disconnect between advertising agencies and consumers. As a fashion blogger described, "You can't communicate product qualities based on a press release written by someone who has never tried the product. That's our work—we know how to communicate an experience [with a brand or a product] to our audiences."

From the creators' perspective, this new media landscape situates consumers at the center of brands and their communications. Thus, creators feel compelled to propose a more "authentic" communication between brands and consumers on the basis of their "knowledge" to promote brands and products' qualities. This knowledge results from their ability to accumulate audiences online through their "technical and digital knowledge" and honest content. As a blogger explains, they can "describe a real experience with the product, . . . something agencies can't do hiring, for instance, TV celebrities."

This is a mutual configuration. Advertisers incorporate creators out of necessity, and as creators are more incorporated into the field of advertisers, they begin to challenge the rules defined by advertisers. Creators feel they may replace agencies' "creativity with authenticity." They are well aware that the traditional advertising model based on the accumulation of audiences by mass media is in crisis with the emergence of digital, and particularly social, media. As a fashion influencer explains, "I think for them [advertising executives] we are a labor force that facilitates another type of reach for products' and brands' promotion. It is a sum of factors: we accumulate audiences on social media, audiences that not always are watching TV, . . . so brands need lots of people talking about them, and here we are." As an experienced advertising executive said, "There is a generational thing. We were not raised with YouTube or Instagram. We were raised with TV, radio, and newspapers. . . . These people [content creators] help us to work for brands in a natural way." It is common for creators to frame their stories and experiences working with agencies around the idea that consumers expect authentic experiences about brands and products, not necessarily "celebrities promoting products they will never use." However, from advertising agencies' perspective, authentic communication does not always mean consumers will go to buy a product. For instance, an executive described the case of an influencer with seven hundred thousand followers who organized a contest on her Instagram account, inviting her followers to go to a store, and nobody went.

Paula, a lifestyle blogger, describes how agencies sometimes experience a lack of creativity in promoting brands, which allows creators to challenge advertising agencies:

> [The brand] Dove was promoting a new product, a deodorant that doesn't stain clothes. When the agency explained to me what they want me to do, it was something so basic, like "I'm going out tonight to a party, but my clothes are stained. With Dove that doesn't happen." Then, I suggested, why don't we try something different? Like, I'm getting obsessed with deodorants that stain my clothes, and then I start trying Dove's deodorant on all my clothes to confirm that nothing happens. Something funny, no? When I sent my media kit to the agency, it described the prices for different types of contents [for example, a Facebook post, an Instagram story, a blog post, a video, and so forth]. They chose the video option, but my condition was to be in charge of the production. Some agencies say yes, some not. I prefer to control the quality of my content.

Paula's description helps us to understand how creators reclaim the power to connect brands and consumers through their practices of content creation. They claim to have better knowledge of what works for their audiences, compared to traditional strategies developed by advertising executives (such as relying on survey data, focus groups, and other sources). Thus, advertising executives are forced to relearn the rules of their field in the face of digital disruption and the power and importance of social media compared to traditional media. Similarly, advertising executives are part of a process in which traditional celebrities do not always represent the interests and demands of consumers. For instance, during a meeting at an agency, there was a discussion in which the client rejected the list of people suggested by the agency to be part of campaign—according to the client, they were not ordinary people but "celebrities." As one advertising executive described, "Sometimes we don't know what to offer to clients, especially when the most important influencers don't have a huge number of followers. They are not celebrities or are celebrities for very specific audiences."

Agencies and creators thus compete together in the field of advertising as cultural intermediaries in shaping consumers' decisions and consumption experiences (Arriagada and Ibáñez 2019). In working together, they constantly negotiate the terms and conditions of collaborations, particularly in relation to the control each actor may have in communicating brands. Creators deploy what Tania Lewis has called "ordinary expertise" (2008, 2) in influencing norms around social and cultural identity. They do this by presenting themselves as authentic experts whose aspirations around consumption are honest and ordinary (Abidin 2016). Advertising executives are challenged when creators ask to be provided clear information and the freedom to display their creativity and knowledge. For instance, a fashion blogger describes her experience with an agency and the difficulties that emerge when executives have no idea how to use a product:

> I have good and bad experiences with agencies. Recently I had to produce a video to promote a hair product, and it was very complicated because the agency had no idea about how to use the product, and I knew how to use it because I had direct contact with that brand. It was difficult because the agency was an intermediary that was not helping me to do my work; on the contrary, they were pushing me to promote the product in a different way than would interest the brand. Finally, I made the video, but it wasn't published because the agency didn't like it. It was difficult.

Struggles in Promoting Brands and Products: Tensions and Boundaries in the Field of Advertising

Through creators' practices of content creation, they compete with advertising agencies in relation to two issues: ethical boundaries and payment for their work. In relation to ethical boundaries, creators make two intertwined arguments. First, they justify their activities as driven by the need to diminish asymmetries of information between brands and consumers. Again, this works as a challenge to advertising agencies, which are driven to create high, and not always realistic, expectations around brands and products. Second, in order for creators to keep their work "authentic" in front of their audiences, they prefer to work with brands that represent their values and identities as creators.

In order to diminish asymmetries in the field, creators leverage their cultural capital to establish an authentic relation between brands and consumers. They compete with agencies in ways to get consumer attention. Though agencies rely on secondary data (for example, surveys, focus group, and other research techniques) or "intuition" to connect consumers' interests with brands values (Ariztía 2015), creators rely on their own experience with products or on video tutorials from other creators. Thus, they confront traditional actors by presenting an authentic experience with the product in front of their audiences and even confront themselves, if they do not like a product. Val, a lifestyle blogger, describes this process of negotiating with herself and the agency about how to communicate about a product she does not like:

> Paco Rabanne organized an event to launch a new perfume, and their agency offered me $350,000 pesos (about US$550) to post a picture on Instagram saying how amazing the perfume was and also making a contest for my followers. . . . At that time, I was moving from my parents' house to live alone. . . . The money was good, and I needed it. However, when I tried the perfume, it was awful. I hated it. . . . I gave it to a friend. . . . I felt terrible because I promoted something I didn't like, and I told myself, "I will never do this again." . . . I felt really bad about promoting something I didn't like.

Creators are establishing new rules about having clear editorial lines when they have to work with advertising agencies for a campaign. For instance, the fashion blogger Francisca protects her content by not promoting products she does not like, seeking alternatives from agencies for branded content that she feels is not close to her identity. She sees being honest with her followers about her relationship with agencies as fundamental, something not common in the Chilean advertising field: "I always warn agencies that I will not post content that fakes products appearing in my life out of nowhere. . . . I will tell them the products I promote were sent by agencies or brands. . . . Sometimes agencies are okay with that, sometimes not. . . . They prefer to avoid that disclosure."

In the field, agencies seek to exert power over creators by avoiding paying for their work. As creators become aware of their positions, they see agencies as competition for brand attention and avoid agencies that may not pay. Indeed, they leverage their cultural capital by becoming cultural intermediaries in the field who may work directly with brands in long-term, paid collaborations. Agencies seek to protect their position of power as intermediaries between creators and brands, using creators as cheap labor. Fran and Daniela—two well-known fashion bloggers in the field of advertising—describe these tensions working with agencies:

> FRAN: I don't like agencies. They don't work well. They want everything for free even though they have cash, millions. . . . So I try to work directly with brands. I think if you have a good product, someone will be interested to pay for them. Agencies only ask for prices and try to avoid paying us.
>
> DANIELA: Sometimes on my Instagram or Twitter account, I write something like, "This month my landlord refused lotions and perfumes as payment. He wanted money." . . . I can't pay my rent with lotions, clothes, or perfumes, you know? I need money to live, not products.

Some creators attribute their difficulties to new agencies that, representing themselves to potential clients as "advertising agencies," do the same work as creators—offering clients online content creation and a number of publications in order to obtain a contract. This phenomenon is described by Laura, a lifestyle blogger, as the best example of how the competition between creators and agencies in a hypersaturated context of commercial messages comes at the expense of the possibilities for creators to make a living: "Five years ago, agencies were doing their job well. . . . They were interested in researching and understanding our work, trying to make good connections between my identity as a creator and a brand. . . . Today that is not the rule. Too many agencies offer everything to potential clients, independently of us, if they are able to do it. They are only interested in making quick cash at the cost of using us as cheap labor force, trying to get the most profit, publishing content elsewhere in order to achieve their compromise with clients."

And so, while advertising agencies have traditionally been the intermediaries between brands and clients, creators are positioning themselves as the intermediaries between advertisers, brands, and audiences. They are part of what Anne Cronin (2004) calls "regimes of mediation," referring to their position in the industry (with clients, regulators, agencies, and consumers) and the mediation they are involved with (for example, of brands' value and of themselves as experts communicating brands' properties).

Conclusion

Creators have begun to challenge the traditional intermediary role of advertising agencies between brands and consumers. They claim their position through expertise based on their authentic style of communication in engaging with their audiences. Advertising executives have to relearn the rules of the field in the context of digital disruption and the power that social media has in relation to traditional forms of media.

In my theoretical framework, I have discussed how creators and advertising executives are situated within the advertising industry as mutually constitutive actors, constantly negotiating rules and boundaries. The field, then, results from constant redefinitions of advertising in the digital age—driven by technological, economic, and cultural changes—through which creators find their niche to accumulate and exert power based on the promise of making a profitable career through their practices of content creation, working together with agencies and brands. This process means that both creators and advertising agencies compete to consolidate their position in the industry. The specific entrepreneurial knowledge deployed by creators challenges the institutional power of advertisers while also validating the economy of online content creation; and advertising agencies must negotiate with them.

Future research may also consider the ways in which both actors are challenged by regulation on commercial content by institutions—for example, the Federal Communications Commission (FCC) in the United States or the Servicio Nacional del Consumidor (SERNAC) in Chile—or by platforms' rules and conditions, which threaten cultural intermediaries with changes in algorithmic configuration that affect the value and impact of their work (Cotter 2019), or by the emergence of "virtual influencers" (Katz 2018). In this context, all cultural intermediaries are exposed to different power forces—from institutions, from other actors, or from technological features—that may at any time begin to compete or reshape the field.

REFERENCES

Abidin, Crystal. 2016. "Visibility Labour: Engaging with Influencers' Fashion Brands and #OOTD Advertorial Campaigns on Instagram." *Media International Australia* 161 (1): 86–100. doi:10.1177/1329878X16665177.

Ariztía, Tomás. 2015. "Unpacking Insight: How Consumers Are Qualified by Advertising Agencies." *Journal of Consumer Culture* 15 (2): 143–162.
doi:10.1177/1469540513493204.

Arriagada, Arturo, and Paz Concha. 2019. "Cultural Intermediaries in the Making of
Branded Music Events: Digital Cultural Capital in Tension." *Journal of Cultural
Economy* 13 (1): 42–53. doi:10.1080/17530350.2019.1652673.

Arriagada, Arturo, and Francisco Ibáñez. 2019. "Communicative Value Chains:
Fashion Bloggers and Branding Agencies as Cultural Intermediaries." In *Lifestyle
Journalism: Social Media, Consumption and Experience*, edited by Lucia Vodanovic,
103–113. London: Routledge.

Banet-Weiser, Sarah. 2012. *Authentic™: The Politics of Ambivalence in a Brand Culture*.
New York: NYU Press.

Barthel, Michael. 2019. "5 Key Takeaways about the State of the News Media in 2018."
Pew Research Center, July 23, 2019. www.pewresearch.org.

Baym, Nancy K., and Robert Burnett. 2009. "Amateur Experts: International Fan
Labour in Swedish Independent Music." *International Journal of Cultural Studies* 12
(5): 433–449. doi:10.1177/1367877909337857.

Bourdieu, Pierre. 1984. *Distinction: A Social Critique of the Judgement of Taste*. Cambridge, MA: Harvard University Press.

———. 1990. *The Logic of Practice*. Stanford, CA: Stanford University Press.

———. 1993a. *The Field of Cultural Production: Essays on Art and Literature*. Cambridge, UK: Polity.

———. 1993b. *Sociology in Question*. Translated by Richard Nice. London: Sage.

Bruns, Axel. 2009. "From Prosumer to Produser: Understanding User-Led Content
Creation." Paper presented at Transforming Audiences 2009, London, September
3–4, 2009.

Carah, Nicholas. 2014. "Curators of Databases: Circulating Images, Managing Attention and Making Value on Social Media." *Media International Australia* 150 (1):
137–142. doi:10.1177/1329878X1415000125.

Cotter, Kelley. 2019. "Playing the Visibility Game: How Digital Influencers and Algorithms Negotiate Influence on Instagram." *New Media & Society* 21 (4): 895–913.
doi:10.1177/1461444818815684.

Cronin, Anne. 2004. "Regimes of Mediation: Advertising Practitioners as Cultural
Intermediaries?" *Consumption Markets & Culture* 7 (4): 349–369. doi:10.1080/10253
86042000316315.

Cunningham, Stuart, and David Craig. 2019. *Social Media Entertainment: The New
Intersection of Hollywood and Silicon Valley*. New York: NYU Press.

Duffy, Brooke Erin. 2017. *(Not) Getting Paid to Do What You Love*. New Haven, CT:
Yale University Press.

———. 2018. "#Dreamjob: The Promises and Perils of a Creative Career in Social
Media." In *Making Media*, edited by Mark Deuze, 375–386. Amsterdam: Amsterdam
University Press.

Gandini, Alessandro. 2016. "Digital Work: Self-Branding and Social Capital in the Freelance Knowledge Economy." *Marketing Theory* 16 (1): 123–141.

Gill, Rosalind. 2010. "Life Is a Pitch: Managing the Self in New Media Work." In *Managing Media Work*, edited by Mark Deuze, 249–262. London: Sage.

Goldhaber, Michael. 2006. "The Value of Openness in an Attention Economy." *First Monday* 11 (6). doi:10.5210/fm.v11i6.1334.

Hearn, Alison. 2010. "Structuring Feeling: Web 2.0, Online Ranking and Rating, and the Digital 'Reputation' Economy." *Ephemera* 10 (3–4): 421–438.

Hearn, Alison, and Stephanie Schoenho. 2016. "From Celebrity to Influencer: Tracing the Diffusion of Celebrity Value across the Data Stream." In *A Companion to Celebrity*, edited by P. David Marshall and Sean Redmond, 194–212. Malden, MA: Wiley.

Jenkins, Henry. 2006. *Convergence Culture: Where Old and New Media Collide*. New York: NYU Press.

Katz, Miranda. 2018. "CGI 'Influencers' Like Lil Miquela Are About to Flood Your Feeds." *Wired*, May 1, 2018. www.wired.com.

Kelly, Aidan. 2014. "Advertising." In *The Cultural Intermediaries Reader*, edited by Jennifer Smith-Maguire and Julian Matthews, 67–76. London: Sage.

Lewis, Tania. 2008. *Smart Living: Lifestyle Media and Popular Expertise*. New York: Peter Lang.

Marwick, Alison. 2013. *Status Update: Celebrity, Publicity, and Branding in the Social Media Age*. New Haven, CT: Yale University Press.

Mediakix. 2018. "Influencer Marketing Survey Results: 2019 Industry Benchmarks." September 1, 2018. https://mediakix.com.

Neff, Gina. 2015. *Venture Labor: Work and the Burden of Risk in Innovative Industries*. Cambridge, MA: MIT Press.

Nixon, Sean, and Paul Du Gay. 2002. "Who Needs Cultural Intermediaries?" *Cultural Studies* 16 (4): 495–500. doi:10.1080/09502380210139070.

Rocamora, Agnès. 2002. "Fields of Fashion: Critical Insights into Bourdieu's Sociology of Culture." *Journal of Consumer Culture* 2 (3): 349–370. doi:10.1177/146954050200200303.

Statista. 2019. "Global Instagram Influencer Market Value 2020." August 9, 2019. www.statista.com.

13

The Political Economy of Sponsored Content and Social Media Entertainment Production

JEREMY SHTERN AND STEPHANIE HILL

As chapters throughout this volume have demonstrated, online platforms are increasingly viable sites for professional entertainment content creation—from established genres and forms of storytelling to new and distinct genres, such as the widespread gameplay "Let's Play" genre and makeup tutorials (chapters 6 and 7). While subscriber numbers and monetization figures are constantly shifting, YouTube reports that the number of YouTubers earning more than $100,000 had, by 2018, grown more than 40 percent compared to 2017 (Spangler 2018). The specific numbers matter less than the larger point that social media content creation is often a professional activity that individuals engage in as part of an identifiable, if emerging, media industry. This is an argument that has been most strongly forwarded by the editors of this volume (Cunningham and Craig 2019) and is shared by other academic and professional experts.

In our case, as critical media studies scholars interested in the politics around media industries and new technologies, taking social media seriously as a media industry means asking questions about the political economy of that media industry. Political economic analysis engages with the balances between capitalist enterprise and the public interest and asks questions about media products and services as commodities (Murdock 2011; Mosco 2009; Garnham 2011; Hesmondhalgh 2012). Political economic analyses of media industries typically adopt historical approaches, reflect on the actual or ideal role of the state in ensuring the public's interest in media industries, and ask fundamental questions about the role of advertising and public relations in setting media agendas. Political economic analyses are, in short, concerned with the power that money has over industrial production and audience reception of media content. Through this lens, power is seen to be structured and privileged by market position (Mosco 2009) and marked particularly by processes of commodification—of turning things that were previously not marketable goods into marketable goods (Murdock 2011).

A political economic lens, then, is one that asks readers to consider the YouTube-sourced figures cited in the first paragraph about the investment flowing into the social media entertainment industry and "follow the money." While there is little comprehensive data on the diverse practices of millions of social media entertainers, early reports on the media ecosystem underline the significance of marketing dollars in supporting the careers of content creators, through platform monetization that includes display advertising, brands deals, and sponsorships (Berkowitz, Davis, and Smith 2019). Very successful influencers have self-disclosed receiving tens of thousands of dollars for each sponsored post that they make (O'Conner 2017). For all that is emerging and innovative about the industrial ecosystem of social media entertainment, the arrangement between content creation and marketing dollars is not new. Advertising and marketing have long been very significant forms of investment in entertainment media production. While the media industry has other sources of income, including subscription models, merchandising, and other forms of intellectual property exploitation, advertising tends to be important to periodic and serialized forms of media such as newspapers, magazines, radio stations, and television channels. As John Sinclair puts it, advertising support is "the motive force behind media industry development" (2012, 1). Advertising dollars have shifted dramatically in response to digital publishing, leaving legacy media with a smaller piece of the pie and a greater dependence on subscriptions. However, advertising still constitutes upward of 30 percent of the annual earnings of newspapers such as the *New York Times* (New York Times Company 2018) and more than 60 percent of earnings for television networks such as Canada's Corus Entertainment (Corus Entertainment 2019). Even movie theaters rely on advertising for significant portions of their income (Cineplex 2018). This relationship between financial support and content production gives advertisers a degree of influence over which stories get told and how, which creators get paid, and what kinds of messages are and are not featured. In short, the political economy of media industries has historically enabled advertisers to have considerable power. Globally, media policy, through rules and enforcement over truth in advertising and the advertising of certain products, has emerged as one form of oversight and counterweight to advertising's influential position. This oversight has often occurred as a response to controversies in which public trust was fundamentally shaken by instances in which advertisers were perceived to have leveraged their financial support to assert editorial control over entertainment content.

Testimonial advertising, sponsored or unsponsored, has been practiced since the mid-nineteenth century, in one form or another, with particular growth as the market for goods shifted from local shops to regional and national campaigns (Petty 2015). Beginning in the 1930s, in the United States, government agencies have needed to step in more than once to combat false testimonials and restore public trust (Schweitzer and Moskowitz 2009). In the early years of television, the relationships between sponsors and content were very close indeed, to the point that many advertisers directly paid for the production of specific shows that they hoped would allow them to target possible consumers of their products (Fahey 1991). Companies such as Procter and Gamble produced their own programming for women directly in their own production studios, emphasizing emotion to increase the appeal of the messages and thereby inventing the soap opera genre. Through companies' own programming and later through advertising produced separately, Procter and Gamble and others exercised a commanding influence on the development of commercial radio and television—a role they are eager to reprise in relation to online media (McGuigan 2015). On radio, corporate advertisers and commercial stations essentially barred labor activists from the air. Government intervention, through policies such as the Fairness Doctrine and, later, under pressure from the civil rights movement, was vital to ensuring that citizen, community, labor, and nonprofit groups gained access to the airwaves (Fones-Wolf 2006). On television, much-watched, brand-sponsored quiz shows of the 1950s faced riotous audience backlash when it was revealed that the results of certain shows were being manipulated in order to manufacture drama and maintain compelling contestants on the show in the interest of maximizing audiences to the brands' advertising messages (Brinson 2003). The fallout from these quiz-show scandals led to government intervention, new media policies, and the establishment of industry regulatory practices that created supposed firewalls between content editorial decisions and advertising sales, which were largely produced separately (Bermejo 2009; Brodmerkel and Carah 2016). This "church and state" division between information/entertainment content and advertising messaging has shifted with the financial hardship that has impacted many legacy media institutions (Couldry and Turow 2014; Casale 2015). With brands renewing their search for trustworthy spokespeople at a time of anxiety over misinformation and cynical consumers, direct sponsorship of content production has reemerged in social media as a viable and appealing business model for creators and advertisers alike.

In this chapter, we specifically examine marketing through sponsored content production. Sponsored content can, by design, take many forms, including product placement and product reviews, but is designed to resemble the style of the publisher's content—whether that publisher is a Instagrammer or a newspaper—and meant to create a favorable impression of the sponsor brand or one of its products (Sonderman and Tran 2013). The return to sponsorship as a popular model of funding content online—particularly through the practice of influencer marketing—revives the controversial media monetization practices that invited new governance of advertising relationships and underlined the vital importance of consumer trust to the advertising industry. We consider sponsored social media content in this historical context, examining how it creates power for advertisers by commodifying social media audiences, analyzing the ways in which media policy and industry regulation provide oversight, and identifying gaps in the current model. On the basis of policy-document analysis and dozens of interviews conducted with social media content creators and advertising executives (cf. Shtern, Hill, and Chan 2019), we situate current practices in sponsored content as part of a historical cycle hinging on consumer trust, with government and industry standards acting as a guarantor, quality assurer, and occasional regulator of trustworthiness. Given the uneasy history of sponsorship in media production, this chapter reflects on the sustainability of the social media influencer economy, or, to put it another way, we ask, Does social media entertainment have a "quiz show" problem?

After a brief literature review, this chapter reviews the influencer content ecosystem and situates it within the larger social media entertainment industry. It provides a political economic analysis of this form of media investment that examines the power dynamics of the social media entertainment industry. We address questions about the way social media creators understand and monetize their audience through influencer marketing. In the process, we aim to underline the old and new ways in which sponsored content empowers advertisers by commodifying audiences. We discuss the current media policies and self-regulatory framework governing sponsored content production. In conclusion, we argue that the historical context suggests that an erosion of public trust may lead to a greater role for interventionist media policy in the social media entertainment production industry in the future. The term *influencer* is not embraced by all content creators but is consistently used by the marketing industry. In this chapter, the term is used interchangeably with *creator*, as the creators interviewed would be considered influencers from an industry and policy perspective. Rather than arguing for a return to strict separation between advertising and editorial (an event that seems unlikely at the time of writing), this chapter suggests that the proliferation of collaboration with advertising partners raises new questions about the way to achieve public policy goals in a transnational context dominated by commercial concerns.

Media Policy, Advertising, and Social Media: Background and Context

Social media websites primarily earn revenue from advertisements—more than 85 percent of earnings for Twitter, Facebook, and Google come from advertising (Alphabet 2017; Facebook 2018; Twitter 2018). For creators, the proceeds of display advertising such as banners or pre- or postroll video are split with the platform, and that income is combined with funds from other practices, including sponsored content and links, selling their own merchandise, and money donated directly by followers and fans. Of these diverse income streams, the highest potential earnings tend to be from sponsored content—direct partnerships with branded advertising campaigns that can command thousands of dollars for a single post. Content creators who incorporate branded content are known, particularly from the perspective of the advertising industry, as *influencers* and defined by the ways that they "engage with their following in digital and physical spaces, and monetize their following by integrating 'advertorials' into their blog or social media posts" (Abidin 2015). Research in this area has focused on the intimacy created between users and audiences and specifically the ways those dynamics are largely based in highly gendered behaviors (Abidin 2015, 2016) in ways that extend problematic issues of precarious work and uneven income (Duffy 2017). Scholars have particularly characterized influencers as practitioners of "micro-celebrity" (Senft 2008; Marwick 2015) who operate through the deployment of online personas that fuel relationships between the influencers and their audiences and between their audiences and the products that the influencers are paid to promote. Other scholars have focused on the labor of individuals in social media architectures (Coté and Pybus 2007; van Dijik and Nieborg 2009; Fuchs 2012; Postigo 2016). Many of these accounts characterize the work of influencers as part of exploitative marketing practices that put the audience in the position of laborers, but some scholars argue that it is simplistic or "simply wrong" (Jin and Feenberg 2015, 57) to reduce every interaction to a matter of economic exchange. In an environment that encompasses intimacy and mutualism alongside asymmetrical and oblique power relations, it is informative to reflect on the way practices that are vulnerable to misuse are being regulated and the way those regulations stack against attempts to address similar difficulties in different times.

Where advertising is concerned, the primary role for policy is to prevent those who have the means to craft messages from deceiving or manipulating the audiences for those messages toward the ends of whoever paid for the content. However, among scholars of social media, the degree to which audiences composed of individuals who are often themselves active generators of content are vulnerable to being duped is a matter of ongoing debate. Scholars such as Mark Andrejevic (2011), Sven Brodmerkel and Nicholas Carah (2016), and Joseph Turow (2012) argue that technology shapes consumer experience to a degree that Andrejevic has characterized as "revamped strategies for managing and manipulating audiences" (2011, 606), where the commodification of audiences strips them of their power and agency. Critiques of commercial practices tend to reflect the norms of cultures and media, with some regions drawing a stricter line between commercial and public-service content and resisting the place of market forces in cultural development more strongly (Bardoel and d'Haenens 2008). In contrast, Henry Jenkins (2006), Adam Arvidsson (2008), and Sarah Banet-Weiser (2012) have argued that digital media have allowed for an expanded, ambiguous relationship between consumers and companies—one in which members of the public can more freely express their views and in which more companies are more likely to react to those views. Sponsored content tends to face a similar division, with detractors arguing that commodified audiences are being duped en masse by commercial content and supporters arguing that critical consumers and publishers can thoughtfully and responsibly integrate sponsorship—creating a scenario in which all parties benefit. While scholars continue to appraise the critical capacities of consumers, advertising regulations have long enforced baseline levels of transparency and factual accuracy.

It is unclear what would be a reasonable approach to integrate, in spirit or in letter, social media influencers into existing advertising regulation regimes, which have tended to rely on publishers reviewing advertising and struggle to keep up with the scale and frequent changes on online platforms (Casale 2015). There are substantial rules about disclosing online advertising relationships, rules that can be more stringent than requirements for product placement in television or film. Many creators see these requirements as unfairly punishing smaller creators while celebrities and media are not as strictly policed (for a discussion of the governance of sponsored content from creators' perspectives, see chapter 14 in this volume). At the same time, there is growing evidence of widespread abuse or neglect of disclosure rules on social media platforms, without clear direction toward reining in abuse (Wu 2016; Alvarez 2017; Chen 2017). However, the letter of regulations and guidelines is only one dimension of concern around commercialization of content. Scholars such as Alison Hearn (2010) have noted a concerning slant toward positive reviews and ranking online that suggests commercial interests are able to guide online critique in their desired direction without the direct financial leverage. Andrea Hunter (2016) has argued that incautious incorporation of sponsored content has led to a loss of trust between certain bloggers and their audiences—ironically undoing the source of value in the relationship. Trust, sometimes specifically as part of brand relationships, is also a prominent part of literature that extolls the empowerment of media "prosumers" (Bruns 2008; Hatch and Schultz 2010; Arvidsson 2013). The importance of trust leads some scholars to suggest that commercialism itself may present no particular ethical issue for editorial or artistic creators and that poor, inauthentic, or deceptive execution of commercial partnerships are the only real ethical risks associated with sponsored content (Jenson 2011; Casale 2015; Wu 2016). Others suggest that sponsorship practices themselves can facilitate responsible governance "because most brands and advertisers will not tolerate association with such affronts to civility and democracy" (Cunningham and Craig 2019, 8, in reference to extreme right-wing content online). These views turn the quiz-show problem on its head, presenting corporate priorities as reinforcing and protecting responsibility in media through the commodification of audience trust.

The prizing of trust by media producers has been noted by communication scholars such Hye Jin Lee and Mark Andrejevic (2014), who have commented on the "fanification of audiences," and by the advertising industry itself, where practitioners have long been advised to avoid direct selling messages (Pulizzi 2012; Holliman and Rowley 2014). Marketing practices directed at fostering relationships with consumers spring directly from the industry's awareness that consumers who feel manipulated can become cynical and resistant to engagement with brands (Holt 2002; Brodmerkel and Carah 2016). This attitude is echoed on by the Federal Trade Commission (FTC), which reminds businesses that their compliance with advertising standards "protects the credibility of the Internet as a marketing medium" (FTC, n.d.). Influencers are likewise invested in their credibility to both sponsors and audiences as they work to earn a livelihood and grow their channels.

Working in the Influencer Economy

In order to describe and analyze the monetization practices of influencers, this chapter draws on a series of interview studies we have conducted in recent years (cf. Shtern, Hill, and Chan 2019). This section presents emerging themes in our understanding of the professional practices of influencers, primarily based on YouTube, Instagram, and independent blogs, as they are related to monetization.

Most influencer marketing is negotiated informally. However, there is perception of increasing stratification among influencers, attributed to programs like Preferred Partners on YouTube and the behavior of multichannel networks, which set the rules for monetization and provide mentorship for some of their clients. Reliance on informal personal relationships extends to influencers' understandings of their audience, which are primarily gathered through interaction in the chat and comments, rather than through data or analytics. In particular, the following themes are crucial to understanding working in the influence economy: the diverse sources of income that creators access; the importance of personal relationships; monetizing audiences; and content as currency. We review each in turn.

Diverse and Ad Hoc Sources of Income

The monetization strategies of influencers typically involve diverse sources of income collected and negotiated on an ad hoc basis. Many influencers have long-term relationships with some sponsors, but they balance those relationships with display advertising on their channels, merchandise sales, tip jars, subscription services such as Patreon, and the subscription and donation options provided by livestreaming services such as Twitch. It is important to underline that, even for the most successful influencers, sponsored content production is only one among various revenue-generation strategies. Even some creators on YouTube with large audiences can struggle to reliably monetize content, such as parody, that is prone to being flagged for copyright infringement by YouTube algorithms. It is thus crucial to understand that display advertising as a revenue stream can be highly rewarding for certain creators but that the barriers to entry can also be quite specific and high. Creators who might have a smaller but very engaged audience or one that is connected to a desirable demographic may not fit the profile of high earners from display advertising but are often highly appealing to advertisers looking to create partnerships for influence work and sponsored production. From the advertiser's perspective, a creator with a good connection to a desired niche is often more important than total number of subscribers because it allows marketers to be confident in the targeting of advertising content (Main 2017). This preference encourages creators to identify their niche and, as one influencer suggested at an industry event in the spring of 2019, "become a master of one" (Maral 2019) in order to make themselves and their audience most interesting to advertisers.

Personal Relationships

In this space dominated by highly personal relationships, negative reviews tend to be managed very carefully. Most influencers we spoke to felt that falsely positive reviews or inclusion of unexpected, "off-brand" content would hurt their channels and damage their relationships with their audiences. Influencers are equally wary of including negative reviews that might damage their relationship with sponsors or presenting positive reviews that might damage their credibility with their audience. "And also, we don't want to hurt the partnership with that restaurant or that company. In general, we try to be neutral. Even if there's something bad, we still—we'll still state the fact, but we won't be as harsh" (interview with food-industry creator). Influencers trying to balance the authenticity of their content with the need to maintain relationships with sponsors might omit negative content entirely, carefully massage negative opinions into a review that is, on balance, neutral, or avoid directly tagging companies being negatively reviewed. Some influencers who find themselves having critiques of products supplied by would-be sponsors prefer to give their negative review offline to the company rather than post content on it. Our studies with influencers underline that many do feel a sense of obligation toward companies that supplied them with products to feature the product and to avoid taking any actions that might damage the company that supplied the product. Overall, these practices reflect the closeness that frequently develops between influencers and their marketing partners, without indicating direct editorial intervention by advertisers.

Audiences and Monetization

When asked, most influencers we talked to described having turned down opportunities that they felt would be a poor fit for their channel. For example, one of our interviewees recalled, "I remember they reached out, and they were, like, wanted to work. And they had a massive budget, but I was like, 'Everyone knows I love good coffee, and [this] is not good coffee.' I'm such a coffee snob. So I'm like, 'This just wouldn't be authentic. I don't care what the budget is. I just can't talk about it'" (interview with lifestyle creator). Many more told us that they had taken a sponsorship that they later regretted because it was difficult to integrate with their existing content strategy. For instance, a video-game channel focused on a particular game told us, "Anytime I introduced new content that wasn't [that game], there was always some backlash from the viewers." The centrality of brand consistency informs their interactions with potential sponsors and audiences, as well as their choice of platforms. While a creator's brand is self-defined, it is shaped by perceptions of their audience's preferences, which can police the boundaries of that channel's content. Influencers' understandings of their own brand frame and inform decision-making about their channels, giving them a reference point when deciding what content to include, when to take sponsorships, which platforms to make their primary places for content, and how to define which actions constitute selling out. Following Matt Carlson's (2015) analysis of reactions to native advertising—paid-for advertising that resembles a publication's editorial content—on the *Atlantic*'s website, one way of looking at these practices is to suggest that influencers manage their relationships with companies in a brand-to-brand manner, defined by mutualism and an understanding that long-term value is controlled by the goodwill of the audience. Rather than the creator self-censoring to avoid advertiser pushback, this is a case of the creator self-censoring to avoid audience pushback.

Content as Currency

To influencers, "good sponsorships" can be defined not necessarily by size of the payment but by the provision of content suited to the influencer's channel. For beauty and lifestyle influencers, that content might include products to try; for others, it might include access to events, sneak peeks at new games, product launches, or copies of books—all of which could be filmed or photographed to provide content to the influencer's own channel. For many influencers, brand partnerships allow them to bring to their audience access to exclusive or expensive consumer products or experiences that would be otherwise unavailable, thus reinforcing their own status as influencers in that sector while doing the work of influence for their marketing partners. Influencers working in genres that do not revolve around product reviews, such as gamers, still benefit from content that could only be provided by corporate sponsors, including interviews with developers and early access to upcoming games. In addition, several interviewees argued that the money that sponsorships provide allows them to create content of a much higher production value for all of their posts—sponsored and unsponsored. These practices underscore the drive to have a constant supply of novel content to keep up the value of the channel and its creator to its audience.

This snapshot, based on summaries of our previous studies of the influence economy, is intended to map out the industrial practices that are emerging in the sponsored content space. It gives us a sense that value is being created through the commodification of individual creators' audiences, in particular, the trust in the authenticity of the content and creator. It also reinforces the immense utility and appeal that sponsored content production holds for advertisers. There is the potential for audiences to misunderstand or be intentionally misled about whether it is the creator or the advertiser whose messages are being broadcast through sponsored content. Such tensions—over the ambiguity in the power relationships between audiences, media creators, and advertisers—underlie the challenges in regulating digital marketing and sponsorship.

Regulating Sponsored Content: From Television to Social Media Entertainment

Direct sponsorship of content online emerges as an industry standard in a significantly more governed environment than it did in the nativity of radio and television, though that governance is enacted in complex ways that are largely enforced by social media platforms themselves in voluntary agreements (Gorwa 2019). At present, advertising is primarily self-regulated in most developed countries through industry groups such as Canada's Advertising Standards Council and the United Kingdom's Advertising Standards Authority. Strong formal regulation has generally been reserved for specific products, such as pharmaceuticals, tobacco, and alcohol, and for more general ethical questions such as false advertising and disclosure of economic relationships (Harker 1998; Sinclair 2012). Existing advertising regulation and industry standards do have provisions for testimonial and endorsement, including on social media; but actual oversight is spotty, and violations are rampant (Hunt 2017; Johnson 2017). Crackdowns and strict enforcement do occur occasionally; for instance, professional YouTubers in the United Kingdom were made to remove videos of themselves participating in an "Oreo lick race" for the absence of clear commercial intent, despite the creators thanking Oreo in the video and in the text description for being a commercial partner (Sweney 2014). The US Federal Trade Commission has also attempted to enforce disclosure, as the vast majority of sponsored posts failed to meet its standards (Hunt 2017). These efforts tend to reach only the most visible influencers, particularly celebrity accounts, meaning that commercial relationships and interventions can go largely unscrutinized, putting the onus primarily on the critical capacities of consumers. The scale of the practice online, meanwhile, makes it unlikely that standards can be consistently applied, and it is probable that enforcement will happen largely in response to reported misdeeds. This mirrors the challenges of enforcement on social media generally, with regulation tending to defer to social media platforms and their terms of service (Klonick 2017). In the United States, the FTC guidelines for disclosure focus on the accuracy of claims made in advertisements and the authenticity of the relationship between endorsers and the products that they endorse (FTC, n.d.).

The groups responsible for advertising in other Western countries, including the United Kingdom and Canada, reference the FTC guides as the standard for creators trying to comply with advertising guidelines (Ad Standards 2016). The guidelines stress that a key factor in deciding whether disclosure is required is whether "there exists a connection between the endorser and the seller of the advertised product that might materially affect the weight or credibility of the endorsement" (10). The test of whether the connection might affect the credibility of the endorsement is usually whether the audience would "reasonably expect" a connection to exist—so a celebrity in a TV advertisement need not disclose the commercial relationship, but a celebrity talking about a brand in an interview does have to disclose the relationship. In other parts of the world, including Europe and major emerging economies such as Brazil, Russia, India, China, and South Africa, regulation follows a similar pattern, relying on industry standards and prioritizing proactive disclosure of financial relationships (Sinclair 2012). In social media entertainment, where norms and expectations are still very fluid, it is difficult to know when an audience might "reasonably expect" a commercial relationship. All major social media platforms have advertising guidelines that include rules for paid promotion. Many have included structural features, such as boxes that can be checked to indicate that a video or post contains sponsored content (YouTube n.d.). These practices make sponsored content more recognizable and contribute to normalizing sponsored content for viewers—creating standards of transparency at the same time as they try to protect and enable sponsored content as a naturalized, integrated part of online content creation. In theory, these practices should make viewers more aware of commercial relationships and able to take testimonials with a grain of salt. However, the primary selling point of influencer advertising is that commercial relationships are not seen to conflict with the creator sharing a candid opinion of a product or company. Rather, the creator and the company are on the same side, and the pressure to retain the audience's trust is meant to deter lapses in honesty and transparency.

As noted, the practices that commercial actors—and their social media partners—engage in often happen at an informal level that leverages emotion and peer-to-peer relationships in ways that scholars such as Brodmerkel and Carah have described as "'below the line' of public scrutiny" (2016, 158). The informal nature of much of online interaction underlies many recent controversies on the platforms, including those over the abuse of content directed at children (Wakabayeshi and Maheshwari 2019) and a number of scandal-ridden YouTubers whose content shook the faith of corporate partners (see, for instance, PewDiePie and Logan Paul). In Western countries, federal trade and competition departments are unlikely to intervene over sponsorship except in the most egregious and visible cases. When the FTC has intervened over improper disclosure of sponsorship relationships, it has largely targeted celebrity accounts, even though celebrity accounts represent only a fraction of the brand deals posted on social media every day (Stiegard 2017). Industry groups likewise struggle to create clear definitions and guidelines for online advertising (Casale 2015). Recent efforts to define any creator with more than thirty thousand subscribers as a celebrity (Wright 2019) begin to catch up to the way that influence works online. There is a risk that the involvement of competition bureaus could single out individual actors or punish already-marginalized creators. Susan Brinson, in her examination of the quiz-show scandal that marked the end of the sponsorship model in television production, notes the US Federal Communications Commission's (FCC's) "long history of capitulating to industry needs" (2003, 287), which often punishes individuals while largely sparing corporations implicated in unethical practices. In the case of social media entertainment, platforms' attempts to control content to protect advertisers often end up punishing creators by restricting monetization to the least controversial, most advertiser-friendly content (Burgess and Green 2018).

Conclusion

While this is not a comprehensive summary and does not fully address the environment in many parts of the world, including China (treated with the attention it deserves elsewhere in this volume), it does suggest that existing regulatory approaches to commercial endorsements are largely reliant on the self-interest of the parties involved, with the FCC passing responsibility to advertisers and platforms, which pass the responsibility to creators. For creators and advertisers, the fear of a quiz-show–style problem disrupting the sponsorship model seems to motivate a conservative approach to content production to protect the most precious commodity: audience trust. The next few years will probably see the stabilization of stricter guidelines around monetization and increased monitoring by platforms, incentivized by closer government scrutiny and advertiser demands for brand-safe advertising placement. Those shifts may encourage sponsorship as a funding model, as it is vetted on a case-by-case basis, but should increase scrutiny of these practices, which present a compelling pathway for channels that make entertainment content but seem unlikely to present a viable model for diverse and informational media.

The lessons from history for the current situation of the social media entertainment industry are multiple. On the one hand, it is clear that the basic business model of sponsored content production has always been highly appealing to advertisers keen to tailor matches between their product's message and the ideal niche market of potential consumers. On the other hand, however, it underlines the extent to which the real power that content creators have in this arrangement is the trust of their audience; trust in the editorial independence of the content, in the authenticity of the creator's voice; and trust in their belief that that content is being produced primarily for the entertainment and/or edification of the audience and not in the interests of packaging and pricing the audience for sale to marketers' objectives. The quiz-show controversies of the 1950s creators and advertisers revealed that attempts to fly too close to the sun with regard to pushing sponsorship agendas over content authenticity can invite public backlash, formal government scrutiny, and intervention through media policy and, ultimately, can devalue the trust commodity that binds creators and their audiences to advertisers. Advertisers seem to have learned that lesson all too well and have demanded—and received—increasingly granular control over where and when their dollars support content.

Most of the new genres created online—Let's Plays, style tutorials, vlogs—are eminently compatible with, or reliant on, commercial products and sponsorship. Even vlogging—valuable for its frankness and simplicity of production (Abidin 2015)—easily incorporates the branded goods that surround its subjects. In contrast, educational content and content serving diverse audiences were hardest hit when advertisers restricted their spending in response to issues with online content (Burgess and Green 2018). One concern that we have sought to highlight in this chapter is that bad practice in social media sponsored content production could damage public trust and ruin a source of income for mostly honest creators. In online spaces, there have already been high-profile incidents of popular influencers creating controversial and offensive content, leading sponsors, advertisers, and social media platforms to restrict monetization toward the safest, most professional channels (Burgess 2015).

However, another, larger concern that should be underlined is the question of whether sponsorship supports all of the diverse content and media genres, including educational, parody, and journalistic content, in the way that separately produced advertising has done. While our political economic analysis of the influence economy suggests that the commodification of audiences and audience trust in creators' choices is working as a model of empowering creators in certain genres and formats, arguably the audiences for other forms of media content—learners requiring educational content, citizens requiring journalistic content, and critics requiring parody and satire, for example—do not lend themselves toward being commodified through sponsored content deals. Thus, it is important to continue to be reflexive and vigilant in considering the places of sponsored content within the social media entertainment but also to consider the place of that nascent sector within the larger media and communication landscape and to reflect as they evolve together.

REFERENCES

Abidin, Crystal. 2015. "Communicative ♥ Intimacies: Influencers and Perceived Interconnectedness." *Ada: A Journal for Gender, New Media, & Technology* 8. https://adanewmedia.org.

———. 2016. "'Aren't These Just Young, Rich Women Doing Vain Things Online?': Influencer Selfies as Subversive Frivolity." *Society Media + Society* 2 (2): 1–17. doi:10.1177/2056305116641342.

Ad Standards. 2016. "Interpreting the Code." https://adstandards.ca.

Alphabet. 2017. "Alphabet, Inc. Form 10-K for the Fiscal Year Ended December 31." www.sec.gov.

Alvarez, Edgar. 2017. "YouTube Stars Are Blurring the Lines between Content and Ads." *Engadget*, October 2, 2017. www.engadget.com.

Andrejevic, Mark. 2011. "The Work That Affective Economics Does." *Cultural Studies* 25 (4–5): 604–620. doi:10.1080/09502386.2011.600551.

Arvidsson, Adam. 2008. "The Ethical Economy of Customer Coproduction." *Journal of Macromarketing* 28 (4): 326–338. doi:10.1177/0276146708326077.

———. 2013. "The Potential of Consumer Publics." *Ephemera: Theory and Politics in Organisation* 13 (2): 367–391. doi:10.1177/0276146708326077.

Banet-Weiser, Sarah. 2012. *Authentic™: The Politics of Ambivalence in a Brand Culture.* New York: NYU Press.

Bardoel, Johannes, and Leen d'Haenens. 2008. "Reinventing Public Service Broadcasting in Europe: Prospects, Promises and Problems." *Media, Culture & Society* 30 (3): 337–355. doi:10.1177/0163443708088791.

Berkowitz, Irene, Charles Davis, and Hanako Smith. 2019. "Watchtime Canada: How YouTube Connects Creators and Consumers." Ryerson University, May 22, 2019. https://sites.google.com.

Bermejo, Fernando. 2009. "Audience Manufacture in Historical Perspective: From Broadcasting to Google." *New Media & Society* 11 (1–2): 133–154. doi:10.1177/1461444808099579.

Brinson, Susan L. 2003. "Epilogue to the Quiz Show Scandal: A Case Study of the FCC and Corporate Favoritism." *Journal of Broadcasting & Electronic Media* 47 (2): 276–288. doi:10.1207/s15506878jobem4702_7.

Brodmerkel, Sven, and Nicholas Carah. 2016. *Brand Machines, Sensory Media and Calculative Culture*. Berlin: Springer.

Bruns, Axel. 2008. *Blogs, Wikipedia, Second Life, and Beyond: From Production to Produsage*. New York: Peter Lang.

Burgess, Jean. 2015. "From 'Broadcast Yourself!' to 'Follow Your Interests': Making Over Social Media." *International Journal of Cultural Studies* 18 (3): 281–285. doi:10.1177/1367877913513684.

Burgess, Jean, and Joshua Green. 2018. *YouTube: Online Video and Participatory Culture*. 2nd ed. Cambridge, UK: Polity.

Carlson, Matt. 2015. "When News Sites Go Native: Redefining the Advertising-Editorial Divide in Response to Native Advertising." *Journalism* 16 (7): 849–865. doi:10.1177/1464884914545441.

Casale, A. J. 2015. "Going Native: The Rise of Online Native Advertising and a Recommended Regulatory Approach." *Catholic University Law Review* 65:129–154.

Chen, Yuyu. 2017. "Cheatsheet: How the FTC Is Cracking Down on Deceptive Influencer Marketing." *Digiday*, September 19, 2017. https://digiday.com.

Cineplex. 2018. *Cineplex Annual Report 2018*. http://irfiles.cineplex.com.

Corus Entertainment. 2018. *Corus: Annual Report 2018*. https://assets.corusent.com.

Coté, Mark, and Jennifer Pybus. 2007. "Learning to Immaterial Labour 2.0: MySpace and Social Networks." *Ephemera* 7 (1): 88–106.

Couldry, Nick, and Joseph Turow. 2014. "Advertising, Big Data and the Clearance of the Public Realm: Marketers' New Approaches to the Content Subsidy." *International Journal of Communication* 8:1710–1726.

Cunningham, Stuart, and David Craig. 2019. *Social Media Entertainment: The New Intersection of Hollywood and Silicon Valley*. New York: NYU Press.

Duffy, Brooke Erin. 2017. *(Not) Getting Paid to Do What You Love: Gender, Social Media, and Aspirational Work*. New Haven, CT: Yale University Press.

Facebook. 2018. "Facebook, Inc. Form 10-K for the Fiscal Year Ended December 31." www.sec.gov.

Fahey, Patrick M. 1991. "Advocacy Group Boycotting of Network Television Advertisers and Its Effects on Programming Content." *University of Pennsylvania Law Review* 140 (2): 647–709. doi:10.2307/3312353.

Fones-Wolf, Elizabet. 2006. *Waves of Opposition: Labor and the Struggle for Democratic Radio*. Urbana: University of Illinois Press.

FTC (Federal Trade Commission). n.d. "16 CFR Part 255: Guides Concerning the Use of Endorsements and Testimonials in Advertising." Accessed September 11, 2020. www.ftc.gov.

Fuchs, Christian. 2012. "With or without Marx? With or without Capitalism? A Rejoinder to Adam Arvidsson and Eleanor Colleoni." *TripleC: Communication, Capitalism*

& Critique. Open Access Journal for a Global Sustainable Information Society 10 (2): 633–645. doi:10.31269/triplec.v10i2.434.

Garnham, Nicholas. 2011. "The Political Economy of Communication Revisited." In *The Handbook of Political Economy of Communications*, edited by Janet Wasko, Graham Murdock, and Helena Sousa, 41–61. Malden, MA: Wiley.

Gorwa, Robert. 2019. "What Is Platform Governance?" *Information, Communication & Society* 22 (6): 854–871. doi:10.1080/1369118X.2019.1573914.

Harker, Debra. 1998. "Achieving Acceptable Advertising: An Analysis of Advertising Regulation in Five Countries." *International Marketing Review* 15 (2): 101–118. doi:10.1108/02651339810212476.

Hatch, Mary Jo, and Majken Schultz. 2010. "Toward a Theory of Brand Co-creation with Implications for Brand Governance." *Journal of Brand Management* 17 (8): 590–604. doi:10.1057/bm.2010.14.

Hearn, Alison. 2010. "Structuring Feeling: Web 2.0, Online Ranking and Rating, and the Digital 'Reputation' Economy." *Ephemera* 10 (3–4): 421–438.

Hesmondhalgh, David. 2012. *The Cultural Industries*. London: Sage.

Holliman, Geraint, and Jennifer Rowley. 2014. "Business to Business Digital Content Marketing: Marketers' Perceptions of Best Practice." *Journal of Research in Interactive Marketing* 8 (4): 269–293.

Holt, Douglas B. 2002. "Why Do Brands Cause Trouble? A Dialectical Theory of Consumer Culture and Branding." *Journal of Consumer Research* 29 (1): 70–90. doi:10.1086/339922.

Hunt, Elle. 2017. "Social Media Stars Face Crackdown over Money from Brands." *The Guardian*, September 16, 2017. www.theguardian.com.

Hunter, Andrea. 2016. "Monetizing the Mommy: Mommy Blogs and the Audience Commodity." *Information, Communication & Society* 19 (9): 1306–1320. doi:10.1080/1369118X.2016.1187642.

Jenkins, Henry. 2006. *Fans, Bloggers, and Gamers: Exploring Participatory Culture*. New York: NYU Press.

Jenson, Ric. 2011. "Blogola, Sponsored Posts, and the Ethics of Blogging." In *The Ethics of Emerging Media: Information, Social Norms, and New Media Technology*, edited by Bruce E. Drushel and Kathleen German, 213–234. London: Continuum.

Jin, Dal Yong, and Andrew Feenberg. 2015. "Commodity and Community in Social Networking: Marx and the Monetization of User-Generated Content." *Information Society* 31 (1): 52–60. doi:10.1080/01972243.2015.977635.

Johnson, Lauren. 2017. "4 Things Marketers Should Know about the FTC's Latest Crackdown on Influencer-Driven Social Media." *Adweek*, October 10, 2017. www.adweek.com.

Klonick, Kate. 2017. "The New Governors: The People, Rules, and Processes Governing Online Speech." *Harvard Law Review* 131 (6): 1599–1670.

Lee, Hye Jin, and Mark Andrejevic. 2014. "Second-Screen Theory: From the Democratic Surround to the Digital Enclosure." In *Connected Viewing: Selling, Streaming and Sharing Media in the Digital Age*, edited by Jennifer Holt and Kevin Sanson, 40–61. London: Routledge.

Main, Sami. 2017. "Micro-Influencers Are More Effective with Marketing Campaigns than Highly Popular Accounts." *Adweek*, March 30, 2017. www.adweek.com.

Maral. 2019. "Niching Down for Your Branded Campaign | Shan Boodram." YouTube video, May 15, 2019. www.youtube.com.

Marwick, Alice 2015. "Instafame: Luxury Selfies in the Attention Economy." *Public Culture* 27 (1(75)): 137–160. doi:10.1215/08992363-2798379.

McGuigan, Lee. 2015. "Procter & Gamble, Mass Media, and the Making of American Life." *Media, Culture & Society* 37 (6): 887–903. doi:10.1177/0163443715584100.

Mosco, Vincent. 2009. *The Political Economy of Communication*. London: Sage.

Murdock, Graham. 2011. "Political Economies as Moral Economies: Commodities, Gifts, and Public Goods." In *The Handbook of Political Economy of Communications*, edited by Janet Wasko, Graham Murdock, and Helena Sousa, 11–40. Malden, MA: Wiley.

New York Times Company. 2018. *The New York Times Company 2018 Annual Report*. www.nytco.com.

O'Connor, Clare. 2017. "Earning Power: Here's How Much Top Influencers Can Make on Instagram and YouTube." *Forbes*, April 10, 2017. www.forbes.com.

Petty, Ross. 2015. "The Historic Development of Modern US Advertising Regulation." *Journal of Historical Research in Marketing* 7 (4): 524–548.

Postigo, Hector. 2016. "The Socio-Technical Architecture of Digital Labor: Converting Play into YouTube Money." *New Media & Society* 18 (2): 332–349. doi:10.1177/1461444814541527.

Pulizzi, Joe. 2012. "The Rise of Storytelling as the New Marketing." *Publishing Research Quarterly* 28 (2): 116–123. doi:10.1007/s12109-012-9264-5.

Schweitzer, Marlis, and Marina Moskowitz, eds. 2009. *Testimonial Advertising in the American Marketplace: Emulation, Identity, Community*. London: Palgrave Macmillan.

Senft, Theresa. 2008. *Camgirls: Celebrity and Community in the Age of Social Networks*. New York: Peter Lang.

Shtern, Jeremy, Stephanie Hill, and Daphne Chan. 2019. "Social Media Influence: Performative Authenticity and the Relational Work of Audience Commodification in the Philippines." *International Journal of Communication* 13 (2019): 1939–1958.

Sinclair, John. 2012. *Advertising, the Media and Globalisation: A World in Motion*. London: Routledge.

Sonderman, Jeff, and Millie Tran. 2013. "The Definition of 'Sponsored Content.'" American Press Institute, November 13, 2013. www.americanpressinstitute.org.

Spangler, Todd. 2018. "YouTube Sets Stricter Requirements for Creator Partners in Response to Advertiser Concerns." *Variety*, January 16, 2018. https://variety.com.

Steigrad, Alexandra. 2017. "FTC Issued Warnings to 45 Celebrities over Unclear Instagram Posts." *WWD*, May 8, 2017. https://wwd.com.

Sweney, Mark. 2014. "YouTubers Ads for Oreo Banned for Not Making Clear Purposes of Videos." *The Guardian*, November 26, 2014. www.theguardian.com.

Turow, Joseph. 2012. *The Daily You: How the New Advertising Industry Is Defining Your Identity and Your Worth*. New Haven, CT: Yale University Press.

Twitter. 2018. "Twitter, Inc. Form 10-K for the Fiscal Year Ended December 31." www.sec.gov.

van Dijck, José, and David Nieborg. 2009. "Wikinomics and Its Discontents: A Critical Analysis of Web 2.0 Business Manifestos." *New Media & Society* 11 (5): 855–874. doi:10.1177/1461444809105356.

Wakabayashi, Daisuke, and Sapne Maheshwari. 2019. "Advertisers Boycott YouTube after Pedophiles Swarm Comments on Videos of Children." *New York Times*, February 20, 2019. www.nytimes.com.

Wright, Mike. 2019. "Anyone with More than 30,000 Social Media Followers Considered a Celebrity, Advertising Watchdog Rules." *The Telegraph*, July 3, 2019. www.telegraph.co.uk.

Wu, Tim. 2016. *The Attention Merchants: The Epic Scramble to Get Inside Our Heads*. New York: Knopf.

YouTube. n.d. "Paid Product Placements and Endorsements—YouTube Help." Accessed September 11, 2020. https://support.google.com.

14

Creator Rights and Governance

STUART CUNNINGHAM AND DAVID CRAIG

Creators generate significant value not only for platforms but also for emerging digital and creative economies by cultivating millions of online communities of interest, testing and proving new and emerging business models, and providing robust feedback in seeking to improve platform service. Yet the symbiotic relationship of creators and platforms (especially YouTube, Instagram, and Twitch and increasingly Facebook, Twitter, and Snap) has been one embraced with considerable ambivalence by platforms. When YouTube executives write corporate history, they minimize the failure of YouTube's early and ongoing attempts to embrace professional content and tend to marginalize the centrality of SME creators to YouTube's success and brand identity (Kyncl and Payven 2017; Allocca 2018). Our history of SME (Cunningham and Craig 2019, 39–62) shows that the relation between established media and platforms, especially YouTube, has been a constant shuffling between courting professional media and being rebuffed by them and that social media platforms' business models are increasingly more interdependent with SME creator culture.

The "new regulatory era" (Cunningham and Craig 2019, 266) we now are in presents as a clear and present danger for creators. In the wake of the "techlash" (Smith 2018), policy makers are rethinking the fundamental legal models of platform regulation. But in the welter of deficits that platforms are being held to account for—threats to democracy, privacy, traditional media sustainability, user and consumer rights—creators' livelihoods and speech rights are never included. When Facebook's Mark Zuckerberg and Google's Sundar Pichai appeared before the US Congress to answer for platform malfeasance (Kelly 2018), there was no mention by the CEOs or their politician-interrogators of creators. In subsequent white papers by key members of Congress developing policy options, creators were conspicuously missing (Warner 2018). The European Union passed Article 17 in 2019, a new copyright directive that holds platforms liable for third-party intellectual property on their sites, ignoring the interests of creators, who were "virtually unanimous" in their dissent. As Dr. Grandday, a leading creator activist, remarked, "The sad thing is that us YouTubers have no lobby groups or unions that can fight for us and speak to politicians directly for us. Most politicians have no idea about the troubles YouTubers face with copyright, or what type of content the typical YouTuber even produces" (quoted in Alexander 2019a).

This chapter develops a creator-centric account of industrial and governance issues in social media entertainment. The interests of creators are examined in the "top-down" context of the exercise of platform governance and efforts, by platforms and the state, to improve it. Those interests are also canvassed from the "bottom up"—how creators and creator advocacy are organizing and acting collectively to improve prospects for creators in this emerging industry.

Earlier scholarship around platforms and creators focused on critique of the "formalization" of the vernacular and the informal. Scholars have mapped YouTube's early history in a "fall from grace" or "declinist" narrative, claiming that the originating communal visions of these platforms have been compromised by the encroachment of commercialism. This scholarship has been unequivocal about YouTube's seemingly being poised to become yet another cog in the mainstream media industry. Jin Kim (2012) describes this shift as the "institutionalization of YouTube from user-generated content to professionally generated content." José van Dijck describes YouTube's evolution from homecasting to broadcasting and "toward viewer-based principles and away from community-oriented social networking" (2013, 117). In the wake of these changes, according to van Dijck, "YouTube is no longer an alternative to television, but a full-fledged player in the media entertainment industry" (127). Joanne Morreale tracks the trajectory of the short-segment comedy program *Annoying Orange* "from user-generated content to television series and cultural phenomenon" and argues that "the case of *Annoying Orange* exemplifies the processes whereby everyday prosumer content on the web becomes fodder for commercial media and demonstrates how YouTube, while presenting itself as a site for participatory culture, has become an arm of traditional media" (2013, 115).

More recent work featuring creators operating on other platforms like Instagram has focused on precarious labor and again made the argument that SME is much more like traditional media industries than offering anything new (Mann 2014; Duffy 2017). "Myths" such as amateurism, creative autonomy, and collaboration serve to "conceal the hierarchical, market-driven, quantifiable, and self-promotional realities of the blogosphere" (Duffy 2015, 61). The structure of this argument is less about decline and more about rebutting claims that SME offers innovation or difference in the media space.

This chapter intervenes in these narratives to argue that critical analysis needs now to recognize SME as in rapid formation as an emerging industry. We wish to attend to issues that actually *support* the further formalization of industry measures in order to buttress creators' careers and livelihoods and the potential many creators offer for progressivity and civic advance in platform culture. This argument preserves some of the core insights of the previous strands of critical studies but grounds and focuses them on working toward better governance of cultural outcomes (including industrial justice and regulatory and support measures).

Analytical Frameworks

The seeming gross power asymmetry between online creators and platforms offers an opportunity to test the Foucauldian understanding of power that informs our theoretical framework, including Foucault's (1991) distinction between power and domination. Power is relational, contingent, unstable, and reversible, whereas domination, a specific subset of power, is one-way, supervening, and controlling. Insights from network economics (for example, Ballon 2014) further support this Foucauldian account of power. The same network effects that accords platforms enormous power also enables better-connected, networked possibilities for horizontal, grassroots, peer-to-peer connectivity and communicative and organizational capability. Thus, while there may be a greater tendency toward oligopoly in platform capitalism, there is also expansive opportunity for peer-to-peer, horizontal, and potentially also democratic voices and self-expression. This analysis allows us to suggest that the kind of power exercised by the big digital platforms is a textbook example of the Foucauldian concept of power.

While fully cognizant of the winner-take-all network effects of the platform oligopoly, we have shown how SME has become a conduit for new voices and has augured an efflorescence of expression globally, while addressing the interests of underserved communities (Cunningham and Craig 2019). Creators work with the ambivalence of commercialized brand culture (Banet-Weiser 2012) while often engaging in representational and cultural activism. The gameplayer Markiplier secured twenty million subscribers while also raising over US$3 million for charity. The Vlogbrothers' Project4Awesome has encouraged legions of creators in their Nerdfighter community to raise funds and awareness for social causes for over a decade. Jerome Jarre's #LoveArmy social media activism helped raised millions for Mexican earthquake victims, Somalian famine sufferers, and Rohingyan refugees. YouTube launched the Creators4Change program, which frames and supports global multicultural creators engaging in transformational social and civic work (Craig and Cunningham 2017).

In this chapter, we examine governance that platforms and the state (we focus mostly on the United States) exercise from the "top down" and creator power and assistive advocacy from the "bottom up." We draw on original interviews with policy professionals at the major US policy agencies—Federal Trade Commission (FTC), Federal Communications Commission (FCC), US Copyright Office, and National Telecommunications and Information Agency (NTIA)—as well as activists and policy experts at Re:Create Coalition, Electronic Frontier Foundation, and the Center for Democracy and Technology.

"Top-Down" Creator Governance

Top-down creator governance refers to the exercise of power over creators. This power may be seen in both state agency and platform regulation and policy. State agency governance over creators may be exercised through direct regulation or policy "guidance," as illustrated by FTC guides on influencers' brand endorsements. More readily, state governance over creators is indirect, namely, *through* platform regulation, as with the provisions of the Children's Online Privacy Protection (COPPA) laws. Our mapping of state governance of creators affirms what Ithiel de Sola Pool described in *Technologies of Freedom* (1983):

multiple agencies with overlapping and underdetermined areas of jurisdiction. The challenges of regulating platforms have contributed to increasing fissures within Western policy regimes, especially between the United States and the European Union and between Western and non-Western regimes, particularly China. These fissures reveal conflicts over values and policy, with creators often caught in the fray.

Platforms may also allow the state to "govern at a distance" (Rose and Miller 2010), while often serving their own interests. As Lawrence Lessig (1999) and Sandra Braman (2006) insist, tech systems engage in latent and invisible forms of policy making that are often more effective than any state action. These forms vary in transparency and automation, including changes in algorithms, programmatic filters, demonetization, content ID systems, partnership programs, user interfaces, and, most notably, armies of anonymous content moderators reviewing takedown notices. On this latter note, as Philip Napoli and Robyn Caplan (2017) show and as Tarleton Gillespie reminds us in *Custodians of the Internet* (2018a), platforms have always sought to minimize awareness of moderation and curation, operating under (and hiding behind) safe-harbor provisions. But the new regulatory era is driven by the inescapable reality that platforms have become, as Gillespie notes, "essential public forums," and "their choices affect livelihoods, elections, and even life or death" (quoted in Rosenberg 2018).

Scholars continuously wrestle over policy solutions. "Digital constitutionalism" (Suzor 2019) is a framework based on the public values of the rule of law that may legitimately set limits on the power of platforms, thus potentially serving the interests of creators and users. This framework proposes that, if platforms are to secure their social license to operate, they should conform to fundamental minimum procedural standards or have such minimum standards imposed on them. Protecting this system would be adequate due process safeguards, including the availability of explanations of why a decision was made and an appeals process that allows for independent review and attempted resolution of disputes.

However, as Terry Flew (2018) argues, any regulation of the platforms is perforce going to be a form of coregulation or "soft law." The very identity of these platforms is inextricably tied to users as primary generators of content. While they curate and moderate at enormous scale, they must remain open to the distribution of user-generated content to a degree that would never be tolerated by traditional publishers or media broadcasters. This gives rise to the principle that "accountability and attendant punitive actions need to be exercised in measured ways to ensure that free expression is not unduly restricted. . . . The most serious breaches of laws and norms should typically be handled through legal and regulatory mechanisms and less serious breaches through self-regulatory private mechanisms" (Picard and Pickard 2017). In other words, free speech is the correlative principle to digital constitutionalism.

Platform governance, whether for self-regulation or as proxy for the state, has repeatedly proven problematic for creators, especially with regard to content moderation. On the one hand, platforms were absolved of oversight of third-party content, if they meet certain conditions, through the "safe harbor" provisions of the Digital Millennium Copyright Act (DMCA). As a result, the FCC has yet to entertain oversight over content issues with platforms, which also reflects how state regulation over content matters have always been fraught with First Amendment concerns. In our background interviews with FCC policy makers, the FCC continues to resist direct oversight over platforms, referring to them as "edge providers"—companies that provide online applications, content, or services but are not critical to the technological function of the internet. As Gillespie (2018a, 2018b) and others have repeatedly shown, platforms are centrally engaged in content moderation through a mix of latent technological innovations and overt shifts in policies and practices. YouTube's automated ContentID system, framed by underlying US copyright law, was designed to thwart legal action from legacy media.

The consequence of ContentID on creators has been paradoxical. On the one hand, creator content may be removed or demonetized for using legacy media intellectual property (IP). On the other hand, platforms neither license nor own creator content, and creators are not signed exclusively to platforms. This affords creators the agency to engage in communicative, content, and commercialized practices across multiple platforms. Furthermore, creators across diverse platforms and modalities (film, image, text) rarely subscribe to the protocols of IP control, although they may do so later to pursue varying strategies of licensing and merchandising. In part, this reflects how creators are not engaging in conventional content production. Rather, they generate more discursive formats and verticals that reflect the communicative affordances of social media platforms to foster greater engagement with their fan communities. Vlogging, Insta and Snap stories, tweets, and livestreams represent content innovation that is quite different from film, sitcoms, and music. One example is how gameplayers monetize their streams while using underlying videogame IP.

For this reason, creators lack the protections afforded by copyright directives and platform content ID systems. As platforms like Facebook have introduced video players, creator content has been "freebooted" for profit, essentially a platform affordance for piracy and plundering (D'Onfro 2015). In the case of one prominent creator, "Facebook's freebooting 'piracy' problem just cost Casey Neistat 20 million views" (Heine 2015). Facebook has since introduced a content ID system comparable to YouTube's, similarly designed to protect legacy media. Creators repeatedly experience rampant piracy, automated takedown notices, and false flags, with conditions growing worse with the advent of livestreaming across these platforms (Masnick 2016).

The debates over copyright and content moderation have taken a sharp turn that illustrates how platform governance has opened fissures between Western policy regimes. In 2019, the European Union passed Amendment 17, a copyright directive that holds platforms responsible for policing and removing infringing copyrighted content *before* upload. This provision contravenes the US safe harbor provisions. More notably, creators would be directly affected, which is why YouTube's chief business officer, Robert Kyncl, has encouraged creators to "speak out" about the proposed law (Hale 2018b). In this instance, platform self-governance and creator agency are aligned against state-based regulation, further evincing the complex, often contradictory, conditions around SME governance.

Platform self-regulation, often in reaction to threatened government intervention, public backlash, or advertiser flight, can sometimes create even more havoc for creators. In 2017, investigative journalists revealed that advertising was appearing programmatically alongside YouTube videos featuring terrorist organizations and neo-Nazis. In a panicked overreaction to advertisers withdrawing from the site, YouTube's "brand safety" response introduced a set of "filters" to promote more "ad-friendly content." This led to what became known as the "Adpocalypse." To secure monetization, creators had to indicate whether their content belonged in a list of categories that were acceptable to advertisers. Notably, most advertisers do not want their ads to be included with content categorized as political, sexual, or violent. But these categories prove broad and vague, blocking advertising for public service announcements against domestic violence or pro-LGBTQ advocacy. If creators did not mark their content categories, these videos would remain demonetized and undergo a human review process by anonymous censors hired by the platform. Even if the video was later cleared for monetization, most creators reported losing up of 90 percent of the revenue they might have earned under the filterless system.

Platform response was well intentioned if radically blunt. The Adpocalypse led to the demonetization of civic-minded and marginalized creators along with extremist content. For example, Casey Neistat and #LoveArmy's fundraiser for the victims of the Las Vegas shooting was removed because of the platforms' automated flagging mechanism, designed to minimize the spread of conspiracy videos about the event. LGBTQ creators have continued, years later, to claim that YouTube's filters represent taxonomic tyranny and perpetuate social injustice by classifying their content as sexual and therefore unsafe for brands (Bardo 2018). Creators like Philip DeFranco, whose civic-minded videos address topics like the Parkland teenagers and gun control, Myanmar refugees, and the arrests of journalists, see these practices as not only shutting down their livelihoods but inhibiting their free-speech rights and their communities' right to know and participate. The effects of the Adpocalypse continue to reverberate through creator careers and livelihoods.

In the United States, creator governance by state agencies includes oversight from the FTC, the FCC, the US Copyright Office, and the NTIA. Operating from diverse jurisdictional interests, these agencies often exert arbitrary influence over creators. While FTC endorsement guidelines demand that online creators be transparent about branded content, creators describe these regulations as "unfair and discriminatory because television shows, music videos, NBA stars and Kardashians get a pass for publishing the same content" (Glazer 2018) and as examples of double standards (Guthrie 2018). The FTC disclosed that these regulations were in response to petitions filed by activist consumer-rights organizations, like Public Citizen, yet another array of stakeholders and policy influencers operating in this space that can crowd out creators' voice.

FTC practices have historically targeted legacy media companies, advertising firms, and platforms but not individual creators. For example, Warner Bros. was fined for failing to disclose payments to creators for promoting its video-game IP (FTC 2016). However, in late 2017, warning letters by the FTC were issued to individual creators who were perceived to be in violation (Fair 2017). This suggests that state-based regulatory oversight may be advancing beyond organizations to target individual actors.

"Bottom-Up" Creator Governance

In this section, we consider how creators are organizing and acting collectively around issues of creator governance. Through industry and the market, creators are exerting influence over platform governance. Creators' influence might be disproportionate to their raw numbers, given that they manage very substantial communities of interest, rather than represent simply themselves in numerical aggregate, or present as an underclass of below-the-line workers, as championed by production studies (Mayer, Banks, and Caldwell 2010). But they also do not fit easily into standard above-the-line categories, as we shall see. Legacy media industry guilds and unions have—even if framed by their own interests—issued appeals to creators to join their ranks. Media and digital rights organizations advocate for some, albeit limited and in some ways misaligned, issues around creator governance.

The level of difficulty of organizing creators is indexed in the failure of the Internet Creators Guild (ICG), the only organization to date dedicated solely to creators. The SME thought leader and Vlogbrother Hank Green (2016) started the ICG in 2016 to support any creators who are "making all or part of their living making stuff on the internet, or are working toward that goal." It was wound up in 2019, unable to make headway against the isolation of creators, their global spread, and the manic work routines that make much sole-trader and small-business practice in general so hard to organize for collective action. The issues remain immediate and intransigent: "networks and studios using illegitimate copyright claims to take down 'huge amounts of content,' record labels allegedly taking 70 percent of every dollar spent on YouTube Premium subscriptions, and brands mandating that creators hide how much they're paid for sponsorships, making it harder for everyone to be paid fairly" (Alexander 2019b). The outgoing ICG director Anthony D'Angelo said, "The space needs health care. It needs fair contracts. I'm certain that collective action is the only way to achieve those goals" (quoted in Alexander 2019b).

On the other hand, in Germany in 2019, the YouTubers Union joined forces with one of the biggest traditional labor unions in the world to launch a campaign to pressure the platform to enter into industrial negotiations. Up to that point, the "union" was a loose association of about twenty thousand members in a Facebook group. But "with deep resources, legal expertise and a track record on labor issues, IG Metall gave the YouTubers Union the kind of legitimacy and urgency it needed to command more attention" (Solsman 2019).

Despite setbacks in the United States, the potential influence that individual voices have through leadership credibility and amplified network effects is potent. For example, in a 2015 blog post titled "Theft, Lies and Facebook Video," Green pointed out that Facebook measured anything longer than three seconds as a "view" (regardless of sound), including those videos that have played automatically in someone's news feed as they scroll past. "This might seem a little like this is a victimless crime, but it fundamentally devalues the #1 metric of online video. The view is the thing that everyone talks about and it's the thing creators sell to advertisers in order to make a living" (Green 2015b). Green's critique was confirmed when the platform revealed that, for two years, it had dramatically overestimated platform watch time between 60 and 80 percent, leading to a backlash from overcharged advertisers and brands (Vranica and Marshall 2016).

Creator practices of sustainability and risk maintenance operate as a form of bottom-up governance. Creators have bypassed platform control and governance by pursuing multiplatform strategies of entrepreneurship, community interaction, and content circulation. Even with disproportionate FTC intervention, influencer marketing remains a more viable and lucrative practice for some creators, in which advertisers often approach creators directly to use, mention, or promote their products, brands, and services. Estimates of the size of the "influencer economy" (Halzack 2016) vary wildly, with contradictory claims that this space is "booming" if also "collapsing under the weight of its own contradictions" (Cush 2016) and "under attack but still working" (Tobin 2018). Influencer marketing has often been narrowly limited to the realm of lifestyle creators, particularly on Instagram, although other platforms have raced to catch up. YouTube acquired FameBit, a self-service influencer marketing agency designed to "connect YouTube creators with marketers" (Ha 2016).

Creator power is now exerting significant influence on platform fortunes. Among many reasons why Twitter shuttered Vine was that the platform "burned the trust" of its creators by refusing to engage in shared partnership agreements as YouTube does (Constine 2016). Vine's top creators protested at Vine offices in efforts to save the platform (Lorenz 2016), before ultimately decamping to competing platforms. While attempting to benefit from Vine's mistake, Musical.ly scaled rapidly in part by providing limited forms of remuneration for native creators through virtual goods (Robehmed 2017). After merging with the Shanghai-based ByteDance, the platform was replaced overnight by its other platform, TikTok, which openly courts creators to grow the platform (Flynn 2018).

Platforms respond to creators' influence through an array of contradictory, often reactive practices. Once limited to invitation only, YouTube opened its partnership agreements to all users, only to rescind the offer, introducing new limits on partnership agreements on the basis of subscriptions and view time "in response to advertiser concerns" (Spangler 2018). YouTube also introduced a suite of revenue models for creators, including channel memberships and merchandise (Perez 2018). These models helped the platform circumvent advertising concerns, compete with other platforms like Patreon that offered creator subscriptions, and entice creators to stay in house or, rather, on platform. YouTube's subscription platform, YouTube Premium (formerly Red), according to Green (2015a), has been "good for creators," although the platform has since introduced advertising and shuttered much of its programming. The leading creators the Vlogbrothers were also key to the development of YouTube's community button, the platform's latest attempt to emulate the social networking affordance of Facebook, which constitutes one of five ways the Vlogbrothers have "pioneered YouTube as you know it" (Dryden 2017).

Creators are now accorded the status of "partners" across nearly every platform. Mimicking YouTube, Facebook has had to introduce new services for creators (Cohen 2018). Snapchat, which has long been resistant to empowering its native creators, has shifted to a creator-centric strategy (Weiss 2018a). Commercializing Twitch creators are afforded multiple revenue streams, along with their own camp and con(ference) (Segarra 2018). Twitter, in addition to purchasing its own influencer firm, Niche, launched "creator originals" designed to help Twitter creators produce more sponsored content (Weiss 2018b).

Advocacy can rebalance power asymmetry. The field of media and digital rights advocacy is expansive, as evinced by the nearly one hundred activists, organizations, and media firms submitting on international internet policy to the NTIA (2018). These organizations intersect with creator governance issues, albeit in limited and often misaligned ways. Agencies such as the Electronic Frontier Foundation continue to place emphasis on copyright and fair use, based on Lawrence Lessig's Creative Commons model, which champions the cultural politics of remix culture, leaving less attended the now more central concerns around the problematics of regulation and free speech to which we have previously pointed. As the director of the Center for Democracy and Technology's Free Expression Project, Emma Llanso (2018) claims, "Copyright fights have been a huge driver in internet policy for the last fifteen and twenty years, but that has skewed regulatory discussions both in terms of what regulatory frameworks we have, and also it presents a limited sense of what users are fighting for. Free speech online is a huge issue, and it covers everything people do online—from posting on social media to being a full-time creator with limited labor rights."

While copyright remains an everyday operational issue for many creators, focusing on copyright ties questions of creator governance to narrow rights battles with legacy media. In this new regulatory era, SME advocacy must attend to strategic issues of speech rights and the need for creators' distinctive voice not to be drowned out in the noisy clamor around platforms' threat to democracy, the plight of established media, and the rights of users, citizens, and children. The director of the Re:Create Coalition, Joshua Lamel (2018), claims that ContentID is a "flawed system but still the best technological solution to deal with infringement issues to date," but the peril is in empowering platforms to approach all governance matters through technological solutionism (Morozov 2013). ContentID is problematic going forward, according to Llanso (2018), because it "is an example of how industry self-regulation has affected what regulators are thinking is possible to do not only in the broader sphere of copyright regulation but also in other areas deemed problematic."

Creators' industrial relationships are not solely with platforms; rather, like other forms of media talent, they operate liminally within a competitive array of industries and multisided markets, including film, television, music, publishing, advertising, and marketing. According to Kevin Erickson (2018), director of the Future of Music coalition, while platforms still have the upper hand, changing industry dynamics have arguably worked in favor of native online musicians. On the one hand, he sees his and comparable creator organizations as holding platforms accountable for how they operate. "There's an asymmetry of power that plays out in terms of the rates, contracts, policies, and practices . . . which are not being chosen to advance the interests of creators as a class but to advance commercial interests." Nonetheless, "labels and contracts are improving because artists actually have more leverage than before historically because of common ground around policy and the shifts in power."

The pressures exerted on legacy media industries by platforms and creators have contributed to Hollywood unions' interest in creators. Screen Actors Guild–American Federation of Television and Radio Artists (SAG-AFTRA) represents 160,000 film and television actors, journalists, radio personalities, recording artists, singers, and voice-over actors, with aspirations to include creators. According to SAG's national executive director, "protections for creators are absolutely necessary as [the industry] continues to grow, because right now, the odds are stacked against movers and makers" (Hale 2018a). Nonetheless, unions' overtures to creators are fraught with complications, as creators are difficult to identify while operating across diverse platforms, verticals, and business strategies. SAG-AFTRA signed a deal with Zeus, an emerging subscription video on demand (SVOD) platform solely designed for creator content, which has secured deals with a subset of creators, most of whom aspire to break into the legacy media industries.

This alignment of interests between creators and traditional media talent is as welcome as it is problematic. SAG's efforts are not focused on platforms, whether YouTube, Facebook, Twitter, or Instagram, nor would SAG secure much leverage with advertisers. Alternatively, as writers and directors, creators might align with these unions only to experience similar misalignment around status and relationships to power. For example, the Digital Writers Union (n.d.), a division of the Writers Guild of America East, has signed "thousands of creative professionals who create digital media." Nonetheless, nearly ten years after the union's founding, most of the guild members are journalists employed by digital news organizations, like *Gawker*, *Vice*, and *Slate*. Creators might fit better within the Producers Guild of America (PGA), except that the PGA is not a labor union but is aligned with the interests of media conglomerates, networks, and studios and not writers, directors, or actors. The PGA New Media Council targets media executives, while focusing on platforms and technology, like SVOD platforms or video-game publishers.

Perhaps the oddest coalition would be creators and Teamsters, until consideration that the Teamsters already represent an eclectic array of media professionals and craftspeople, like editors and story analysts, not to mention Silicon Valley bus drivers (Dale 2017). Similarly, tech employees are organizing in response to the precariousness of labor conditions in the gig economy (that many of these firms helped initiate). Organizers like Tech Workers Coalition and Tech Solidarity are fueling a nascent movement in response to perceived collusion by tech firms with Trump administration policies (Coren 2017). As traditional unions like the AFL-CIO pivot from manufacturing to the service sector, professional workers, including software engineers, have seen unions as a viable bargaining option. In this regard, creators may experience better alignment with makers and coders than with actors or writers.

Conclusion

This chapter has traversed the ongoing exercise of top-down power in creator governance. What might appear to be gross power asymmetry may, to some extent, be mitigated by possible implementation of models of digital constitutionalism underpinning higher standards and practices of content moderation, including recognition of creator rights; by platforms' impacts on creators being sometimes unintended; and by state actors often "governing at a distance," and very unevenly, rather than through direct censorship (as in China and in other authoritarian polities). The Foucauldian calculus of power is further clarified in the treatment of "bottom-up" creator governance, through which we have discussed gathering efforts of creator activism and advocacy. The view from the bottom up surfaces creators' power derived from network effects, market forces, and industrial formation and has canvassed the challenges of formal collective action, including the degree of alignment of creators with media and digital rights organizations. Our discussion evinces Foucault's (1991) notion of power as relational, contingent, unstable and reversible, with power asymmetry based on what appears as the supervening power of platforms mitigated to some extent by multistakeholder, multi-industry relations often playing out outside the remit of platforms or evincing the relative dependency of platforms on creator buy-in.

We align our scholarship normatively with advocacy for creator rights. Jack Conte, cofounder and CEO of Patreon, a subscription site designed for creators, summed it up best in a "creator manifesto" in late 2017. Conte (2017) asked, "What will it be like to be a creator in 2028?" Creators, he said, would be "even more" culturally, politically, and economically powerful than they are today. They will be "amplifying their leverage" through better systems and organizations. Most importantly, they will be "fully integrated into the fabric of society as a workforce (health insurance, lending, financial systems, pensions, and other benefits traditionally tied to employment)." For this to happen by 2028, platforms will have to develop much more effective self-regulation that recognizes the centrality of creators to their operations and formalize their interdependencies, and states will have to act to ensure that these conditions are met.

REFERENCES

Abidin, Crystal. 2015. "Communicative ♥ Intimacies: Influencers and Perceived Interconnectedness." *Ada: A Journal of Gender, New Media, and Technology* 8. http://adanewmedia.org.

Alexander, Julia. 2019a. "YouTube Creators Are Still Trying to Fight Back against European Copyright Vote." *The Verge*, March 27, 2019. www.theverge.com.

———. 2019b. "YouTubers' First Organizing Attempt, the Internet Creators Guild, Is Shutting Down." *The Verge*, July 11, 2019. www.theverge.com.

Allocca, Kevin. 2018. *Videocracy: How YouTube Is Changing the World . . . with Double Rainbows, Singing Foxes, and Other Trends We Can't Stop Watching*. New York: Bloomsbury.

Ballon, Peter. 2014. "Old and New Issues in Media Economics." In *The Palgrave Handbook of European Media Policy*, edited by Karen Donders, Caroline Pauwels, and Jan Loisen, 70–95. Basingstoke, UK: Palgrave.

Banet-Weiser, Sarah. 2012. *Authentic™: The Politics of Ambivalence in a Brand Culture*. New York: NYU Press.

Bardo, Sal. 2018. "YouTube Continues to Restrict LGBTQ Content." *Huffington Post*, January 16, 2018. www.huffingtonpost.com.

Braman, Sandra. 2006. *Change of State: Information, Policy, and Power*. Cambridge, MA: MIT Press.

Cohen, David. 2018. "Facebook Is Testing Several New Products for Creators on Its Platform." *Adweek*, March 19, 2018. www.adweek.com.

Constine, Josh. 2016. "The Reasons Why Twitter Won't Let Anyone Save Vine." *TechCrunch*, October 30, 2016. https://techcrunch.com.

Conte, Jack. 2017. Twitter post, December 29, 2017. https://twitter.com/jackconte/status/946794483416367104.

Coren, Michael. 2017. "Silicon Valley Tech Workers Are Talking about Starting Their First Union in 2017 to Resist Trump." *Quartz*, March 24, 2017. https://qz.com.

Craig, David, and Stuart Cunningham. 2017. "How Social Media Stars Are Fighting for the Left." *The Conversation*, February 21, 2017. http://theconversation.com.

Cunningham, Stuart, and David Craig. 2019. *Social Media Entertainment: The New Intersection of Hollywood and Silicon Valley*. New York: NYU Press.

Cush, Andy. 2016. "The 'Influencer' Economy Is Collapsing under the Weight of Its Own Contradictions." *Gawker*, December 5, 2016. http://gawker.com.

Dale, Brady. 2017. "The Economic Justice Fight inside Silicon Valley's Commuter Buses." *Observer*, June 4, 2017. https://observer.com.

de Sola Pool, Ithiel. 1983. *Technologies of Freedom*. Cambridge, MA: Harvard University Press.

Digital Writers Union. n.d. Home page. Accessed August 30, 2020. www.digitalwritersunion.org.

D'Onfro, Jillian. 2015. "Here's a Look at Just How Big a Problem 'Freebooting' Is for Facebook." *Business Insider Australia*, August 4, 2015. www.businessinsider.com.au.

Dryden, Liam. 2017. "5 Ways the Vlogbrothers Have Pioneered YouTube as You Know It." *PopBuzz*, May 8, 2017. www.popbuzz.com.

Duffy, Brooke Erin. 2015. "Amateur, Autonomous, and Collaborative: Myths of Aspiring Female Cultural Producers in Web 2.0." *Critical Studies in Media Communication* 32 (1): 48–64. doi:10.1080/15295036.2014.997832.

———. 2017. *(Not) Getting Paid To Do What You Love: Gender, Social Media, and Aspirational Work*. New Haven, CT: Yale University Press.

Erickson, Kevin. 2018. Director, Future of Music Coalition. Interview with David Craig, July 6, 2018.

Fair, Lesley. 2017. "Three FTC Actions of Interest to Influencers." Federal Trade Commission, September 7, 2017. www.ftc.gov.

Flew, Terry. 2018. "Platforms on Trial." *Intermedia* 46 (2): 24–29.

Flynn, Kerry. 2018. "'Bridge the Gap between China and Here': To Grow Beyond Lip-Syncing Teens, TikTok Seeks Out Creators." *Digiday*, August 10, 2018. https://digiday.com.

Foucault, Michel. 1991. "Governmentality." In *The Foucault Effect: Studies in Governmentality*, edited by Graham Burchell, Colin Gordon, and Peter Miller, 87–104. Brighton, UK: Harvester Wheatsheaf.

FTC (Federal Trade Commission). 2016. "Warner Bros. Settles FTC Charges It Failed to Adequately Disclose It Paid Online Influencers to Post Gameplay Videos." July 11, 2016. www.ftc.gov.

Gillespie, Tarleton. 2018a. *Custodians of the Internet: Platforms, Content Moderation, and the Hidden Decisions That Shape Social Media*. New Haven, CT: Yale University Press.

———. 2018b. "Regulation of and by Platforms." In *The Sage Handbook of Social Media*, edited by Jean Burgess, Alice Marwith, and Thomas Poell, 254–278. London: Sage.

Glazer, Mikey. 2018. "Social Media Influencers Stump for More Seamless Product Placement." *The Wrap*, February 6, 2018. www.thewrap.com.

Green, Hank. 2015a. "Is YouTube Red Good for Creators?" *Medium*, October 23, 2015. https://medium.com.

———. 2015b. "Theft, Lies, and Facebook Video." *Medium*, August 3, 2015. https://medium.com.

———. 2016. "Introducing the Internet Creators Guild." *Medium*, June 16, 2016. https://medium.com.

Guthrie, Scott. 2018. "Product Placement Double Standards Affecting Influencer Marketing." *Sabguthrie.info*, May 29, 2018. https://sabguthrie.info.

Ha, Anthony. 2016. "Google Acquires FameBit to Connect YouTube Creators with Marketers." *TechCrunch*, October 12, 2016. https://techcrunch.com.

Hale, James. 2018a. "SAG-AFTRA National Director Wants to Protect Online Creators, Says Industry Is 'Very Unfair and Unbalanced.'" *Tubefilter*, August 15, 2018. www.tubefilter.com.

———. 2018b. "YouTube's Robert Kyncl Urges Creators to Speak Out against Proposed EU Copyright Law." *Tubefilter*, September 5, 2018. www.tubefilter.com.

Halzack, Sarah. 2016. "Social Media 'Influencers': A Marketing Experiment Grows into a Mini-Economy." *Washington Post*, November 2, 2016. www.washingtonpost.com.

Heine, Christopher. 2015. "Facebook's 'Freebooting' Piracy Problem Just Cost Casey Neistat 20 Million Views." *Adweek*, November 12, 2015. www.adweek.com.

Kelly, Erin. 2018. "Senators to Zuckerberg: We May Need to Regulate Facebook to Protect Privacy." *USA Today*, April 10, 2018. www.usatoday.com.

Kim, Jin. 2012. "The Institutionalization of YouTube: From User-Generated Content to Professionally Generated Content." *Media Culture & Society* 34 (1): 53–67. doi:10.1177/0163443711427199.

Kyncl, Robert, and Maany Peyvan. 2017. *Streampunks: How YouTube and the New Creators Are Transforming Our Lives.* London: Virgin Books.

Lamel, Joshua. 2018. Director, Re:Create Coalition. Interview with Stuart Cunningham and David Craig, June 18, 2018.

Lessig, Lawrence. 1999. *Code and Other Laws of Cyberspace.* New York: Basic Books.

Llanso, Emma. 2018. Director, Centre for Democracy and Technology's Free Expression Project. Interview with Stuart Cunningham and David Craig, June 19, 2018.

Lorenz, Mic. 2016. "'We Knew Vine Was Dead': Vine's Biggest Stars Tried to Save the Company, but They Were Ignored." *Business Insider*, October 29, 2016. www.businessinsider.com.

Mann, Denise. 2014. "Welcome to the Unregulated Wild, Wild, Digital West." *Media Industries* 1 (2). doi:10.3998/mij.15031809.0001.206.

Masnick, Mike. 2016. "Facebook Launches Its Own Version of ContentID, Which Will Soon Be Abused to Take Down Content." *TechDirt*, April 13, 2016. www.techdirt.com.

Mayer, Vicki, Miranda Banks, and John Caldwell, eds. 2010. *Production Studies: Cultural Studies of Media Industries.* New York: Routledge.

Morozov, Evgeny. 2013. *To Save Everything, Click Here.* New York: Public Affairs.

Morreale, Joanne. 2013. "From Homemade to Store Bought: Annoying Orange and the Professionalization of YouTube." *Journal of Consumer Culture* 14 (1): 113–128: doi:10.1177/1469540513505608.

Napoli, Philip, and Robyn Caplan. 2017. "Why Media Companies Insist They're Not Media Companies, Why They're Wrong, and Why It Matters." *First Monday* 22 (5). doi:10.5210/fm.v22i5.7051.

NTIA (National Telecommunications and Information Administration). 2018. "Comments on International Internet Policy Priorities." www.ntia.doc.gov.

Perez, Sarah. 2018. "YouTube Introduces Channel Memberships, Merchandise and Premieres." *TechCrunch*, June 22, 2018. https://techcrunch.com.

Picard, Robert, and Victor Pickard. 2017. *Essential Principles for Contemporary Media and Communications Policymaking.* Oxford, UK: Reuters Institute for the Study of Journalism, University of Oxford. https://reutersinstitute.politics.ox.ac.uk.

Robehmed, Natalie. 2017. "From Musers to Money: Inside Video App Musical.ly's Coming of Age." *Forbes*, May 11, 2017. www.forbes.com.

Rose, Nikolas, and Peter Miller. 2010. "Political Power Beyond the State: Problematics of Government." *British Journal of Sociology* 61 (1): 271–303. doi:10.1111/j.1468-4446.2009.01247.x.

Rosenberg, Scott. 2018. "What We're Reading: How Content Moderation Defines Tech Platforms." *Axios*, July 29, 2018. www.axios.com.

Segarra, Lisa. 2018. "Twitch Is Launching a Creator Camp to Make You a Better Streamer." *Fortune*, July 24, 2018. http://fortune.com.

Smith, Eve. 2018. "The Techlash against Amazon, Facebook and Google—And What They Can Do." *Economist*, January 20, 2018. www.economist.com.

Solsman, Joan. 2019. "YouTubers Union Has Big Demands. Google Won't Negotiate." *CNET*, August 23, 2019. www.cnet.com.

Spangler, Todd. 2018. "YouTube Sets Stricter Requirements for Creator Partners in Response to Advertiser Concerns." *Variety*, January 16, 2018. https://variety.com

Suzor, Nicolas. 2019. *Lawless: The Secret Rules That Govern Our Digital Lives*. Cambridge: Cambridge University Press.

Tobin, Jim. 2018. "Influencer Marketing Is under Attack: Six Reasons It Still Works." *Forbes*, June 1, 2018. www.forbes.com.

van Dijck, José. 2013. *The Culture of Connectivity: A Critical History of Social Media*. New York: Oxford University Press.

Vranica, Suzanne, and Jack Marshall. 2016. "Facebook Overestimated Key Video Metric for Two Years." *Wall Street Journal*, September 22, 2016. www.wsj.com.

Warner, Mark. 2018. "Potential Policy Proposals for Regulation of Social Media and Technology Firms." White paper/platform policy paper. www.warner.senate.gov.

Weiss, Geoff. 2018a. "Snapchat to Place Renewed Emphasis on Creator Community, Unveils Second Series with Patrick Starr." *Tubefilter*, June 21, 2018. www.tubefilter. com

———. 2018b. "Twitter's Niche Moves into Non-branded Content with Josh Peck, Miel Bradouw, More." *Tubefilter*, April 30, 2018. www.tubefilter.com.

ACKNOWLEDGMENTS

Our first thanks go to our contributors—all twenty-one of them—who have agreed to put social media entertainment and the creator culture it has spawned under the microscope. Needless to say, without their expertise and commitment to the project, we would not have a book to put before you.

Eric Zinner, our editor at New York University Press, has been a strong supporter and a source of always-valuable advice. Editorial assistant Dolma Ombadykow has been consistently helpful through the process of preparation. We thank them both and thank as well the anonymous reviewer who sharpened our thinking about the project.

We take this opportunity to thank Dr Adam Swift, who has worked (again) with us on this project and has contributed meticulous editorial oversight.

The Digital Media Research Centre in the Creative Industries Faculty at Queensland University of Technology has been an enormously stimulating environment, as has the Annenberg School for Communication and Journalism at the University of Southern California.

This book is an output from the Australian Research Council (ARC) Discovery Project 160100086, "The New Screen Ecology and Opportunities for Innovation in Production and Distribution," for 2016–2018, awarded to Stuart Cunningham. David Craig also received funding from Shanghai Jiao Tong University's USC-SJTU Institute of Cultural and Creative Industry and from Zizhu National High-Tech Industrial Development Zone, via the Zizhu New Media Management Research Center.

ABOUT THE CONTRIBUTORS

ARTURO ARRIAGADA is Associate Professor at the Universidad Adolfo Ibáñez School of Communications and Journalism (Chile), where he conducts research at the intersection of media, technology, and society. His particular areas of interest include social media and labor; social media and political communication; and platform economy and promotional culture. His work has been published in the *Journal of Communication, Journal of Cultural Economy*, and *International Journal of Communication*. This research has been funded by Chile's National Fund for Scientific and Technological Development (Project 11150095).

SARAH BANET-WEISER is Professor of Media and Communications at the London School of Economics. She is the author of *Empowered: Popular Feminism and Popular Misogyny* (2018) and *Authentic™: The Politics of Ambivalence in a Brand Culture* (NYU Press, 2012), among others. She is the coeditor of *Commodity Activism: Cultures of Resistance in Neoliberal Times* (NYU Press, 2012) and *Racism PostRace* (2019). She is the coeditor in chief of the ICA journal *Communication, Culture and Critique*.

NANCY K. BAYM is Senior Principal Researcher at Microsoft Research and Research Affiliate in Comparative Media Studies/Writing at the Massachusetts Institute of Technology.

JEAN BURGESS is Director of the Digital Media Research Centre, Queensland University of Technology. Her most recent book is *Twitter—A Biography* (with Nancy K. Baym; NYU Press, 2019).

DAVID CRAIG is Clinical Associate Professor at USC Annenberg School for Communication and Journalism and Visiting Professor in the Institute of Cultural and Creative Industries at Shanghai Jiao Tong

University. With Stuart Cunningham, he is the coauthor or coeditor of multiple books, journal articles, and chapters about the social media entertainment and *wanghong* industries. Prior to academia, in addition to LGBTQ media activism, Craig was a Hollywood producer and network programming executive responsible for over thirty projects that garnered over seventy Emmy, Golden Globe, and Peabody nominations.

STUART CUNNINGHAM is Distinguished Professor of Media and Communication at Queensland University of Technology. He is coauthor (with David Craig) of *Social Media Entertainment: The New Intersection of Hollywood and Silicon Valley* (NYU Press, 2019) and coeditor (with Terry Flew) of *A Research Agenda for Creative Industries* (2019).

BROOKE ERIN DUFFY is Assistant Professor at Cornell University, where she holds faculty appointments in the Department of Communication and the Feminist, Gender & Sexuality Studies Program. She is the author of *(Not) Getting Paid to Do What You Love: Gender, Social Media, and Aspirational Work* (2017) and *Remake, Remodel: Women's Magazines in the Digital Age* (2013). Additional information about her work can be found on her website, www.brookeduffy.com.

MOHAMED EL MARZOUKI is Assistant Professor of Communication at the Illinois Institute of Technology. His research focuses on youth citizenship and digital media in North Africa and the Middle East.

DAMIÁN FRATICELLI is Associate Professor of Semiotics of Networks at the Buenos Aires University, Argentina. He is author of *The Triumphant Decline of Comedy TV Shows* (2019).

ZOË GLATT is a doctoral candidate in the Department of Media and Communications at the London School of Economics (LSE), where she is conducting ethnographic research into the lives and labor of aspiring and professional YouTube creators within the growing online video industry. She is Managing Editor of the ICA journal *Communication, Culture and Critique* and Graduate Student Representative for the Association of Internet Researchers (AoIR). Additional information can be found on her website, www.zoeglatt.com.

STEPHANIE HILL is a PhD student in the Joint Graduate Program in Communication and Culture at York University and Ryerson University in Toronto, Canada. She is a recipient of the Joseph-Armand Bombardier Canada Graduate Scholarships (CGS) Doctoral Scholarship.

SANGEET KUMAR is Associate Professor in the Department of Communication at Denison University, Ohio. He is the author of the forthcoming book *The Digital Frontier* (2020).

BRENT LUVAAS is Associate Professor of Global Studies and Modern Languages and Graduate Faculty Member in Communication, Culture and Media at Drexel University. He is the author of *Street Style: An Ethnography of Fashion Blogging* (2016) and *DIY Style: Fashion, Music, and Global Digital Cultures* (2012) and coeditor of *The Anthropology of Dress and Fashion: A Reader* (2019). He is also the blogger behind *Urban Fieldnotes* (www.urbanfieldnotes.com). Follow his latest project on digital street photography on Instagram at @streetanthropology.

JUNYI LV is a PhD student at the Annenberg School for Communication and Journalism, University of Southern California. She studies rhetoric, argumentation, and social media entertainment.

SRIRAM MOHAN is a doctoral student in the Department of Communication Studies at the University of Michigan, Ann Arbor. He is the coeditor of *Global Digital Cultures: Perspectives from South Asia* (2019).

HECTOR POSTIGO is Associate Professor of Media Studies and Production at Temple University. He is the author of *The Digital Rights Movement: The Role of Technology in Subverting Digital Copyright* (2012) and the coeditor of *Managing Privacy through Accountability* (2012). Postigo was an Annenberg Fellow at Stanford University's CASBS and cofounder of Culture Digitally. Additional information about his work can be found at www.hectorpostigo.com.

ASWIN PUNATHAMBEKAR is Associate Professor and Founding Director of the Global Media Studies Initiative in the Department of Communication Studies at the University of Michigan, Ann Arbor.

He is the coeditor of *Global Digital Cultures: Perspectives from South Asia* (2019).

MEGAN SAWEY is a doctoral student in the Department of Communication at Cornell University, where she studies digital labor, the role of technology in companionship, and the intersection of commodification and companionship. She is advised by Brooke Erin Duffy. Additional information about her work can be found at www.communication.cals.cornell.edu/people/megan-sawey/.

CARLOS A. SCOLARI is Professor of Analysis of Interactive Digital Communication and Coordinator of the PhD Program in Communication at the Universitat Pompeu Fabra, Barcelona. He is the author of *Media Evolution* (2019) and *The Laws of the Interface* (2018).

JEREMY SHTERN is Associate Professor and a founding faculty member in the School of Creative Industries at Ryerson University in Toronto, Ontario. He is coauthor of two books: *Media Divides: Communication Rights and the Right to Communicate in Canada* (2010) and *Digital Solidarities: Communication Policy and Multi-stakeholder Global Governance: The Legacy of the World Summit on the Information Society* (2010).

JOSÉ M. TOMASENA is a Mexican writer and PhD candidate in the Communication Department at the Pompeu Fabra University. He is the author of the novels *The Trail of the Bodies* (2019) and *Cobra's Fall* (2016).

JARROD WALCZER is a media and communications doctoral candidate at the Queensland University of Technology's Digital Media Research Centre in Brisbane, Australia. He is also an adjunct instructor at Moravian College in Bethlehem, Pennsylvania. His research explores the impact that toy unboxing creator culture has had on YouTube and the children's media industry in the United States.

ELAINE JING ZHAO is Senior Lecturer in the School of the Arts and Media at the University of New South Wales, Sydney. She is the author of *Digital China's Informal Circuits: Platforms, Labour and Governance* (2019).

INDEX

Page numbers in italics indicate Tables